GEORGE O'BRIEN
A Biographical Memoir

JAMES MEENAN

GEORGE O'BRIEN
A Biographical Memoir

GILL AND MACMILLAN

First published 1980 by
Gill and Macmillan Ltd
15/17 Eden Quay
Dublin 1
with associated companies in
London, New York, Delhi, Hong Kong,
Johannesburg, Lagos, Melbourne,
Singapore, Tokyo

7171 1035 4

For Annette

Printed and bound in Great Britain by
Bristol Typesetting Co Ltd, Barton Manor, St Philips, Bristol

Contents

Preface

THIS book has been written in the belief that some memoir of George O'Brien should be available to the very many people who met him either as his students in University College, Dublin, or as associates in one or other of his many activities. It is based on his written recollections, on his remembered table-talk and on the reminiscences of many of his friends. Few letters or engagement books survive.

The recollections were not written for the usual reasons, of expressing a point of view or of recording events that seemed important to the writer. They do both the one and the other; but their primary object was quite different. It will appear that George O'Brien's life, outwardly tranquil and assured, was overshadowed by recurrent periods of severe depression. His recollections were first written around 1948 on the suggestion of his medical adviser who was concerned much more with his mental than with his physical well-being. There were all too many unpleasant or painful memories. It was thought that his mind might be in some sense liberated if he took a stock-taking of his life and cleared away many things that were best forgotten. It will be seen how badly that was needed.

Into the first version he put everything, great or small, important or trivial (as it might appear to a reader, not indeed to him) at considerable length. He was much more concerned with the unpleasant things that happened to him than with the pleasant : the recollections are, as it were, a dial that reflects the clouds and only rarely the sun. He then, about 1950 or so, wrote a second version largely based on the first but shorter in that a great deal of the resentments of the original draft was excluded. Finally, around 1951 or 1952, as it would seem, a third copy was typed which was very nearly a clean copy of the second, usually differing only in the sequence of narration. Unfortunately, about a quarter of the third draft is missing which perhaps does not matter greatly as the second and surviving third drafts resemble each other so clearly.

The question presents itself at once : did he intend these recollections to be published? There are a number of considerations that suggest he did not and that he regarded what he had written as a kind of catharsis rather than as a formal autobiography. Even in the second and third drafts there is still a great deal of trivia and of excursions into a number of subjects that aroused his curiosity without impelling him into a serious study. Moreover and, rightly or wrongly, this seems decisive, he did nothing to bring the recollections up to date though he had still twenty years of active life left to him when he had finished the third draft. If he intended a formal biography, one feels, he would have used his leisure to continue it to some obvious ending point such as his retirement from the College in 1961 or the loss of his Seanad seat four years later. To those who may think that, no matter what his intention may have been, the complete text should now be published, it may be answered that even the second draft runs to about 250,000 words, a formidable proposition to put to any publisher.

This has involved a series of judgements on what and where to quote and where not to quote. The following rules have been adopted and, one hopes, consistently followed. Quotations are taken from the third draft, from the second only where the third is not complete and never from the first. Nothing has been quoted from either draft when it is clear that he had altered his judgement in later years. Also, many of his most salty comments have not been repeated. He was a highly controversial figure when Dublin was an angrier and a more quarrelsome place than it is today (or it may be, the anger and the quarrels have passed into different spheres of daily life). He had a keen eye for the phrase that could wound most deeply; and he retorted pungently on his critics. But although most of them are now dead, their children are not and their feelings must be respected, all the more because, by an agreeable irony, many of those children were subsequently among George's most devoted and admiring students.

The existence of the recollections has demanded the composition of something more than a limited memoir. Whether it is successful or not, the picture that emerges is not at all what many will expect. Most of those who remember George O'Brien knew him in the 1940s and 1950s: they would know little of his life between the wars. In those years he mixed in many matters and with many people in a society that still commands interest. It seems right that he should be allowed to speak for himself in these matters. One result is that a high proportion of the book is concerned with his life before he joined the College staff in 1926: another is that many cherished anecdotes of his sayings and doings in College must be regretfully discarded. There is one other matter that must be mentioned. His later students knew him as a respected professor with an assured status. They would have known little of his early set-backs and would have little suspicion of the constant struggles from which his life, even to nearly the end, was never secure.

He belonged to a period that has now passed into history. He was born into a world that was ruled from Europe. He was middle-aged when the entry of the Soviet Union and the United States into the second war spelt the end of a European domination that had lasted for centuries. He bore the marks of his youth. He was born into an orderly and ordered world, the world of the pound sterling and the rule of law. He was also born into a Dublin still governed by distinctions of class, religion and politics. These do not matter much, if at all, today. They did when he was growing up. The picture that he draws may appear irrelevant, perhaps sometimes repellent. It should not obscure the reality of a profoundly good and loyal man who suffered greatly from adversity but retained the magnanimity to rise above it and become an example to others.

Those who did not know him must form their own judgement. Those who did have formed their judgement long ago. Everybody had their own George. To those who met him he gave the unspoken lesson that even the worst reverses can be overcome by constancy and courage and that one must never, never, allow oneself to be overborne by abuse and clamour into saying what one does not believe to be true. Political Economy was not the profession of his first choice but it had for him standards of professional honour and conduct no less rigorous than those of the Bar. To know him was a privilege and a constant joy.

A*

Acknowledgments

I must express my deep gratitude to Mr John Lynch who lent me his copies of the first and second drafts of the recollections and to Mr John Gaynor, solicitor, for his loan of the third. I received constant encouragement from Paddy Lynch whose interest in the venture never flagged. There were very many others, too numerous to name, in the College and elsewhere, who volunteered reminiscences or anecdotes. Only too often, considerations of space prevented the use of their material.

I

Childhood 1892-1900

GEORGE O'BRIEN was born in Dublin on January 26th, 1892. His father, Richard, then proprietor of the Wicklow Hotel, married twice, having two sons and one daughter by the first marriage. George was the only child of the second marriage. His half-brothers and half-sister were many years older and had left home before he was born. His father died in 1906; from then until his mother's death forty years later, as a youth and a grown man he was the only child of a widowed mother.

Richard O'Brien had a varied career. He had run away to sea 'from his unhappy home and unkind step-mother' and had travelled widely at a time when travel, even within Europe, was restricted to the rich and the adventurous.

> My father was a self-made man. Entirely as a result of his own energy, enterprise and exertion, he became the owner of a successful hotel, which was my childhood home. From small beginnings he built up a good business, educated a fair sized family and left a respectable fortune. I think he did a good life's work. He was a typical Victorian business man. He wanted no advice or assistance from anybody. He was prepared to shoulder all the risks and take all the responsibilities of business, but he wanted to be left alone.

His son's recollections of him are uniformly happy. 'He was an old man, with a white beard, walking on a stick. I think he had worked too hard, worried too much and played too little. . . . He was very kind to me and I have nothing but pleasant memories of him.'

> I am sure that if my father had had a good education he would have been a success in some of the professions. He had a very

good brain and was interested in things of the mind. He had a good taste in music, drama and furniture. He was a very constant theatre-goer and, luckily, encouraged me to follow in his footsteps. As a child I was taken to many operas, concerts and plays. . . . In his later years he was a voracious but judicious reader. My early education was derived largely from the numerous newspapers and magazines that he used to bring home. If broadcasting had existed in his time I am sure he would have been a very keen listener both to talks and music.

Inevitably, in view of his early death at the age of fifty-eight, his figure is shadowy, but it is a kindly and beloved shade. He was a Catholic though not, it appears, devout : he only resumed the practice of religion in his last years to please his wife. His son, who himself was to experience years of indifference, felt that he was an agnostic at heart. Lastly, in an age when one's religion usually determined one's politics, Richard O'Brien was a unionist. Perhaps he was not much of one; he refused to swathe the hotel in red, white and blue for the relief of Ladysmith (though that may well have been because a number of his customers would have taken deep offence) but he was definitely not a nationalist. George must have been one of the few Irish Catholic boys of his age who was not brought up on the catalogue of Ireland's wrongs or the hatreds of the Parnellite split. This, like other aspects of that small family life, was to affect him later.

Looking back on it now, I cannot help feeling that my mother was to blame for not insisting on his taking more holidays. Perhaps she had tried and failed. I think it more likely that she did not think about it at all. In later years, when she and I lived together, she never understood the need for rest and recreation. She let me work as a student without much regard to the possible effect of overwork on my health. I think that she was probably equally blind to the bad results of my father's incessant labour.

His mother, thus equivocally introduced, was some eleven years younger than his father. She came from County Wicklow, of a family that had been recently converted from protestantism as a result of a mixed marriage. Her son recalls that 'she had nothing like his (father's) brains, and whatever brains she possessed she did not strive to develop'. And again : 'She was sensitive on the subject of never having been to a good convent school. My father warned me, when I was quite a small child, never to hurt her feelings on this subject.'

Relations with his mother were to affect him all his life. They were not easy. There seems to have been a lack of understanding —on both sides, perhaps. Above all, it would seem that there was an absence of overt affection which, in the circumstances of his life, was to be badly needed.

My mother was very religious in a devotional way. She was a complete contrast in this to my father. . . . I was, of course, greatly influenced on this subject by my mother and my nurses . . . I have no doubt at all that my mother loved me very deeply. . . . But she seemed afraid, either by reason of shyness or fear of spoiling me, to make any outward sign of affection. I never was petted, fondled or kissed like other children. Indeed I was quite surprised, later in life, to see the way in which children were treated by their parents. My father was a little more inclined than my mother to indulge and spoil me. But I was never a spoilt child in the usual sense of the term. Indeed, I think I was brought up with a certain Spartan austerity, in which, of course, there was no trace of cruelty. If I was never petted, I was never punished.

This did not change as he grew up. Part of his recollections of school at Weybridge was that his mother came over to a prize-giving and was disappointed that he had won many, but not all, of the prizes. Later, recalling his years in College and the King's Inns, he remarks in a perceptibly harsher tone that she allowed him to strain himself by over-work.

It seems a sadly negative picture. If the mother was shy so certainly was the son even in adult years. Both mother and son, one feels, paid a heavy price as a result.

Years later, he wrote that he would have preferred it if he had been given the baptismal name of Polycarp, the patron saint of his birthday. 'I share,' he wrote, 'the Church's attachment to the significance of festivals and anniversaries, and I regard it as proper that one should venerate the saints whose feasts coincide with events in one's life or after whom one is named'. All his life he was highly conscious of anniversaries and coincidences, a

trait which he shared (as he observed) with Cardinal Newman.
In addition, St Polycarp had been consecrated by St John to
whom George had a 'great devotion because of the peculiarly
intimate relationship that existed between him and Our Lord . . .
I have come to believe that, if there is anything at all in the
intercession of saints—which is an essential element of Catholic
faith—his intercession should be unusually effective'. So he wrote
in his later fifties, when he had resumed the practice and regained
some of the spontaneity of his faith.

In fact, he was given the names of George Augustine Thomas.
The first name may have been suggested by then recent events.
A few days before his birth, the Duke of Clarence, who as eldest
son of the Prince of Wales stood second in the royal succession,
died of influenza. His only brother, Prince George of Wales,
accordingly became heir-presumptive to the throne which he was
later to ascend as King George V. Granted the politics of the
O'Brien family, it seems at least possible that the choice of first
name was not fortuitous. George, however, in his retrospect
looked back to St George, not yet, at the time he wrote, demoted
in hagiography. 'St George's principal claim to fame was his
achievement as a dragon-killer. I have killed a few dragons in
my time—not the serpentine scaly sort but biped dragons in
lounge suits and academic dress'. Those who read further will
be able to supply the names. The other two patrons were given
their due, perhaps over-due, significance. St Augustine 'shared
with me a saintly mother, a sinful youth, the grace of repentance
and a vocation of learning'. As for the last name, divided between the doubting Apostle and the Angelic Doctor, he plumped
for the second 'who would be a very suitable patron for a university professor'. In fact he rarely if ever used the second or
third names. They were revived in the pages of *The Catholic
Bulletin*, with a clear intent to annoy him, by some of the dragons
just mentioned who, it was understood at the time, added a
soutane to their diversity of disguises.

The O'Brien family had no roots in Dublin. None of his
grandparents had lived in the city, neither his father nor his
mother had been born there. None of his relatives had been there
for more than a generation. This would not be unusual today
when the city's population has been swollen by decades of immigration; in the later years of the last century it grew slowly

and with very little immigration. There is some irony in the fact that one whose life was to be confined to the city should originally have had such tenuous ties with it.

He was proud to recall that he had been born in the heart of the city, the Dublin equivalent of a Cockney, born within hearing, not of Bow bells, but of those of St Patrick's. He has an evocative reference to hearing those bells on empty Sunday evenings. It establishes a link across the years between him and all those who remember the same chimes from their youth. There was something in a boyhood in Dublin which marked it out from any other city. George's reference perhaps recalls his first understanding that Dublin exercised a spell and a fascination for those who knew it that few cities of the world, however populous, rich or powerful they might be, could ever remotely equal.

It is not so very long since the Dublin in which he lived began to disappear, but it already seems as remote as Doctor Johnson's London. Physically, the city hardly changed at all until the last decade of his life. New suburbs were created in the fields of Crumlin and Donnycarney but these were not areas that he often visited. The city proper, lying between the two canals, hardly changed at all except to grow a little seedier as the decades dragged on, but it experienced little of the changes that became so common, and so resented by Dubliners, in the sixties. If James Joyce had returned to the city before his death in 1941 he would have seen little that he had not known, the lurching trams, the distinctive electric light standards, the rows of small houses with a horse of Hanover or an Infant of Prague over the fanlight of their hall-doors. This was George's Dublin also.

He was proud to be a citizen of that decaying but enduring city. Above almost all things, he was a Dublin man, and one sometimes feels that he was always quite content to live in its streets and squares, that his illness was a convenient excuse for not leaving it. It is difficult to think of him visiting Cork : it is quite impossible to think of him visiting Belfast. He had the true feeling of the Dubliner for those two cities, not contempt, still less hostility, but a plain lack of interest tinged with suspicion.

One remembers meeting him in Earlsfort Terrace on an evening before the war. He had driven out beyond Inchicore and had walked along the canal to some lock. He remarked how striking it was to lean up against the bridge and to reflect that there was nothing between him and America. This was not said as a joke nor was it intended to dismiss some couple of millions of his countrymen. It was rather that in his heart he would have approved of an Aurelian wall being built around the city or a revival of the old Pale to defend it against what lay outside. For him as for many, Dublin was indeed no Athens nor was it Rome; it was crowned neither with violets nor with laurels; but it was a city that had power to capture the hearts of those who lived in it.

His recollections of childhood were almost uniformly happy. He spent most of his days in Merrion Square to which his parents had obtained a key. St Stephen's Green was not then as well laid out as the Board of Works has since made it nor was it well patrolled. Merrion Square, surrounded almost completely by houses in family ownership, was regarded as safe for younger children. Every summer the family took a furnished house at the sea, sometimes Howth more often Dalkey. The sun always shone, there was plenty of boating and bathing, there were band recitals in Sorrento Park every Saturday night. In 1904 they rented a house in Kingstown, 8 Marine Terrace, which stood in an attractive row, since partially destroyed, overlooking the East Pier. Later, after his father's death, there were holidays for a few weeks in England or Scotland. These ended with the outbreak of war: as things turned out, they were never to be resumed. He never left Ireland and was rarely more than thirty miles from Dublin after 1917. That was not at all in his mind then. 'I always enjoyed my English holidays and my Irish excursions very much and I looked forward to travelling abroad a great deal when the war came to an end.'

If the summers were spent by the sea, much of each winter, before he went to school, was spent on farms. It may seem strange to those who remember his later views on Irish agriculture that he spent months at a time on farms in the north county Dublin and in the Dublin mountains. One of those winters, he recalls, was spent near Tallaght. Attendance at Mass at the Dominican Priory there so impressed his imagination that he decided that he would become a monk when he grew up. 'I do not think,' he adds, 'that this resolve was very firm because it melted away when we left Tallaght, of which I have nothing but pleasant memories. I have never since flirted with a religious vocation'. The reaction cannot be thought to be unexpected. Elsewhere he records that when by himself he played at saying Mass and giving sermons.

Between the seaside and the farms, he was not much at home during his early childhood. Apart from the occupations just noted, he had several of the more usual interests of Edwardian boyhood. It was still the age of steam : the building of express engines for the railways and of Atlantic liners approached its zenith. He accumulated the catalogues of Messrs Basset-Lowke, postcards of the latest engines of the Great Western or the London North-Eastern or of the latest contestants for the Blue Riband of the Atlantic. 'My principal interests lay in railways, ships and travel. I looked forward to seeing many parts of the world. . . . The impression of my early years is of uneventful enjoyment.' The next sentence reads : 'I think that the very happiness of my early years was responsible for some of my misfortunes in later life'.

The autobiographer is entitled to cast backwards and to find in his past the ultimate causes of his present. A biographer runs considerable risks in doing so. Nevertheless a couple of points may be made here, though they will be made again. In all these recollections, there is no mention at all of any companions of his own age. He did not, it seems, experience the normal adjustments which are imposed on even extreme youth by mixing with others. He recalls a couple of rebuffs from elders when he tried to join their children at play in Merrion Square. Very many people must have had the same experience at some time or other and have long since forgotten it. He may have forgotten it at the time but years afterwards he dredged up these memories as a possible cause of his extreme shyness in later years.

In his assessment, the matter went deeper than an incident of personal relationships. He came to feel that when he was young he had been preserved from, or cut off from, the less attractive side of life. He refers to writers, such as Kipling and Saki, whose childhoods were so unhappy that they were affected for the rest of their lives.

They became suspicious and defensive. I, on the contrary, remained singularly innocent of the evil of mankind until much later. I assumed that people generally were as kind and good as my relatives and their servants. . . . I believed that reason would prevail and justice would always be done. I grew up innocent of the evil dispositions of man. My illusions might have been shattered if I had experienced hatred or cruelty or jealousy in my home. I never did, however, encounter these monsters except on the few occasions when I received the injuries, insults or rebuffs which I have described. They may have been, however, small signals of storms to come.

There was one other consequence of spending his early years in an hotel. It may not be readily understood today, but it had an enduring influence throughout his life.

In the closing years of the blessed nineteenth century the line between trade and the professions was much more clearly drawn than it is today. Hotel-keeping was regarded as a comparatively respectable occupation compared, for example, with pawnbroking or owning a pub, but it was unquestionably trade. The gradations of the social hierarchy were so accepted by my own family that I went out into the world under no illusions regarding the disadvantages of being the son of a business man. . . . I was always acutely aware of attitudes of superiority. This was a result of the atmosphere in which I lived during my childhood which was favourable for the development of an inferiority complex. Indeed, I think that my family were unduly sensitive on this point. Actually I never experienced nearly as much inconvenience on that account as I had been led to expect, possibly because I was prepared for the worst and was thankful for small mercies. The removal (to Kingstown) was, of course, a step up in the world. A hotel-keeper whose family lived in a private house was definitely superior to one who lived in his own hotel. The young people of the present generation are blissfully ignorant of those subtleties that loomed so large in my youth.

George rarely allowed himself to forget them before he was well into middle age.

2

At School 1900-10

In September 1900 he was sent to the Catholic University School in Lower Leeson Street. Apart from any other consideration, it was near at hand to the Wicklow Hotel—up Grafton Street, across the Green and fifty yards up Leeson Street, with only two crossings whose perils were then confined to trams and horse-drawn carts and cabs.

We may pause a moment on this scene because it became central to his life and because it has been changed almost beyond the recall of memory. The Green was still largely a residential area. The west side indeed had a number of shops, as George Moore was to note with distaste in *Salve*. There were also several between Grafton Street and Dawson Street. Further along, past the Archbishop's Palace and convenient to the Shelbourne Hotel, the shoe-makers—Stephens and Bourke—lay between the hairdressers—Prosts and Jules. Otherwise, doctors, dentists, barristers and solicitors lived in the houses which nestled between the clubs, convents and churches. The residents were not necessarily fixtures. Eimar O'Duffy, the undutiful son of one of them, recalls that his father lived on the Green 'until the flowing tide of social and pecuniary prosperity carried him further to Merrion Square.' O'Duffy and his companions used the Green as their playground, which was not without some anxiety for their parents because Cuffe Street was far gone into slums and no child was allowed to walk past the hovels of Leeson Lane even in daylight.

Towards the Leeson Street gate were grouped the Loreto convents (the Dominicans had not yet arrived) with their schools and hostels for the girl students attending University College in 86 Stephen's Green. Between them lay St Vincent's Hospital, staffed by graduates of the Catholic University Medical School, the older and more prosperous half-brother of the College.

Down Earlsfort Terrace were the buildings of the Royal University (sometimes an examination hall, sometimes an exhibition hall, as Oliver Gogarty was to remark). They were to be the site of the reconstructed University College from 1917 until the move to Belfield in the later 1960s.

At the corner of Leeson Street lay a cluster of shops. Among them were, inevitably, three public houses (which varied very greatly in respectability), a post office, a newsagent and tobacconist, a fruiterer (for the hospital no doubt) and a chandler's shop with a peculiar musty smell inside and sacks of oats on the pavement outside. Such was the scene as George made his way to school in the last autumn of the nineteenth century. It remained largely unchanged until the seventh decade of the twentieth. It is the scene that thousands will remember as part of their youth. George knew it as schoolboy, student and professor and he was to talk about it with affection in the last week of his life.

The Catholic University School was and is conducted by the Marist Fathers. It had been founded by Cardinal Cullen in 1867 to provide a secondary education for students proceeding to the Catholic University. (It was the lack of a secondary education system which the historians of Newman's rectorship have singled out as his greatest handicap). The University, apart from its Medical School, did not prosper and CUS was deprived of its primary purpose. Nevertheless, the relations between it and University College, especially in the first half of the present century, were exceptionally close. At the turn of the century, it catered for the professional and business (sometimes rather grand words) classes. There was, George notes, 'a complete absence of class consciousness or snobbery among the boys'; an observation which would be echoed by those who followed him to CUS in later years.

It is clear that he enjoyed his four years there. His lack of interest in games did not matter: 'I was not unduly given to the worship of football. . . . My memories of CUS are entirely happy ones. Both masters and boys were kind and friendly.' These remarks may explain why CUS has not, as yet at least, engaged the attention of Irish novelists but, again, they would be endorsed by many of his successors in Leeson Street.

Another of his beliefs is best illustrated by quotation. 'Luckily the Irish language revival had not yet reached the secondary schools, so I was spared the frustration and waste of energy that is the lot of Irish schoolboys today.' The next sentence may cause surprise. 'Our time was much better employed learning Greek.' This branch of study had to be abandoned when he left CUS: it was not taught at Weybridge nor at Belvedere. In general studies, he did not do much of note. He enjoyed his four years in CUS and never afterwards spoke of it without affection and respect. In later life he supported the school union and served as its president. This, as will appear in its place, was not solely out of loyalty but his gratitude to his first school was very real.

In 1904 he was sent, not without protests from the President of CUS, to St George's College, Weybridge. This represented a clean break not only with home life but with the friends he had made in Leeson Street. Some of them no doubt, as has been the custom, went on from there to Irish boarding-schools; others stayed their whole time there; very few indeed went to England for further schooling. On the general issue of sending Irish boys to English schools, he was later to hold that they were at a disadvantage in that they lacked friends of their own age when they returned unless, as happened in his own case, they went afterwards to an Irish school or university. Generally, he was inclined to lay down the proposition that Irish boys were either greatly improved or greatly disimproved by being sent to school in England. For many years this was one of his most effective ploys at a dinner table. It was certain to set off an argument. Equally certainly, the argument quickly passed from the abstract plane to the highly personal. Hot and uncharitable words would pass. Everybody at the table enjoyed themselves hugely. The issue is perhaps less important now than it was when the century was younger.

St George's was founded about 1860 by a Catholic nobleman who was later ordained by Cardinal Newman. Lord Petre believed that the existing Catholic schools in England had too much in common with seminaries. Something like a public school was needed, catering particularly for the sons of the traditional Catholics and of richer Catholics who might eventually enter public life. After his death in 1893 *The Tablet* wrote that, indirectly at least, he had spurred the Catholic schools to train their students better 'particularly in the inculcation of a certain refinement which heretofore had been allowed to stand somewhat at a discount.' By the time that George was sent there the school had passed into the hands of the Josephite Fathers. They taught boys to the age of sixteen.

It is notable, perhaps a bit surprising, that he took to his new life like a duck to water. He was 'very contented and happy' during his four years there. 'Indeed, I do not remember looking forward with any keenness to the holidays or with any regret to their termination'; surely the ultimate accolade that any school can be given, though it may also suggest something about his life at home. He did well in class. Compulsory games were lightly enforced. So he came to spend the summer days acting as umpire, which perhaps says more about his ability in the field than for his knowledge of the Laws of Cricket. He did well in his last years in class and won many prizes. His mother, who came over to one of the prize-givings, was disappointed that he had not won them all. This was to be remembered in later years.

It did not spoil his memory of the place.

I have always been glad that I was sent to Weybridge. It gave me a glimpse of England during the great Edwardian period before everything began to go wrong. I have the happiest recollections of long summer days umpiring cricket matches on our singularly beautiful cricket ground, of boating on the Thames, of swimming in our pool in the woods and of long drives in wagonettes on frosty winter evenings to schools in other parts of the Thames valley.

The tone of the school was, as might be expected, highly conservative in political and social matters, infused by the especially intense patriotism of English Catholicism. For George, this influence was greatly strengthened by a friendship during his last two years there.

I came completely under the domination of my great friend Philip, whom I admired and loved so much that I absorbed all his valuations. He was entirely English in outlook, a strong conservative, an admirer of the upper class, to which he himself belonged and, I am afraid, a snob. I have no doubt that my whole attitude towards life was largely coloured by his friendship.

And so,

I came back from Weybridge in 1908 knowing nothing at all about my own country. The priests, the lay masters, the boys and, above all, Philip, had produced between them a very good specimen of an English Catholic Conservative boy of sixteen.

He had now got as far as Weybridge could take him. What was to be done now? It may have been that, originally, there had been some intention of sending him on to another English school. If that had happened his subsequent life would certainly have been very different. Whatever may have been the reason of the decision to bring him home, it could not have been due to any lack of money. His father was dead, but the hotel was being excellently managed. The family derived a comfortable income from it.

The intention may have been that he should go directly from Weybridge to university in Dublin. Here was the first turning point in his life. Almost certainly, his son recalls, Richard O'Brien would have decided on Trinity. His widow, it seems, had no particular views beyond the feeling, which might have been decisive, that Trinity was the natural place to go to. Matters got so far that George was interviewed by the Junior Dean. (One is reminded of Oliver Gogarty calling, with an equal failure to follow through, on the Registrar of the Medical School in Cecilia Street, a decade before). However, his step-brother believed that political feeling did not favour Trinity and would favour it still less when Home Rule had been achieved. He advised that George should be sent to University College. (The College was then, as it had been since 1883, under Jesuit management, but the bill which established it in its present form was going through Parliament in that summer of 1908).

What followed is straight out of *A Portrait of the Artist*. An introduction to the Dean of Studies, still Father Darlington, was secured; and for the first of how many thousand times George mounted the steps of 86 and passed under the lion above its entrance. Father Darlington, some ten years older than Joyce had described him, had retained the combination of a gushing manner and a kind heart. Everything was settled with the smooth efficiency which Irish novelists of the day ascribed to the Jesuits. George was not to go to Trinity. He was to go to Belvedere for two years and then to University College where he would read law.

There will be something to be said later about the consequences of this choice between the two Dublin universities. Here it may be noted that a third choice existed or, by the standards of our time, might have been thought to exist. George might have taken up where his father had left off, as owner and manager of the Wicklow Hotel. This does not appear to have been considered.

At that time, the prestige of the Jesuits stood at a peak in Ireland. It was still remembered that some of them had ignored episcopal instructions in the 1860s and had given absolution to the Fenians. For a generation they had been in charge of the only institution in the country where young Catholics could obtain something approaching a university education on terms that they were willing to accept. More recently, their schools had been remarkably successful in the public examinations for which all Irish secondary schools, Catholic and Protestant, entered their pupils. This was rubbed in by throw away assertions that success in examinations, however impressive in newspaper advertisements (including their own), was not their primary concern. That was the formation of character according to the historic mission of the Society since its foundation. Their labours were directed towards the preparations of their students for the responsibilities which Home Rule, 'only around the corner' in 1908, would bring. As their day school in the capital city, Belvedere was large and bustling. It had (with great justice) a high opinion of itself.

It was a higher opinion than George was prepared to concede. To begin with, at least, he was not impressed either by his teachers or by his fellow students. His recollections offend against a literary canon by their failure to depict the members of the Jesuit community. Father Conmee was still Provincial and died only a couple of months before George left Belvedere. He glitters through the pages of *Ulysses*. He is central to the first book of Conal O'Riordan's *Adam of Dublin* sequence. Only lately his memory has been refurbished by Conor Cruise O'Brien.

But there is nothing from George on this shining figure, exuding urbanity and dispensing favours, a Haroun al Raschid under the top hat and frock coat which the fashion of the day expected from the Church Triumphant.

Two Jesuits are recalled; both were typical of their time. The first was Father 'Willie' Doyle. His fame then rested on his great gifts as a giver of retreats. It was the golden age of Jesuit retreat-giving. The most famous retreat in modern literature had been given, in Belvedere, only a decade before. Across the Irish Sea, Father Bernard Vaughan thundered against the sins of society: there were many who believed that he had received King Edward VII into the Church on the royal death-bed—though it now seems that the monarch's last visitors did not include the equivalent of a Father Huddleston. At home, Father Robert Kane ministered to the simpler problems of the Irish faithful. Father Doyle went up and down the country and possessed an immense prestige.

This did not impress George. He notes that Father Doyle

since his death, has been talked about as a saint. Several books have been written about him and it is said that efforts will be made to canonize him. He made no particular impression on me. He certainly did not strike a casual acquaintance as being in any way unusual.

This seems very negative but it can be understood. In the first place Father Doyle spread the devotion of making frequent pious ejaculations during every day. This would not have been acceptable to George who thoroughly disliked all ejaculations, pious or profane. Worse still was the fact that one of the books written about Father Doyle was Alfred O'Rahilly, then a Jesuit scholastic. This was no passport to George's good opinion. But something deeper may have been involved. Father Doyle was a powerful preacher who appealed to the emotions. As time went on George was more and more fearful of the force of the emotions, not least his own.

It should be added, if only to illustrate the times, that a few years later Father Doyle volunteered for service in France. He became a chaplain to the Dublin Fusiliers and was killed during the battle of Passchendaele in August 1917. He attracted much love and a deep respect from many kinds of men.

The other member of the community who receives mention
was a very different man—Father John O'Connor. For him the
tone of recollection changes abruptly. He was 'the outstanding
figure among the Jesuits: a great judge of character of boys and
young men and a striking personality whom I found very kind
on occasions when I needed his help'. This was high praise
from one who was always fairly balanced in his assessment even
of those with whom he was on terms of friendship. It is not
surprising therefore that these expressions of praise are followed
by what seems a chilling summary. 'He was a peculiar combination of worldliness and saintliness. I suppose his shrewd worldly
wisdom was harnessed AMDG.' No doubt : the combination was
freely and generously given to generations of young people in
their early perplexities. (*Well to know that, dear. Bravo, dear*).
When he wrote the passage just quoted, it would have been fresh
in George's memory that he had received very useful help from
Bloody Bill of the Nine Fingers (these striking soubriquets should
not go unrecorded) in his first campaign for the Seanad. The help
was all the more generous because, until then at least, George
had never been what might be called a practising Belvederian.
Father O'Connor had a further and even greater claim on his
gratitude, as the founder of the school debating society in which
he was to discover and develop his fluency and proficiency in
public speaking.

We turn from the community to the classroom. He did not
take kindly to the change from an English boarding school to an
Irish day school. To this was added a feeling that he was not
particularly popular. (This, at least, is what he wrote in his
recollections forty years later. It is to be taken with some reserve.
One of the touching things about him was that he never expected
to be liked : he had had all too many experiences of rebuffs). It
can be seen certainly that there were many ways in which he
did not fit in. He came late, a newcomer where friendships had
already been formed through years of shared experience. He was
no good at games, in a school that set great store by them. From
Weybridge he had acquired an English way of looking at things.
Worse still, he had acquired an English accent. These were not
acceptable credentials.

Curiously enough the principal friendship that George made
was with the outstanding person in the school—Arthur Cox. It is

well worth while to go back to old numbers of *The Belvederian* to learn how high was his standing. When he left for University College, he was given a special send-off. He was chaired around the school: a special play-day was given in honour of his academic successes. Admittedly this may have something to do with the fact that he was a son of Dr Michael Cox, a close friend of the deputy leader of the parliamentary party, John Dillon. But one is left feeling that that kind of thing doesn't happen often nowadays.

Both in Belvedere and at College George and Arthur Cox kept in close touch. It is also notable that they tended to avoid possible academic confrontations. All his life George had a great respect for Arthur Cox and was always interested in what he thought about the issues of the day. They were not, one thinks, close friends but they had a high opinion of each other. George was touched when Arthur, writing in the centenary history of the Literary and Historical Society, referred to 'George O'Brien, for whose lifetime friendship I am deeply grateful'.

In later years, George attached great importance to the two years in Belvedere. They were a vital link between the years in England and the years in University College. He had gone to Weybridge already far removed from the assumptions and ways of thought in which his contemporaries were reared. This detachment was increased by Weybridge. Belvedere narrowed, though it did not close, the gap. There he learned, without being so taught by anybody in particular, that he had a country whose interests might be very different from those of Great Britain.

All this may be summed up by one incident. A school friend brought him to the Abbey one night. It was his first visit. 'It was typical of the detachment of my family from nationalist Ireland that they had never been to the Abbey and, if they had been, would certainly have regarded it as a joke'. Richard O'Brien's interests had their limits. The play George saw was that maker of rebels, *Cathleen ni Houlihan*. It did not make him a rebel, then or later. It did make him a nationalist, certainly a highly constitutional nationalist of a type that was soon to be out of date, but a nationalist nevertheless.

Nothing in the nature of revolutionary ideas ever came my way. . . . The main current was parliamentary nationalism derived from O'Connell through Parnell and the Irish party. Social problems, apart from the relief of congestion, occupied no part of our attention. The clamant problem of poverty in the slums by which Belvedere was surrounded aroused no curiosity or indignation. Nor were we interested in the great social experiments that were being made by the Government at that very time. We were Whigs rather than radicals. If Home Rule had been achieved in those years, the Irish Parliament would have been a very conservative and respectable assembly—a Catholic version of Grattan's Parliament. It would have been like a meeting of the Repeal Association held in the Old House in College Green.[1]

He was at Belvedere to prepare himself for University College. The regulations then in force, long since discontinued, enabled him to spend his first year preparing for Matriculation and his second in preparing for First Arts. These were exalted quarters in which the seamier side of Irish education, as portrayed by Conal O'Riordan in *Adam of Dublin*, was unknown. Throughout his later life he was deeply conscious of his debt to the Jesuit system of education.

On the educational side I profited from my new school, especially in English and Latin. I experienced a taste of the great Jesuit literary tradition that had been absent at Weybridge. My principal master was a layman who was a barrister and had been an Army officer. He was a man of the world and, though not a great scholar, he had a wide outlook on scholarship. I have very little recollection of my studies which I performed in a rather perfunctory way. I suppose I must have worked satisfactorily enough as I passed Matriculation and First Arts. I had no ambition to get honours at this stage of my education in spite of my success at Weybridge. It was only when I began to study law that I became a serious student.

1. It was difficult indeed to generalise about political feeling at that time or later. *The Belvederian* for 1915–16 chronicled the death of two former students in Easter Week—Joseph Plunkett, executed after court martial as a signatory of the Proclamation of the Republic, and Reginald Clery, who was a member of the Dublin Veterans' Corps (better known as the Gorgeous Wrecks) who were ambushed in Haddington Road. The same issue contained a list of Belvederians at the war which covered six pages. At that time many Irish school magazines would have shown much the same picture.

There was one other part of the years at Belvedere which he felt deeply enough to recall.

I think I matured considerably. I experienced something in the nature of a conversion on the spiritual side of my life. In my last years at Weybridge I had become very lax and slack in my religious duties. I observed all the outward signs of devotion but was inwardly very arid and cold. My passionate friendship with Philip distracted my mind from everything else. It was really a relationship that contained a good deal of paganism.

The return home brought a change of mood. 'During my time in Belvedere there was a retreat which brought me back to repentance and good behaviour'. The reader may feel that there was something special about retreats in Belvedere; but the results were impermanent. 'I soon drifted into careless ways again. I was appointed junior prefect of one of the sodalities and gave the impression of being as sincere as any of the other boys, but, in fact, I became very lax'. Whatever about retreats, it seems that sodalities in Belvedere were much the same as they were everywhere else.

This is the first occasion on which he mentions his attitude to religious beliefs and practice. There will be more to be said later. He did not, he says, derive any guidance from Belvedere 'where very little religious instruction was given except to the younger boys'. The reason was not the absence but rather the pervasiveness of belief.

The apparent lack of emphasis on dogmatic instruction really reflected the depth of underlying assumptions that were never questioned. . . . Certainly, nothing happened in Belvedere to weaken or interrupt the Catholic influences which had moulded me in my home and in my previous schools. If I was lax it was in practice, not in faith; and my laxity was entirely my own fault. In the sphere of religion, my youth passed without controversy or conflict.

In later life he had no doubt about the greatest gift he received from Belvedere. In his first year there, the Debating Society was established by Father O'Connor. The first auditor was, almost inevitably, Arthur Cox. The committee was composed of George, E. T. Freeman, Andrew Horne and Noel Purcell.

It met on Friday evenings and I do not think I missed a single meeting for the two years I was in the school. It was here that I first learned to speak in public without stagefright or embarrassment, and it was in preparing my speeches that I began to learn something about current Irish politics, on which I had been hitherto entirely ignorant.

In his second year, 1909–10, he was elected auditor and read his address on *The Repeal and Home Rule Movements in the Nineteenth Century*. This suggests some quickness in mastering his subject. It also suggests a good sense of timing. The first general election of 1910, in January, had ended in the Irish party holding, so far as a count of heads could do so, the balance of power. All things considered, a history of Home Rule suited the time. It also suited the platform—John Dillon, MP, Vice-Chairman of the Irish Party, Tom Kettle, one of its most brilliant younger supporters and Dudley White, junior counsel to the Attorney-General and, at that moment, fresh from his triumph in the once celebrated case of *Cooke v The Midland Great Western Railway*. For all three the future then shone, deceptively.

In the most immediate sense, it did not suit the time at all. The meeting was fixed for May 10th. Four days before, King Edward died unexpectedly.

I imagine that the Jesuits must have been perplexed what to do : whether to annoy their nationalist friends by putting off the meeting or their loyalist ones by proceeding with it.

Readers will remember that the same dilemma faced the Abbey Theatre that week. Like the Abbey, the Jesuits went ahead.

I got through the evening without feeling the slightest pang of anxiety or stagefright. My poor mother, who was in the audience, suffered an agony of nervous tension. She need not have done so, because the thought of breakdown or failure never entered my head. Indeed I must have appeared 'cocky' to the audience with my self-assurance and my English accent.

The English accent soon faded : all too soon he was to lose the self-assurance. There were two things that he learned once and for all from the Belvedere debating society. One was a fluency and clarity which was never to desert him through years of speaking and debating. The other was less happy. In his first year, he had in some way fallen foul of the mood of the debating society and had sat down in silence at a debate in which the other speakers had been loudly applauded. The reason is not given in his recollections; and, whatever it was, it did not prevent his election as auditor. But it was one of a number of little things which were stored up and were to be remembered in less happy days.

> This bitter experience possibly had the result of making me a little bit suspicious of people generally. I have never ceased to expect a hostile attitude; and that very expectation may have bred a defence mechanism which reinforced a natural shyness.

Experiences five years in the future made his memory only too retentive of slights, important or otherwise.

At the time, the incident should have been overlain by the triumph of his address. He had gone to Belvedere to prepare himself for a university career. He had done so most successfully. The future must have seemed secure and fair when he entered University College in the autumn of 1910.

B

3

University College
and the King's Inns 1910-13

AT that time, University College was in the throes of one of
the many transformations which have marked its history. For
decades, the Catholic bishops had opposed the attendance of
Catholic students at Trinity College. They had, with varying
degrees of enthusiasm, established the Catholic University which,
with Newman as Rector, opened its doors in 1854. The University
did not possess and never obtained the power to award degrees.
Its faculties of Arts and Science were not successful. On the
other hand, the Medical School in Cecilia Street prepared its
students for recognised examinations conducted by bodies such
as the Royal College of Surgeons. It grew and prospered when
the other branches of the University, in 86 St Stephen's Green,
were almost dormant.

In 1879 the University Education (Ireland) Act established
the Royal University. This institution was solely an examining
and degree-giving body. Its object was to provide a means
whereby Catholic students might obtain degrees. In response
to this measure the Arts and Science faculties were re-organised
as University College Dublin. In 1883 the bishops entrusted the
management and direction of the College to the Jesuits.

In 1908 the Irish Universities Act established University
College as a constituent college of a new National University
of Ireland with a full range of faculties. The Medical School,
which by then enjoyed considerable prestige, was joined with
it. It was expressly laid down that the new University and the
new College should have no religious affiliations though, as a
matter of course, it was then taken that the atmosphere would
be as Catholic as that of the Queen's University of Belfast, set
up at the same time and on the same conditions, would be
Presbyterian.

What was certain in 1908 was that the Jesuit control of the College had been ended. What seemed equally certain was that control had passed to the parliamentary party which had procured the passage of the Act. This was to be belied very soon, by events which could not then have been foreseen. But the belief did not help the new College. The transfer, as it seemed, of control over the higher education of Catholics from the Society of Jesus to the Irish Party did not inspire confidence or respect. A clear majority of the people might well be enthusiastic for Home Rule; but they reserved the right to have their own opinion of some of the members of the Home Rule party.

These matters would have been above the head of any student crossing the Green to 86 in the autumn of 1910. There was one difference between George and most of his fellows. Most of them would not have gone to Trinity anyway. George might well have done so; and from many points of view there was a great deal to be said for going to College Green. Just then, Trinity was passing through one of the greatest periods of its distinguished history. A university that could point to Mahaffy and Tyrrell, Purser and Joly, to name only some, need fear no comparison anywhere in the world. The splendour of its Tercentenary celebrations in the summer of 1892 was still fresh in memory. A Catholic young man, even if he had no place in the social and political order for which Trinity then stood, might well believe that his career would be more assured if it were commenced in such glittering company. He might not aspire to the *cursus honorum* of his fellow-students, the parliamentary representation of the University and the Lord Chancellorship of Ireland, or at the very least, a seat on the Bench. But he could do very well for himself. Many Catholic, many Jesuit, schoolmasters thought so then and much later; and, turning a deaf ear to the warnings of the Bishops, agreed with parents who felt that their children's future would be better assured in College Green than in St Stephen's Green.

George summarized his own opinion some forty years later.

I have already expressed the view that I would have been more at home in Trinity College. In spite of that, I am always glad that I did not go there. In the long run and at the deeper level I have gained far more from University College than I would have gained from Trinity. I would have fallen in too readily with the prevailing assumptions and would, possibly, have developed an anti-Irish and perhaps even an anti-Catholic bias. My slight degree of independence may have added to the benefits which I derived from my association with University College.

One may reflect on the antipathies which lay close to the surface of Irish life in those days. No doubt, the religious issue was by then more a legacy from the past than a continuing element. The political issue was much more acute. Very naturally, in those days Trinity was regarded and regarded itself as a bastion of English rule in Ireland. As an institution, whatever about the opinions of individual members of its staff and graduate body, it held itself aloof from the currents of nationalist thought which began to flow at the end of the nineteenth century. Readers of *Ave* will recall the speech of Yeats in which he attacked its indifference to the literary revival. The enthusiasm with which it greeted the British victory in South Africa was remembered by a much wider audience. All this happened a long time ago and it would not be worth recalling today except to remind the reader that in the second decade of the century a choice between Trinity and University College involved a great deal more than a choice between one university and another.

The choice had been made for George. He was now to meet hopes and prejudices, loyalties and hatreds, which were new to him. Belvedere had done something to instruct him on the tensions and issues of life in Ireland. The experience was now to be continued on a larger scale. Nowadays, when the proportion of people living in Dublin and its environs has greatly increased relatively to the rest of the population, the College is about evenly divided between students from the Dublin area and the rest of the country. In 1910 about two-thirds of the student body came from the country. The variety of origin brought an even greater variety of character.

In those first sixteen years of the century as it moved out from Royal to National, it had received, suffered and in a sense nurtured many Irishmen of remarkable quality—men who were to be dangerous or saintly or brilliant or fanatical;

intellectuals, talkers, soldiers, novelists, patriots, priests; all dyed-in-the-wool Irish, Christian brother-trained or Jesuit-trained—egoists all, eccentrics many, gifted and wilful men, and one of them certainly—and he the least useful and the proudest—a genius.[1]

So wrote Kate O'Brien of the College to which she came in 1916. It seems as good a picture as can be found of that out-pouring of hopes and fears to which the older university had been for so long a stranger.

Another novelist, more exactly contemporary with George, put the matter in another way.

It's something new in universities—no traditions about it at all. Trinity's just a second-rate Oxford. Quite as musty and not half as magnificent. You'd only stifle there. It's a mere Rathmines university, if you know what I mean. The National's new. It might be a bit shoddy, but we might make something of it.[2]

Kate O'Brien was concerned with what she thought the College was; O'Duffy with what he thought Trinity was not. They are not to be taken as objective observers. But O'Duffy captures the growing impatience with the pretensions of a regime in Ireland which was losing the capacity or even, as it seemed, the will to rule. The students of contemporary St Petersburg can hardly have had a stronger sense of the need of change, of *res novae*, than those of Dublin in the last faltering days of the Castle.

Nothing in George's life so far had prepared him for these ways of thought or feeling. It increased his sense, already too acute, of isolation.

Although I was in the very thick of student activities, I was, to some extent, an outsider. There was an influential circle in the College whose members, I felt, disliked me. They had all come from homes where there was a tradition of national-ism. They had absorbed ideas as children which I had only begun to learn when I went to Belvedere. They had all been to Irish schools where nationalism was part of the air they

1. *My Ireland*, Batsford, 1962, p. 112.
2. Eimar O'Duffy, *The Wasted Island*, Martin Lester, n.d. p. 111.

breathed. My background was different. In my home, Irish politics did not exist; and, in Weybridge, nationalism was regarded as vulgar, nearly as 'caddish' as Lloyd George. Although I have no doubt that I had become a sincere nationalist, and that I looked forward to the coming of Home Rule with the same certainty and the same hopes as my fellow students, my outlook on many things was different from theirs. I was like the convert to Catholicism, who is never really regarded by the Catholics who have been brought up in the Church, as quite the same as themselves. In some indefinable way I did not 'belong'. My nationalism was an intellectual conviction, not an emotional attitude. It was constructed on alien foundations. It did not go to the roots of my being. . . .

I had none of the hatred and distrust of Protestants which was felt by some of the other students, especially those from Ulster of whom we had quite a number. I met so many Protestants with my family that I could scarcely regard them as enemies or persecutors. Nor did I dislike the landed gentry for their iniquitous behaviour in the past. None of my immediate relations had been agricultural tenants and I was unaware of the bitterness engendered by the Land War. There were no tales of evictions in my family legends. Far from disliking the gentry I admired them at a distance for their style and elegance. My ideals in architecture and art were all based upon my admiration for the classical models of the eighteenth century which I associated in my mind with the landed aristocracy. Georgian Dublin was my spiritual home. . . . It was no accident that the student whom I got to know best and with whom I spent a good deal of time and took long walks with was Ambrose Davoren. Although Ambrose came from a higher social level than I did, his outlook was the same as mine. His background was one of a large house, a good deal of money and good society. Instinctively we came together and got to know each other very well. I was told on one occasion by another student, who regarded the information in much the same light as he would have regarded the news that some of his friends had horns or a tail, that Ambrose was a Unionist. I do not know whether he was or not because we never discussed politics, but I certainly did not care. That indifference probably explains the reason for my unpopularity which, while it was not actively displayed, certainly existed. I would probably have made more friends if so many Catholics who had been to English schools had not gone to Trinity College. These students would have shared my outlook and valuations to a greater degree than my actual fellow students.

These passages speak for themselves. It seems right to turn aside for a moment to write of Ambrose Davoren. He was to go on to be called to the Bar and to be one of those who volunteered when the war broke out. His contemporaries loved him. To Maurice Healy, he 'might well have been christened the Chatterton of the law. He cannot have been much more than twenty-three when he died, but he was the close friend of the old Lord Chief Baron, who talked to him as an equal. He treated law as Yehudi Menuhin treats his violin; he compelled it'. To Arthur Cox, he was 'a classical scholar in the best sense, not pedantic but almost reliving the clear light of the ancient Greece he loved.' Like so many of his generation in Ireland he was fated to be killed, at 'Plugstreet Wood' in July 1917 in the European civil war. It would have been more fitting if he had fallen, like so many others from Dublin, in the bright air of the Dardanelles and in sight of Troy than in the mud of Passchendaele.

To return to George, the reasons for antipathy may have been as he describes. There may very well have been an element of shyness on both sides. There may have been something else, to which Eimar O'Duffy made allusion, which was common enough in the College and in the country for years to come. Writing of an advanced nationalist in the College of his time, which was much the same as George's, O'Duffy notes how he regarded some students as

> . . . traitors to Ireland, a category in which he also placed everyone who had ever been in England, everyone who admired English literature, everyone who spoke English without a pronounced Irish accent, everyone who parted their hair or brushed their clothes. . . .[1]

George's sole objective was to be called to the Bar after the

---

1. *The Wasted Island*, p. 259.

prescribed course of lectures and dinners at the King's Inns. No thought had been given to what degree should be taken in College. This led to a degree of blundering which would be irretrievable nowadays. No one had advised him what would be the best course to follow. No one had told him even the difference between an honours degree and a pass degree. He started by entering for a pass degree and switched only when he learned that his colleagues at Belvedere had opted for one or other of the honours groups. In those simpler days it was possible to be so casual about these matters.

Having discovered that there was a difference between honours and pass he decided to enlist for the honours group X, in Legal and Political Science, which 'appeared to be the most nearly relevant to my legal studies. This was one of the most momentous decisions of my life. The legal subjects in the group specially appealed to my taste and talent'. The Legal and Political group was a bit of a misnomer at that time. Denis O'Keefe had not yet come to College to make his course in Politics one of the outstanding experiences of undergraduate life. The first of the two-years course in the group was composed of History (in which John Marcus O'Sullivan was professor) or Logic (Fr Shine) or Ethics (Fr Cronin), Political Economy (Fr Finlay) and the National Economics of Ireland (Tom Kettle) and (one records without comment) a course in Latin. The second year was made up of a continuation of the two economics subjects with courses in Jurisprudence and International Law (James Murnaghan), Roman Law (also James Murnaghan), Constitutional History, Constitutional Law and the Law of Evidence (Swift MacNeill), and the Law of Property and the Law of Contract (Arthur Clery).

At his degree examination in September 1912 he came first in the group. With an overall eighty-three per cent, he was comfortably ahead of James Meagher who was the only other first honour. Prizes were awarded to the first honours with the best performance in any group. He tied for one with Arthur Cox. The prize was not remarkable, being eighteen pounds, but one feels that that particular *ex aequo* gave him a special pleasure. (Another prize winner that autumn was Patrick Hogan).

The overall mark may seem high by the standards of the present day. In more ways than one, it will repay breaking down.

He got ninety-seven per cent in Property and Contract. That, of course, was Arthur Clery's marking which was always in a class of its own. He got eighty-eight per cent in Roman Law and eighty-four per cent in Jurisprudence and International Law from James Murnaghan, who, in marking scripts at least, was not renowned for generosity. The other subjects yielded marks which would be thought good today but were well below the height of those mentioned—seventy-four per cent in Political Economy and National Economics from Finlay and Kettle, and another seventy-four in Constitutional Law from Swift MacNeill. It may seem odd that his lowest marks, if over seventy per cent can be called 'low', were in the subjects of which he was later to become professor. But he was not then interested in economics.

For that reason he did not contemplate a Masters degree. His eye was not on the King's Inns. He did enter on the course leading to the LL.B., and sat First Law in June 1911. He was first in a small group which included Henry Molony, the future senior counsel. So well he might have been because his over-all mark was ninety-five per cent. He entered for the degree examination in June 1913 but did not sit, presumably being more concerned with the Senior Victoria and the Brooke. It would have been an interesting contest if he had; the other contestants were Arthur Cox (who, of course, came first), John A. Costello and Ambrose Davoren.

His professors 'were a rather distinguished lot of men'. James Murnaghan was to be one of the first judicial appointments under the Free State and sat in the Supreme Court for many years. Swift MacNeill was much senior to the others, being old enough to remember the troops leaving Dublin for the Crimean war. He sat as MP for South Donegal from 1887 to the collapse of the parliamentary party in 1918. In the House of Commons, where he was known as 'Pongo', his principal interest was the abolition of the birching of young ratings in the Royal Navy. What was more to the point, he had a reputation as an expert in parliamentary procedure, as indeed any member of the party needed to be. At this time, in 1910, he was tipped as first Speaker of the restored Irish House of Commons.

Of the other professors, Father Finlay will appear so frequently in later pages that little need be said here. At this time he was already over sixty, with a long lifetime of work to his name, par-

B*

ticularly as Horace Plunkett's most important supporter in the co-operative movement but also as an intermediary in almost every conceivable branch of social importance. He was to have a decisive influence on George's career. There remain, contemporaries of each other and just over thirty at this time, Arthur Clery and Tom Kettle.

Of Clery, whom he did not like in later years, George wrote :

> Clery was a bachelor who liked the society of young men. He used to invite us to very pleasant dinner parties where we met some of his own generation. He was kind to us and I appreciated his friendship at the time. I learned later that he was very bigoted against the British and against protestants and a great extremist in politics, although he took no active part in revolutionary movements. I am afraid he influenced some young men in the direction of his own views and that he sowed the seeds of a good deal of bitterness.

There was more to it than that, if an intrusion may be permitted. Most certainly Clery was a complicated person. In youth he behaved himself as a man of fashion; a couple of years before George met him he espoused the practices and ideals of the more extreme Gaelic Leaguers. To the end of his life in 1932, he was kind and encouraging to generations of students : for many of them, he practically was the College. Certainly he became cynical as he grew older : the acceptance of the Treaty was a heavy blow; Mr de Valera's entry into the Dáil even heavier. Some cynicism spilled over into his talks with students. But that is very little to put against so much.

What, almost certainly, was in George's mind when he wrote the words quoted, was that Clery's favourite pupil was John Costello and, for some reason which lies buried in the politics of the Literary and Historical Society (the college debating forum), George was never at his ease with John Costello. It is particularly true of that generation of students that their relations with each other in College had consequences in later life.

> Tom Kettle did not pretend to be a profound student of economic theory. He was a politician and a man of affairs with a first-hand knowledge of current Irish economic problems. In this respect he resembled Father Finlay. He had been

a member of Parliament and a successful journalist. His class was so small that his lectures were really conversations in which he did not hesitate to express opinions on many subjects far outside the field of economics. On fine afternoons in May, he and his students used to go to Stephen's Green where he would lecture in the open air, near where his bust now stands. . . . Kettle was 'a professor of things in general' from whom I learned a great deal about history and literature.

This was to be one of the most frequent reminiscences of his time in College. It was sometimes so expressed as to imply that everybody else in that small group had gone to the War and had been killed. This was an exaggeration : more to the point was that at this stage in his life Kettle was unhappy and disappointed. He had rather fallen into drink, and his appearances in the chair of the L. & H. of which he had been an outstanding auditor only a decade before were sometimes embarrassing. In a couple of years he was to go to the war, believing that Ireland, now promised Home Rule, had a duty to succour small nations such as Belgium. What he would have done, or wished to do, had he returned was a theme for his contemporaries for decades after he was killed in 1916 in the last stages of the battle of the Somme. They all, with one possible exception, adored him and revered the memory of his better days. Fifty years after his death, when the Somme had long passed out of memory, the survivors organised a memorial Mass for the repose of his soul. He must have been a deeply attractive man.

This opinion, it seems, was not wholly shared by Arthur Clery who had been his contemporary at Clongowes and in the College. 'They got on each other's nerves', wrote William Dawson, who was one of their group in the L. & H. He added a sentence which may sum up the matter. 'Perhaps Clery had the higher regard for his friend's ability and Kettle had a greater affection for his friend'.[1]

Kettle and Clery, George records, were the only professors who took much notice of their students. 'Our other professors influenced us only through their lectures. There was nothing of that intercourse between them and us that would have constituted the education by conversation that is such a valuable feature of

1. Arthur Clery; *Studies,* March 1933.

a complete university'. The only instance of conversation with Father Finlay was when he asked what he should read for his degree examination. The answer might have been expected. 'He told me to read J. S. Mill. This was the only piece of personal advice I ever received for my economics examination. It constituted the sum total of my tuition'.

Whatever the deficiencies of professional tuition may have been, the students 'made up for the lack by a good deal of mutual education of one another'. It was the more easy to do this because the College, and its classes, were so very small. In 1911–1912 the combined faculties of Arts, Science, Law and Commerce (all housed in 86) totalled fewer than five hundred. In September 1912, nine students sat for the honours degree in Political Economy; two in the Economics group and seven in Legal and Political. (There were no general students and, as yet, no candidates in Commerce). Moreover, many of this small band were people of quite exceptional distinction.

> I need mention only Tom Bodkin, Maurice Healy, Patrick McGilligan, Arthur Cox, Kevin O'Higgins, Patrick Hogan, John Costello, Denis and Aubrey Gwynn and Cecil Lavery to indicate the quality of the student body.

(He might have added Conor Maguire, Cahir Davitt, Jim Magennis, Edward Freeman and Ginger O'Connell).

> We were few enough to get to know each other very well, even if some of us did not like each other very much. Indeed, some of the developments in the political history of Ireland in the years since the Treaty grew out of the affinities and dislikes of my contemporaries. Old alliances and old quarrels re-appeared in the wider field of public life. . . . In spite of a certain amount of coolness between some of us, we had known each other so long that we developed a kind of free-masonry, uniting us against strangers. . . . We had the common tie of the same youthful memories and the same academic loyalties. We were a band of brothers, even if the family was rather disunited.

Their meeting places (he recalls) were the steps of the National Library and the Café Cairo (in Grafton Street, where Scholl's now stands). The Library could still accommodate students : its steps were, as they had been in Joyce's day, the place to discuss everything in general. For a couple of decades after this, the steps were still used on sunny afternoons: for many into the middle of the century, they are the best remembered part of student life. The Café Cairo was rather for people such as Denis Gwynn and Eimar O'Duffy who brought out *The National Student* and, a little later, Michael Tierney and Ginger O'Connell.

The centre of activity, however, was the Literary and Historical Society. Perhaps it was not quite the society that it had been at the turn of the century, when it counted Joyce and Kettle, Clery and Con Curran and Hugh Kennedy among its members. But the later years of the first decade of the new century and the early years of the second formed, at the least, a barely subsidiary peak. The College was still small enough for it to be a genuinely debating society.

> Its members did not practice debating for its own sake. We all took it for granted that, if Home Rule was achieved, we would be among the politicians of the new Ireland. A Home Rule Parliament in College Green in those days would, no doubt, have been dominated by the Irish Party, which would have earned the credit for its establishment. . . . We, in the College, had many connections with the Irish Party. . . . We all confidently expected that in a short time we would be exercising our oratory, not in the dingy precincts of the old Physics Theatre in 86, but in the 'Old House in College Green'. It was because of this hope that we took our debates so seriously. We had heard that future prime ministers were picked out because of their performances at the Oxford Union, and we believed that, when the chair at 'the L. & H.' was taken by distinguished visitors, such as John Dillon, some future Irish prime minister might attract influential attention if his oratory aroused sufficient admiration. Debating took such a large part of our energies that I remember Arthur Cox saying to me that there were only three positions for which we were being fitted by our education—prime minister, leader of the opposition and Speaker of the House of Commons.

There was to be a Dail, not a House of Commons. Its achievement was to be effected by means that could not have been foreseen in 1911. It has rarely set great store by oratory or debating. But the members of the L. & H. were right in essentials.

In normal times there is a very gradual and indeterminate transition from the lower to the higher ranks of professional and political life. But when a revolution succeeds, a new generation suddenly takes the place of the old. In Ireland the Treaty produced such a revolution. . . . The result was that the youth of my generation grew up to a situation where openings were unusually wide and opportunities unusually common. The part played by my generation in the College in the New Ireland is shown by a debate that took place in 1913 between the Literary and Historical Society and the Law Students' Debating Society. The L. & H. was represented by Arthur Cox, John Costello, Conor Maguire and me. All of us had, I suppose I can say without vanity, distinguished careers. Our little team included a future prime minister, a future chief justice, a future president of the Incorporated Law Society and a future senator. The four of us were present at a dinner given by the L. & H. in 1951. My feelings on that occasion were composed of a mixture of pride in my contemporaries, of consciousness of approaching old age and of awareness of the loyalty and continuous tradition of the College graduates.

These were years in which voting power counted in every May, however important oratory may have been for the rest of the year. He proposed Arthur Cox for the auditorship in 1912. This was an indication of his standing, but the majority (until then unprecedented in the number of votes cast on each side) by which Cox defeated John Costello was more probably due to the exertions and blandishments of the candidate than of his proposer.

It must be said that George did not shine in this particular context. The year before, in 1911, the election had been fought between Paddy McGilligan and John Ronayne with such ferocity that the Solicitor-General was brought in to adjudicate on the votes. The decision turned on his ruling about some spoiled votes. There has always been a strong tradition that one of those spoiled votes was George's and (far worse) that he had spoiled his vote through stupidity rather than perfidy.

If anybody had ventured to predict that one of the parties to this (1912) contest would have become prime minister of an Irish Republic his prophecy would have been received with some scepticism. If a hearer had chosen to believe that the prophecy would come true and had been asked to say which of the candidates was destined for this distinction, he would have unhesitatingly chosen Cox. I do not think that anybody would have chosen Costello, who matured late and whose elevation was the result of unforeseen political circumstances.

George's highest, indeed his only, office in the Society was that of Correspondence Secretary under Arthur Cox. In the same year he won the Silver Medal for Oratory. The Gold was won by M. J. Ryan. To anybody who ever heard the two men speak, this will appear a remarkable result.

His true stronghold was the Legal and Economic Society which was founded by him and Arthur Cox. It was a small society, largely composed of the members of the Legal and Political and the Political honours groups. It discussed papers; it held serious debates. It was 'by comparison with the L. & H., highbrow. It aimed at the serious discussion of serious subjects and everybody spoke as well as he possibly could'. The distinction between the two societies is very clear. George was its auditor in 1913–1914. He was succeeded by Cecil Lavery, which is a fair indication of the high standing of the society. Unfortunately it perished in the political excitements of succeeding years and was not revived when calmer times returned. It was always a great grief to George that its minute-book disappeared in the wreck.

And so, in the autumn of 1912, he took his degree and turned from the College, for ever as he then expected, to complete his studies for the Bar.

He became a student of the King's Inns in the autumn of 1910. *The Irish Law Times* noted the admission of 'George A. T. O'Brien, third son of Richard O'Brien, late of 8 Marine Terrace, Kingstown'. His certificate was signed by Daniel O'Brien.

The King's Inns was, in some ways, a more congenial atmosphere than the College. The buildings dated back to the eighteenth century and had that air of aristocratic dignity which appealed to me so strongly. The ceremonial procedure at dinner, the elaborate uniforms of the servants, the procession of the Benchers, the gallery of portraits of judges in the dining hall—all these things satisfied some sense of order and security.

There was also the experience of meeting new people and encountering different ways of thought. Many of the students at the Inns came from Trinity and, of them, several came from the north of Ireland. George was too much of a Dubliner to be much interested in anybody who came from the northern side of the estuary at Malahide; but dinners at the Inns had a solvent effect.

Those years were the time when the Home Rule struggle was at its most intensive phase. Feeling between nationalists and unionists was very bad, and the country was heading for civil war, led by the bad example of arming in Ulster. But I cannot recollect any disturbance of the friendly relations between the students in King's Inns, whose families must have been on opposite sides of the great political controversy. The atmosphere was much more congenial than that of the College to my somewhat tepid nationalism.

The Inns widened the circle of his acquaintances. His closest friend in the Inns was Charles Bewley.

Bewley was the son of a prominent Dublin doctor of the Quaker community. He had been at Winchester and Oxford, where he won the Newdigate and became a Catholic. When he returned to Dublin to read for the Bar he elected to do his lectures in University College instead of Trinity College, where one would have expected him to go on account of his family connections. This choice was, I think, a symptom of the 'cussedness' that made him, at times, difficult to his friends. He was a very brilliant and accomplished young man, but his talents were not forensic and he never really shone as a law student or as a barrister. One morning, after a lecture in College, he came up and spoke to me. I suppose I appeared less alien to him than the other students. After that we became great friends and our friendship lasted for many years.

The passage may be thought to tell nearly as much about its author as about its subject. The closing words, as will later appear, are very definitely words of limitation.

His approach to the law course at the Inns was very different from his detached attitude to Political Economy in College. 'I worked very hard for these examinations. For two summers, 1912 when I was working for the degree and 1913 when I was working for the Brooke, I had practically no holiday and very little outing or exercise'. The result justified the strain, in so far, that is, as it could be justified by results. He won the Junior Victoria in 1912 and the Senior Victoria and Brooke in 1913. The hat-trick had been achieved only once before. Perhaps, even then, the winning of the Brooke was not taken to be any guarantee of a successful career at the Bar. It is plain that George did not see things in that light. The Brooke and the Victoria prizes were, like the degree, fences that had to be cleared ahead of everybody else. He did not count the cost to himself.

In later years he came to believe that the strain of work for these examinations had little or nothing to do with the break-down which was only two years in the future. 'The cause operating through my student years that may have helped to lead to that disaster was not my over-work but the intense worry that I would not get first place. My principal opponent for the Brooke (Bewley, who came second) lived in Merrion Square. I used to walk around the Square to see if the light was burning in his study at night'. Much later he discovered that the light he had taken to be in a study was in fact a stairway light which was kept burning all night. 'All through life I have been worried by equally groundless causes'.

Some readers may reflect that the true point was not whether the worry was groundless or not but rather that he should have felt any sense of worry at all. Plenty of people have got on very well in the world without getting honours or first places in examinations. In older universities, in healthier societies, the importance of examinations would have been minimised by a sense of assurance and belonging. But that was the trouble. He did not feel that he belonged anywhere: he was always insecure.

There was another aspect of the matter which must be mentioned here. In his account of the years at Belvedere and College, there is little or no reference to his mother. His life had been busy and self-absorbing. Now, in recalling this period of pressure, a sense of resentment appears. He came to feel that his mother should have realised what was happening and insisted on some relaxation of strain. But,

> my poor mother displayed the same thoughtlessness that I suspect she had displayed towards my father in earlier summers. She did not seem to realize the need of relaxation and comfort. She was intensely ambitious for my success. She had tasted blood and it was hard to satisfy her appetite for reflected glory.

On the same page of his typescript he records that, around this time, his mother sold the house in Marine Terrace and moved to 40 Northumberland Road. (In those days barristers usually lived within the canals, presumably so that they could use the services of the Legal Express, an agreeable horse-drawn van which brought their bags from their homes to the Four Courts every morning and returned them in the evenings). Moving house in middle age is rarely pleasant : it is even less so when the move is in the wrong direction. No social comparison between Marine Terrace and Northumberland Road is intended, though there may have been some sacrifice of amenity. What was certainly sacrificed to her son's career was the circle of friends that she had acquired in Kingstown, and (it would seem) did not replace during the thirty years of life that was left to her. On this, the comment runs :

> She made these sacrifices for my sake. I think it pained her a great deal. She was always prepared to make sacrifices for me, but was not prepared to indulge me in small ways. She allowed me to work very hard, without any rest or change, during those long summers.

There was no such alloy in the gold of the other great success of his time in the Inns. He at once joined the Law Students' Debating Society. It met on two evenings each week, one being devoted to legal debate and the other to general subjects. In 1911–12 he won the silver medal for general debate and was elected Correspondence Secretary. In the next year he won the gold medal for general debate and the medal for impromptu speaking. He is recorded, perhaps unexpectedly, as speaking in favour of the admission of women to the legal professions. He was a member of the committee for 1913–14 but did not stand for the auditorship on the ground, he says, that he was engaged in his work for the Brooke.

If the promise of success could be judged by academic performance and debating skill, the years at the Inns were as triumphant as they appear to be happy. Reviewing them forty years later, he wrote :

> Everything pointed to my having an outstandingly successful career. Superficially, to the casual observer around the Four Courts in 1914, no young barrister looked more likely to succeed than I did. I had won all the prizes in King's Inns and had played a prominent part in the Law Students' Debating Society where I had won several medals. I was a fluent public speaker with no trace of stage-fright or nervousness. I had no influential firms of solicitors backing me, but I had a few solicitor friends and was in the way of gaining more by the numerous introductions I received from D. J. O'Brien and my friends on the Leinster Circuit. I had a small independent income, enough to enable me to afford to tide over the difficult early years when a young barrister's fees are small and not too numerous. Yet the casual observer would have been wrong.

4

The Bar 1913-16

HE was called to the Bar by Ignatius O'Brien, then Lord Chancellor, on November 1st 1913. The day of one's call is usually a day to be remembered, perhaps a little hazily, as a milestone in one's life. In his case, memory was only too sharp.

It was typical of the curious lack of knowledge of the airs and graces of life that distinguished my family that not one of them thought of having a little party to celebrate the event. This was not due to lack of kindness or good-will. It reflected indifference to any sense of the importance of the occasion.

As he felt that something should be done about it, he brought his mother to a quiet dinner in the Metropole restaurant. 'My principal memory of the day is that of a splitting headache which may have been prophetic of what fate had in store for me'. All too many of the milestones in George's life were painted black.

It is hardly necessary to repeat that in pre-war Ireland the path of advancement lay almost completely through the three traditional professions—the Church, Medicine and Law. One could, of course, go into the Indian civil service or the colonial service. Irish Catholic schools prepared their students for both of them with great success, as any school annual up to, though not after, 1918 will show. If, however, one wished to stay in Ireland, business was a closed and small circle and land was tightly held. By any standard the professions were the most attractive careers. They were well remunerated, they possessed (in Dublin if not in Belfast) a higher social standing than trade or manufacturing. Above all, Catholics might hope, given some luck, for advancement in them. In George's case the obvious choice was Law, where the handicaps of religion counted for less than elsewhere.

In 1913 the Irish Bar seemed to have reached a plateau of prosperity. The price cycle had turned upwards, and farmers benefited not only from favourable prices which were to go still higher during the war but from the improvements in production and marketing which had been introduced, through the co-operative movement, by two people with whom George was to have a great deal to do—Horace Plunkett and Father Finlay. Added to all this was the effect of Wyndham's Land Purchase Act of 1903, perhaps the greatest victory gained by Ireland over the British Treasury throughout the entire period of the Act of Union. Its generous advances in cash seeped through the country, raising (to borrow a later phrase) all boats on its swelling tide. By all this the Bar gained doubly. Landlords had been bribed so lavishly to sell out that titles had to be refurbished and marriage settlements, long buried under masses of mortgages, regained their credibility. The tenant-purchasers began to ascertain and delimit their rights against each other and against members of their own families. The higher Courts were fully occupied with questions arising out of the grafting of roots of title; the lower Courts with the proving or disproving of rights of way.

There were not only the attractions of practice, there were then considerable hopes of preferment. The country had no lack of judges to resolve these matters of title. The judicial establishment in 1913 comprised the Lord Chancellor, two Lords Justices of Appeal, two Judges of the Chancery Division, a Land Judge and nine Judges of the King's Bench—fifteen in all, flanked by two Judicial Commissioners. In addition, there were sixteen County Court Judges and, for the cities, five Recorders. Even allowing that the needs of thirty-two counties were thus served, it may seem an ample provision. But, as Arthur Balfour had remarked both as Chief Secretary and Prime Minister, the one issue which would always unite Irish nationalists and Irish unionists was any proposal to reduce the judicial establishment.

Judicial remuneration, granted the then purchasing power of money and low taxation (1s. 2d. in the pound income tax and no sur-tax), was generous, much more so than under native government. The Lord Chancellor drew £6,000 a year, the Lord Chief Justice £5,000, the Lords Justices £4,000 each and the puisne judges £3,500. And there was always the chance of a peerage—not always welcomed as we shall see.

These were the golden days of preferment. The changes of government at Westminster made the sun's rays more glorious still. For over nineteen years until the end of 1905 the Conservatives had been in office with one brief interlude. Now the Liberals were in. They had to look after their own, those rare birds by then, the Ulster Liberals. But they also had to listen to their allies, the Irish nationalists. The parliamentary party, with a self-denial which has been often forgotten, had pledged itself not to accept any office from government until Home Rule had been won. This gesture did not extend to its supporters.

As the vast majority of Protestant barristers belonged to the unionist party, the small number who did not so belong had a marvellous time. The Ulster Liberals, in particular, reaped a rich harvest. It used to be said that, during Lord Aberdeen's term of office as Lord Lieutenant, it was good to be a Home Ruler, better to be a Presbyterian Home Ruler, but best to be a tubercular Presbyterian Home Ruler. It so happened that an unusually large number of judgeships fell vacant during this period, with the result that barristers with the right political complexion found themselves elevated with a rapidity that bore no relation to their professional achievements. . . . As the supply of Protestant Liberals became exhausted, Catholics came in for their share of promotion.

Between January 1915 and November 1917 there were eight judicial appointments in Ireland, six in the High Court and two in the County Courts.

In those days judges still held office for life. This irremovability created difficulties for government, especially when the course of promotion was vexed by the formation of the first Coalition in May 1915 and the supersession of Asquith by Lloyd George in December 1916. On the earlier of these occasions, Asquith had written that 'the occupants of the Irish Bench—especially the antiquated and infirm—stick to their places like wax'.[1]

1. Asquith's irritation was caused by the persistent efforts of James Campbell (then, with Carson, MP for Dublin University, and a strong Irish unionist) to obtain promotion to the Bench when the first Coalition was formed in May 1915. Eventually in December 1916, when Asquith

Then as now, the centre of the Bar was in the Law Library in the Four Courts. The Irish barrister paid a subscription to the Law Library and to its dressing-room. To quote Maurice Healy, who had been called in 1910.

> I forget whether either institution exacted an entrance fee, but the annual subscriptions were two guineas and one guinea respectively. For the guinea paid to the dressing-room your wig and gown were minded and, when necessary, mended for you : clean bands were laid out every morning. When you went to Sessions or Assizes you found the robes you had doffed the evening before awaiting you in the country, having been sent by parcel-post from the dressing room. ....
>
> ... The main chamber of the new Library was a long hall divided by pillars into bays; a gallery ran around three sides of the room, one end being occupied by the staircase. Law reports and text-books were stored in the bays. Seating was provided in the bays, in the gallery and in a smoking-room. The seats could be occupied by anybody except against their owners; in this way accommodation was provided for two to three hundred members of the Bar.[1]

A clerk at the door, then John Campion, guarded the door and dealt with solicitors, informing them (not always with complete accuracy) of the whereabouts of whatever member of the Bar was sought. The tradition of the Library was that any member, however junior, in any difficulty on some point of law or procedure, might approach any other member, however senior,

1. *The Old Munster Circuit*, Dublin. Browne & Nolan, pp. 45–47.

---

was overthrown by Lloyd George, he became Lord Chief Justice. (See Heuston, *Lives of the Lord Chancellors, 1885–1940.* Clarendon Press, Oxford, 1964.

This did not satisfy Campbell who achieved his appointment as Lord Chancellor in place of Ignatius O'Brien in June 1918. It was understood at the time that O'Brien had driven down to the Four Courts and was robed and ready to go into Court when he was informed of his removal.

More again may be added. O'Brien was offered a peerage by way of solace. He accepted it unwillingly and took the title of Lord Shandon. It was suggested in the Law Library that a more suitable title might have been Lord Stepaside. In the same line of thought but in a more cruel vein, it was further suggested that, as his marriage had been childless, an even better title might have been Lord Stillorgan.

and ask for advice and guidance. It was the right of the junior to ask : it was the duty of the senior to help.

The Library thus described was destroyed in the explosion which wrecked the Four Courts in 1922. Its replacement stands in another part of the building, and is differently laid out. It is hardly necessary to say that George never doubted the superiority of the old over the new. What appealed to him particularly was the sociability and good talk of the Library—qualities in which there cannot have been much falling off.

> I found the Library a very congenial place. In spite of a good many personal animosities and jealousies, the atmosphere was friendly. Professional *ésprit de corps* was very high. Political and religious differences did not prevent amicable relations in the Library. In the smoking-room and dressing-room much good conversation and many amusing stories were to be heard. To mix on terms of equality with my elders taught me a great deal about the way of the world. . . . I have no doubt at all that my experience at the Bar broadened my mind and prevented me being a mere academic specialist. The three years that I spent at the profession made me a man of the world. If fate had not decreed otherwise I think I would have become very fond of the Library and the geniality and good fellowship of the profession.

He adds, very typically

> Possibly, the attraction would have diminished as I grew older and the novelty began to wear off. Perhaps my agreeable memories arise from my own inconspicuous career. I was not successful enough to arouse the demons of jealousy that plagued some of my friends.

He devilled with Dan O'Brien, later a County Court Judge and later still, under the Free State, the 'railway judge'.

> I used to go to his house (in Kildare Street) every evening and obtained a glimpse of the hard life to which a successful barrister is condemned. He dined about six and was at his desk by seven. He never went to bed before one or two o'clock. He rose early, dealt with a heavy morning post and hurried to the Four Courts where he remained all day.

Perhaps part of the burden of work was created by his own character. He was deeply scrupulous and liable to change his view of a case submitted to him. If so, as George used to recall, his devil, who had already posted an opinion in the pillar-box outside the RDS in Leinster House in time to catch the eight o'clock collection, would be sent out again with a different opinion to catch the collection at midnight. It was not for nothing that he received the soubriquet of 'Anxious Dan'. He had a very varied practice as any junior had to have in those days; and he was thought to be a first-class person to devil with. From him, George learned ' not only a lot of law, but a lot of worldly wisdom in the treatment of solicitors and clients'. Through him also, George was introduced to several members of the Bar who were rising to, or had already attained, high place in the profession.

It was also through Dan O'Brien that George decided on his choice of circuit. No one, it seems, had told him that it would be wise for a very junior barrister to make himself known outside Dublin just as no one had told him the difference between a pass and an honours degree. As the judicial system then stood there were, to begin with, the courts of Quarter Sessions. Originally, they were for the discharge of criminal cases but they were developed so that civil matters up to a certain sum, might be heard before them. The County Court Judge was *ex officio* the chairman of Quarter Sessions as well. He went his round four times a year. An appeal from his decisions lay to the next going Judge of Assize (the Assizes were held twice a year) who reheard the entire case. Any member of the Bar might appear in any County Court, though for anybody to attempt ubiquity would obviously be both eccentric and unprofitable. But only members of the appropriate Circuit might appear at Assize without a special fee. Moreover, once a member of the Bar had chosen a circuit he was in practice bound by his choice. Mobility was not encouraged. The best known case in this regard is cited by Maurice Healy in his book on the Munster Circuit. Edward Carson, already a member of the Leinster Bar, applied for the permission of the Munster Bar to transfer to it. The application, Healy is at pains to record, was not on account of any difference between Carson and the Leinster Bar nor did the Munster Bar refuse it on political or personal grounds. But refused it was.

Perhaps it should be said that the Leinster Bar had nothing to do with the geographical limits of the province of Leinster. Its assize towns were Wicklow, Wexford, Waterford, Clonmel, Nenagh, Maryborough, Kilkenny, Carlow and Naas. It catered for the needs of several thriving towns set in a fertile and prosperous countryside.

The rules of the Leinster Bar laid down that every probationer had to travel around one circuit before he could face election. At that particular time the process of election was not as straightforward as it might have been. 'There had recently been a blackballing of a candidate on the grounds that he was suspected of unprofessional conduct and there was a certain amount of trouble in the air'. It was the first of many times of his life that he was to be troubled by the black-balling of others. So far as he was concerned, he had a smooth passage and was elected without any difficulty. The only criticism of him, he recalls, was one which will fall unexpectedly on the ears of those who knew him later. He lit a pipe before the members of the Bar mess had finished breakfast.

His patron and mentor on the circuit was Bob Kinahan, 'a very successful junior member of the circuit who seemed to take a liking for me, although we were as different as chalk and cheese in almost every respect'. If it was an attraction of opposites it was to endure long after Kinahan's death in 1921.

He was himself a unionist who treated Home Rule as a joke. His great heroes were the Dublin Fusiliers. He was a complete West Briton. Although he indulged freely in all kinds of amusements, he was a devout Catholic. The greatest offence one could commit in his presence was to eat meat on Friday in a public dining-room. This, he said, was 'letting the side down'. . . . He was hail-fellow-well-met with all sorts and conditions of people.

Kinahan had been one of the great group of students at University College around the turn of the century. (He figured in *A Portrait of the Artist*, not altogether flatteringly, as Moynihan). His name was to appear in George's table talk for many years in connection with two stories. The first concerned Kettle, who did not drink at all during his years in College. Walking down from a dinner at the Inns some years later with

Kinahan and others, he accompanied them, as often before, into a public-house at the corner of Denmark and Mary Streets. On this occasion, as on others, he was challenged to take a glass of whiskey. For whatever reason he did so; and in the later years of his too short life he did so only too often. The story, as George told it, went on to describe Kinahan's remorse when the news came through of Kettle's death on the Somme. The connection between the public-house and death at Guinchy was never challenged. And, as George liked on occasion to point his stories with a moral, he would go on to warn his guests never, never, to press a drink on anybody who didn't want one. The story and its moral was often told to students who, dining with their professor for the first time, were uncertain whether they should opt for wine or seek safety in a soft drink, a glass of stout being plainly inappropriate.

The second story formed a pendant to the first. During the summer Assize of 1921 (which must have been a very light one) Kinahan fell ill at Maryborough. The circuit moved on to Kilkenny but a couple of his brethren stayed behind with him. He seemed to be recovering but one afternoon he sent one of them down to the church to find out whose feast-day it was, as he was sure he would not survive to see another. It was the feast of St Apollinaris. 'I can die happy,' Bob said, 'I have invoked his name every day of my life'. He did die that day.

The story may not be true at all or even in part;[1] for the matter of that, the first story may not be true either. They may be nothing more exact than the folklore of the Bar; but it gives an engaging picture of a carefree life and the close loyalties of a shared profession. It was no wonder that a young man should be attracted by its manner, or that the young man should begin to drink a bit. At that time, there was not much else to do in the country towns of Ireland, after the mess dinner had been eaten and the briefs read.

The reference to drink comes into his recollections many years later. Clearly it was not even the phantom of a problem at this

---

1. Pedantry insists that the feast of St Apollinaris, Bishop and Martyr, is celebrated on 23 July. Kinahan died on the 21st July. He was buried from Harrington Street church on the 23rd. Many of his brethren are recorded as having attended the funeral. It seems safe to assume that the story was born before the mourners had dispersed.

time. His practice was growing, assisted by introductions from Dan O'Brien and Bob Kinahan.

I think I can say at this distance of time that I did the little cases well. I had a good knowledge of law, immense self-confidence and considerable experience of public speaking. One thing led to another. I came to know new solicitors in various towns and I began to get a few cases on my own account. In the course of a couple of years I had held at least one brief in every one of the nine counties on the circuit.

By now, the war had broken out, but it had not yet affected the easy-going country life. It had not yet claimed the lives of friends: that was to come with the Dardanelles and the Somme. If anything, it had augmented the prosperity of the countryside. The old ceremonial and customs continued unchanged. The Judges of Assize were still driven through the streets wearing their robes, preceded by trumpeters and escorted by detachments of cavalry and mounted police. Little, if anything, had changed in over a hundred years.

The Irish Bar still retained some of the traditions of the days and ways described by Sir Jonah Barrington. . . . The circuit travelled with its own butler, wine and library and we lived as a band of brothers like officers in a mess. We were invited in turn to dine with the judges who travelled around the circuit. This was an admirable method of introducing young barristers to the judges and made for the solidarity of the profession. I was fitting in splendidly with my new surroundings. I liked the railway journeys and the hotel life and enjoyed making new friends and acquaintances. Everything pointed in the direction of my becoming a successful and, I think, popular member of the circuit.

Very soon all these occasions of pleasure were to be taken from him.

On March 27, 1914 a small vessel, the *Aletta* of 336 tons gross was lying in the Waterford river being discharged of a cargo of coal. A young man, John Mackay, was one of a group of dock labourers who were unloading on to the quay. The men in this group went aboard and ashore by means of a ladder. At low tide, the vessel being below the wharf, the ladder was upright and perfectly safe. At high tide it was horizontal and the men had to cross it on their hands and knees.

The men had gone off work at about 10.30 p.m. and returned at 11.00 p.m. The ladder was then horizontal. Mackay who, it was common case, was quite sober, was the last to return. A splash was heard. His body was recovered three days later. He was earning twenty-five shillings a week, of which he gave ten to his father. The father sought compensation for his loss. The case was sent to George to advise proceedings.

He had a choice of procedure. The safest and most obvious was under the Workmen's Compensation Act of 1897. Alternatively he could go under Lord Campbell's Act, whereby the representatives of a person killed by the wrongful act, neglect or default of another might sue for damages. This course might be more risky but it would give him a jury.

George points out that the most that he could expect to get under Workmen's Compensation was £150 while he might expect much more under Lord Campbell's Act. In fact he sued for £1,000 and his client eventually got £270. But, as he adds, that was not the point. He went, he writes, by way of Lord Campbell's Act because he had never heard of Workmen's Compensation. That the winner of the Brooke and both Victoria prizes should never have heard of Workmen's Compensation may seem a surprising comment on the courses then given in the King's Inns. However that may be, he advised proceedings under Lord Campbell's Act. The case was heard before Madden J. and a special jury in Waterford in March 1915.[1]

The findings of the jury were summarised in the House of Lords eighteen months later by the Lord Chancellor. They were :

1. That it was reasonably practicable to use a gangway as a means of access from shore to ship.

2. That the ladder employed was not secure nor reasonably safe for the purpose.

3. That at the time of the occurrence it was not so placed as to be a safe means of access.

4. That Mackay died as the result of a fall from the ladder.

5. That the non-use of a gangway in accordance with the

---

1. *Mackay v J. H. Monks (Preston) Ltd.* 2 I.R. (1916) 200, 241 : 2 I.R. (1917) 622 : 1918 I.L.T.R. 13.

statutory regulations was the proximate and direct cause of the death of Mackay.

6. That the neglect of the defendants to provide a reasonably secure and safe means of access was the proximate and direct cause of the death of Mackay.

7. That the defendants did provide a gangway suitable to be employed by those in charge of the vessel.

The case turned, not on the facts as found by the jury but on the statutory regulations mentioned in the fifth point. These regulations had been made under a section of the Factory and Workshops Act of 1901. They laid down that, in the circumstances in which the accident occurred, a gangway should be provided. In fact a gangway was available but it was not provided until after the accident. The defendant's counsel took the point that the regulations did not refer to ships. The Shipping Federation had in fact decided to make this a test case of shipowner's liability. This brought the Seamen's Union into the fray so that the issues were much greater than appeared at first sight, or than would have been raised by a Workmen's Compensation case. Mr Justice Madden ruled that the point about the regulations could not be decided in Waterford, in the absence of authorities and that the plaintiff should move for judgement, on the findings of the jury, in the High Court in Dublin.

The case was argued before the King's Bench in June 1915. George was led by two seniors, de Renzy and Lupton. The Court was composed of the Lord Chief Justice (Cherry), the Lord Chief Baron (Palles) and Gibson J.

The Court held, Cherry dissenting, that the regulations were *ultra vires* and dismissed the action. This went to the Court of Appeal in November 1915 and February 1916. The Court of Appeal was composed of the Lord Chancellor (Ignatius O'Brien) sitting with Ronan and Molony, LL. JJ. On this occasion George was led by Lupton and Dan O'Brien. The Court of Appeal upheld the judgement of the King's Bench.

George's direct involvement in the case ended at this point, but it will be useful to complete the account of its progress to the final tribunal of appeal. The Union and the Federation were determined to fight to the end. Accordingly *Mackay v Monks* came before the House of Lords in July 1916. Judgement was given in the following October. Their Lordships divided three

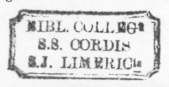

to two. The judgement of the majority, (the Lord Chancellor Finlay, Lord Atkinson and Lord Parker of Waddington) was that the regulations were *intra vires*. Lords Parmoor and Wrenbury dissented. Judgement was accordingly entered for the plaintiff. The receipt of £270 may not have compensated him for the loss of his son : in terms of value it might not, in view of war-time inflation, have been all that much more than he would have got, a lot more quickly, under Workmen's Compensation. But the law had been clarified.

The effect on George was catastrophic. By October 1916 he had all but abandoned his career as a barrister. He suffered a blow to his self-confidence which was never to be fully healed. He had no doubt of its importance to the course of his life. It occupies a pivotal place in his recollections.

The loss of confidence in his judgement stemmed from the framing of the action. Almost certainly he was asked by his seniors why he had not followed the well-beaten path of Workmen's Compensation. There is a passage in Gibson's judgement which is much to that effect. He could well have thought of himself as a young man who had caused a lot of unnecessary trouble to the Bench and to his seniors at the Bar.

He did not believe that they in fact took all that much trouble. There were consultations before the hearing in the King's Bench, oddly enough in de Renzy's house, 3 Burlington Road, where he himself was to live twenty years later. But neither senior was present when it came to the hearing and George was left to argue the case for five days by himself.

I was kept on my feet, being most unfairly interrupted and heckled by the Bench for two or three days. My seniors never appeared. I was left to carry a most fractious and troublesome baby. . . . The court was hostile and did not give me a fair chance to reply to their questions. The three judges were old or ailing and did not, I am convinced, really grasp the issues in the case. I was conscious of the presence of some of my contemporaries at the Bar who were torn between jealousy at my having such a big case and pleasure at the deep water in which I was immersed. I knew that some of my relations were in the public gallery.

These sentences were written much later when a better sense

of proportion might have been expected. When all was said and
done, he had not done so badly. He had borne the heat and
burden of the King's Bench for several days on his own. He
might have had cause for complaint against his seniors but that
is a complaint which many juniors before and after his time have
had. He had divided the court in the King's Bench; and the
Chief had held for him. He suggests that Gibson was originally
in his favour but was swayed by the masterful Chief Baron.
Reminiscences of the time agree that that happened often enough.
In the heel of the hunt his argument had been upheld by the
House of Lords. Taken all round, he had not done badly for a
barrister of less than two years standing.

So might many a junior have consoled and comforted himself.
George did not.

> In the end I had failed. My judgement had proved unsound;
> my arguments unconvincing. My faith in myself must have
> been severely shattered; my self-confidence undermined. I
> had received a slap in the face from which I never recovered.
> This was the turning point in my life.

The reader must be reminded once again that these sentences
were not written at the time but thirty-five years later when he
had been an established professor for over twenty years and had
just been elected as the parliamentary representative of his university. If he could write then in such manner, how could he
have felt at the time?

Certainly it appears to have been the immediate cause of the
breakdown from which he suffered in the next two years, from
which he never wholly recovered. That will be considered shortly.
Here, it is proposed to complete the account of his time at the
Bar. His self-confidence dwindled rapidly during the remaining
months of 1915. 'I reached the stage where I hoped I would
not receive any business involving an appearance in Court. I tried
to induce my clients to settle their actions and argued with
prisoners that they should plead guilty.' The contrast with twelve
months earlier is pathetic. But 1916 was no better. His stage-
fright returned in full measure. To restore himself, he went to
Bundoran for some weeks in the Long Vacation, the last summer
holidays he ever spent at any distance from Dublin. There he
met Denis Henry, soon to be the first Lord Chief Justice of

Northern Ireland, then at the height of his career at the Bar. 'I told him my symptoms. He was sympathetic and tried to reason with me. He said that he never rose to speak without being nearly paralysed by stage-fright.' George returned to Dublin determined to make a fresh start.

But the old demon had not been laid. The Michaelmas term was ghastly and the Hilary term worse. . . . My condition was becoming known in the profession and solicitors were giving me even fewer briefs than they had hitherto given me.

James O'Connor, by now Attorney-General (the readiness of senior people to give what advice and help they could is notable), advised him to go to Glasgow to consult an osteopath in whom he had great confidence.[1] Dan O'Brien advised against this, warning George that his departure would be taken in the Library as a sign of a break-down. In those days, perhaps no one really understood what was wrong. Shell-shock was still a new concept and derided by many doctors: its application to civilian life was not yet generally contemplated. His symptoms would have been attributed to too much drink. To go to Glasgow was an escape or perhaps a flight; but his misery was so great that he even consulted William Carrigan about joining the Army. So, early in 1917, he went to Glasgow for treatment and remained there until coming up to Easter. He did not then return to the Library. He decided to take a long rest. In normal times he would have gone abroad, but this was impossible with the war entering its fourth year. He had to remain in Dublin with his failure. Later, he returned to Glasgow on what was to be his last journey outside Ireland.

He stayed there until the end of 1917. The time had now come for an effort to return to practice. He decided to take the plunge at the Gorey sessions, where he had been reasonably successful, at the beginning of the Hilary term of 1918. He planned to go down on the train that barristers took, leaving Westland Row at 6.15 a.m.

As the afternoon of the day preceding the sessions passed, I became more and more nervous and anxious. In the evening,

1. A then fashionable theory held that deformation of the skeleton and consequent interference with the adjacent nerves and blood vessels was the cause of most diseases.

C

about eight o'clock, I went to Price's the chemist's shop, in the hope of getting some sedative . . . I cannot remember the details of the conversation I had with the gentleman in the shop, who was an old friend. . . . Whatever passed between us, I decided that I could not make the requisite effort next morning. I returned home and told my mother that I had abandoned the intention of attending the sessions. I think we both understood that the end of my legal career had definitely arrived.

The date, as he was at pains to discover decades later, was 14 January 1918. He was not yet twenty-six. His career lay in ruins.

In later years, he consoled himself with such reflections as:

I do not think I really possessed the qualities requisite for success at the Irish Bar. I do not think I would have been a great success even if my health had remained good. My skin was too thin to bear with equanimity the interruptions, impertinences and snubs that fell daily on the barrister from some of the rougher customers on the bench. I had a certain pride that would have prevented me from being subservient to solicitors and their clerks, whom I could never have courted or flattered for their support. I was not a really good mixer, being rather reserved and shy. My attainments were academic rather than practical. I would not have figured well in the rough and tumble of every-day practice.

All that may have been true enough though it certainly contains an element of special pleading. Nevertheless, in many ways he remained in heart and in mind a barrister.

My legal training has coloured—possibly not for the better—my attitude to the professorship and to the subject which I am paid to teach. No economic problem ever seems to be finally settled. There is no generally recognized court of appeal. My legal training has made me impatient of controversies which seem to lack generally accepted hypotheses and which fail to reach binding conclusions. I assume that every disputed issue must be capable of a definite solution. This is the attitude of a lawyer and especially of a lawyer trained as I was in the positivist tradition.

It is also, perhaps one might add, the attitude of a man who had come of age before 1914.

The wounds healed slowly; perhaps they never completely healed. In his later years, however, he cherished his links with the Bar and kept them in good repair. Years afterwards the Leinster Bar invited him to their annual dinner. He accepted with alacrity and talked about the dinner, and the kindly thought of his hosts, for weeks afterwards. He frequently dined at the Inns, noting with alarm the juvenescence of Benchers. In College his closest ties were with those students who were also reading law. To the end he read the law reports in *The Times*. He could be relied on to have mastered the details of any case, such as the Portuguese bank-note case, which brought legal and economic issues together. A practising barrister he had ceased to be : he remained a well-informed and inquisitive junior.

Years later I sat beside him at a meeting of the Academic Council. He had some proposals which needed approval. They were not controversial but, being complicated, they might have been thrown back to us for re-drafting. He was anxious. Once on his feet he was clear and concise. Everything was agreed without discussion. Walking away from the College I was inspired to say 'You opened the case well today.' I don't think that, in all the years I knew him, I ever said anything that pleased him more. He stopped and beamed. He reminded me of what I had said for ages afterwards. For one golden moment he was again the young barrister leaving the Court after a case well argued and won.

As this writer sees it, George's greatest achievement as a man was to accept defeat at a time when it is hardest to bear and to build for himself a new and distinguished career on the ruins of the old. That will be described in the pages that follow. But one point may be made. The failure indeed was there, but it is not so clear that in the end, materially at least (which altogether ignores the mental aspect), he lost heavily by it. In 1914 he saw himself, one must assume, as an ambitious junior does, rising in his profession and eventually reaching the Bench. In his short time at the Bar he had seen several people elevated whose qualifications were hardly superior to his except in length of practice. He might well have dreamed in those hopeful years of rising to the very highest places under a Home Rule government. It was as well for him that such dreams were dispelled, however brutally. A few years after his retirement, the old order was swept away : the judicial establishment of the Irish Free State needed no more than nine judges for the Supreme and High Courts. If he had remained in practice, he would surely have been regarded as being too young for preferment when the new system was established in 1924. It is highly unlikely that he would have been offered a judgeship under Mr de Valera's first administration. His prospects would not have been improved by the change of government in 1948. Mr Costello had his own priorities for judicial preferment, and there is little reason to believe that George would have ranked very high among them. By then George was a successful, well-liked and respected professor and senator. If he had remained at the Bar he might have been an ageing and disappointed senior counsel.

5

The Collapse 1916-18

THE breakdown that has been described was to affect him throughout the more than fifty years of his later life. Its influence waxed and waned. It did not prevent him, as will shortly be seen, from embarking on new and successful activities within a surprisingly short time. In the long run, a rather longer run than he had expected, they were to lead him to a new career, at the University rather than at the Bar. But a great deal of that new career was determined by what had happened to him in 1915. The causes and consequences should be considered at this point.

The seeds of his collapse were present long before he faced the King's Bench or the Court of Appeal. It is clear that he reacted violently to adversity : it is not so clear, but it seems highly possible, that those unhappy days did not themselves create but rather uncovered a sensitivity which was already part of his character. Into his middle twenties his way of life had done little to strengthen his defences against reverses. He was an only child : he seems to have been a solitary child. In his recollections, there is no mention of visits to other families or of childrens' parties or of any other of the innumerable ways in which one learns to meet and cope with one's contemporaries. Perhaps because of that, he seems to have been apt to remember unduly the small slights and set-backs which occur even in the most buoyant childhood. As the son of the owner of the hotel, he was sheltered : he was also, one may imagine, indulged. He was happy to read and to be in his own company. His recollections are not of friends of his own age but only of his home and, even there, of a father whom he was soon to lose.

This may have brought uncertainty and anxiety when, as he grew up, he had to move in wider circles. Clearly, he had enjoyed his years at CUS and Weybridge. He had more difficulty in adjusting himself to Belvedere and the College. One feels that there was a great deal to the College that he did not know, into which, perhaps, he did not wish to enter. It comes out, to take an example, in his reference to the steps of the National Library, which echoes the *Portrait of the Artist*. There was more to the steps than he recalls, or perhaps knew. One may illustrate the point by a quotation from Con Curran who knew those steps well in Joyce's day.

> In the College societies, on the steps of the National Library, they plunged into debate. Night after night when the Library had closed, they would continue their interminable discussions, swinging backwards and forwards before their lodgings, loath to separate, unwilling to conclude anything.
> In short they lived as all students since Abelard and Duns Scotus have lived.[1]

In George's time, they lived like that too, and students were so to live twenty years later still. But there is no memory among his contemporaries of his presence after the Library had shut. It is difficult to imagine him walking round and round the Green or up and down the Rathmines Road. He was always rather on the outside looking in. In College he seems to have been unsure of how he stood in relation to his colleagues or how he stood in relation to many of the issues of the day. More deeply perhaps, in a manner that would not have troubled many of his companions, he was unsure of his social standing at a time when the divisions of class, however defined, were still very real. He had no one and no thing to identify with. It seems also that he could not, certainly he did not, look to his home for reassurance.

These difficulties, it may be suggested, were brought to a head by the events of 1915. Amongst those difficulties and in spite of them he had preserved some certitudes derived from his Jesuit education and his legal training, that in the legal system as everywhere else in the world there existed accepted canons of order, of precedent and procedure, that judges could be relied on to decide rightly just as university examiners could be relied on to recognise merit. Once these beliefs were shattered there was little to hold on to. Within limitations which will now be described,

1. C. P. Curran. *James Joyce Remembered.* Oxford University Press, 1968, p. 21.

he was able to rebuild his life. In the writing of his economic histories, in the editing of the *Irish Statesman*, in the society of the Arts Club, he could pass the time agreeably and usefully. There remains the feeling that all these things were a form of escape, that he dared not sit by himself at home. Once he was by himself, he was lonely and insecure. His condition was akin, one is assured, to the hypochondriac or the manic depressive. He was suspicious of himself, of others and of whatever life might bring.

It was part of the burden that these suspicions came and went and came back. He enjoyed long periods of confidence and relative security, from about 1923 to 1933 and again from about 1946 into the middle 1950s, to take two examples that can be singled out. But even when the sunshine of life shone on him most strongly, he was always aware that the shadows might return and engulf him all too quickly. Writing of the late 1920s, he cannot help but look forward from a busy and apparently happy time to the down swing of his life-cycle which awaited him in the next decade. Writing in the early 1950s, when all who knew him would have said that things had never gone so well for him, he reflected that he was being strengthened against the next bout of depression. He was certain that he would have one. He did have one.

Some of his troubles grew worse as time went on. Before he was thirty he had become unwilling to make any long journey : he was not far into his thirties when even a day out in a car might develop its terrors without any warning. Later years brought a fear of being in high places, even of being in upstairs rooms, of small rooms, of crowded rooms. He could indeed cope with these but he was always aware that his power to do so might disappear in a moment. He could never leave things to chance.

This meant a continual struggle with himself and with every circumstance of his daily life. He had to plan his days with a detail which would be inconceivable to happier people. He lived behind entrenchments; he would not venture far outside them; he would not venture out at all unless the way of retreat had been fully secured.

In his recollections, there is no reference whatsoever, after his school-days, to human affection. It is almost as if he had essayed to live without it. This may well have been the most severe strain of all. Behind the outward appearance of a disciplined and highly organised way of life, one may sense a lonely person who was deprived of affection, but whose character would have flowered if he had encountered it. He was not to know the strength that might have been brought by a love returned or by sharing the human adventure of marrying and founding a family. Intellectually formidable, emotionally he was extraordinarily immature. He was fortunate at least in that he escaped the more dangerous consequences of such an imbalance.

This was not inevitable. In his time in the Arts Club, he was, as the phrase then went, 'talked about'. Memories of that time recall two highly attractive girls with whom his name was linked by gossip. Nothing of that appears in his recollections. It may have been that the circumstances of his home life made marriage difficult. It may have been that he used those circumstances as an excuse. However that may have been, the gossip did not get very far. There was not, neither then nor later, any other form of gossip. He was incapable of finding any lasting satisfaction outside the rigid conventions into which he was born.

In that, he was not unusual in his generation. What was perhaps more singular was that he did not make the usual Irish substitution of drink for sex. Certainly, he felt from time to time that he was drinking too much, especially in Arts Club days but also during subsequent periods of depression. However that may be, drink was never allowed to interfere with his duties and, so far as the period of the Arts Club was concerned, it did not prevent an amazingly rapid composition of a long book on an unfamiliar subject.

If he had suffered from some physical disability such as the sudden loss of sight which his friend T. G. Moorhead bore with such dignity, every allowance would have been made for him. He was in fact maimed spiritually in a manner which limited his physical activity but was not at all perceptible to those who did not know him very well. Only too often, allowances were not made and actions were attributed to selfishness or lack of consideration that really flowed from the limits within which he was forced to organise his life.

In the 1920s and much later he was often criticised through a lack of understanding. His professional brethren who had stuck it out at the Bar and had endured the vagaries of the Bench saw no reason to sympathise with a colleague who had apparently run away at the first shot. And, when one uses that metaphor, it comes to mind that all over Europe in the January of 1918 young men were catching trains that would bear them to destinations more grim than a sessions at Gorey. Then and later, there was no sympathy to spare for cases such as his. In a time that was only too used to death and mutilation and that knew little of nervous disorders, his collapse seemed something less than a tragedy. It will appear later that his friendships throughout life were with his seniors and his juniors, only occasionally with his contemporaries. This was not accidental. His seniors might have known about the Court of Appeal but they would not have cared. His juniors would neither have known nor cared.

These difficulties were to plague him throughout his life. What should be said here is that there were many times when there was a gulf fixed between his life as it would have seemed to acquaintances and the reality. The chapters that follow will describe an active and busy way of life. It did not appear so to him, especially during those periods before he got into the College, when he had nothing in particular to do. Writing of one of them, he says

> This was a period of my life when I must have appeared very idle to the casual observer. I had plenty of money, otherwise I could not have kept going. But I had no settled employment or earned income. I was associating with artistic and literary people, with whose outlook I had no deep sympathies. I was, I suppose, lonely and was glad to have the society of pleasant people who were prepared to take me at my face value and not ask too many questions. . . . Indeed I was leading the life of a leisured dilettante, which must have been unpleasing and embarrassing to my mother. My home life became emptier and emptier.

Certainly the decision to abandon the Bar strained still further the relations between mother and son.

> I think we both realized that the end of my legal career had definitely arrived. I was so relieved at the relaxation of the tension induced by the thought of the sessions that I did not devote much thought to the long-term implications of the step

c*

I had taken. I am afraid my mother must have been very disappointed. I can well remember the way in which she took the announcement of my decision. Her attitude was one of annoyance rather than of pity. She obviously blamed me, as most people did, for not 'making the effort' to conquer my nerves, not understanding that the inability to make the effort was precisely the trouble for which I needed a cure. She must have felt that I had let her down with a vengeance.

Almost ten years had passed since he had returned from Weybridge. It had then been decided what profession he should enter; and the necessary route to that goal had been mapped out. Now, after a deceptively promising start, these plans lay in ruins and, in a common point of view, by his default rather than by any stroke of ill fortune. Number 40 Northumberland Road cannot have been a happy house for either the son or the mother. But the son could, and did, keep out of it.

This seems the proper place to discuss some aspects of his private affairs. By far the most important of them was his relationship with his mother. It was of unusual importance. His father died when he was fourteen : his mother did not die until some thirty years after he abandoned the Bar, when he was in his middle fifties. She appears frequently in his recollections, rarely happily, often with the eloquent prefix of 'my poor' mother.

My mother was several years younger than my father. I think he was devoted to her and that he did everything in his power to make her happy. . . . What she lacked in intellect she made up for in charm. She was exceedingly handsome and had beautiful manners. I frequently heard admiring comments made about her charm when she was quite an old woman. She was a little bit spoilt, I think, by my father and by her three step-children who, I must say, behaved exceptionally well. It was all the spoiling that she received when she was young that made her a little difficult to deal with in her old age. She was accustomed to get her way by means of gentle bullying. She led a very sheltered life. My father was a man of very strong mind and decided views. My mother never had to think out anything for herself. The result was that she became a little bit helpless in the affairs of life and found it hard to make up her mind even about small matters.

So it may have been; though some matters soon to be recounted suggest that it was the mother rather than the son who took the decisions. But there can be no doubt about what is said earlier. Those who remember Mrs O'Brien will recall a striking appearance which old age seemed to enhance and a delightfully sympathetic manner of greeting the students who came into her house for a few minutes before they were brought elsewhere for a meal. George rarely brought his students into his mother's house for more than a moment. It could and did occur to some of them that they would have been very glad to have talked more with her. But at that time of life one is incurious about family arrangements. There remains a feeling that Mrs O'Brien would have welcomed longer meetings with her visitors, even if she might well have preferred them to be less immature than the average undergraduate.

In the light of later knowledge I have no doubt that my breakdown was partly caused by my anxiety not to prove a disappointment to her. She was wrapt up in my success in which she would gain some reflected glory. I had, in a way, spoiled her by being too consistently successful as a student. Any achievement short of first place had come to be regarded as a failure. I was most conscious of the embarrassment and shame that my strange illness must be causing her. She was sensitive to the suggestion that what was really wrong with me was TB which we were disguising from our neighbours under the pretence of a nervous breakdown. . . . Even apart from what the neighbours might say, the reality was bad enough. All her hopes were centred on my success and I had become, at least temporarily, an invalid. My anxiety was largely due to my desire not to displease her, not to 'let her down'. Her anxiety grew with every growth in mine.

Things did not improve during the 1920s.

I was really living the life of a rich young man, not making any serious pretence of earning a living. I think my way of living was justifiable in the circumstances, but to the casual onlooker the justification was not apparent. I involved my mother in summers in expensive furnished houses in Greystones. I was impatient when she did not enter with enthusiasm into these schemes which involved her in considerable trouble and expense. She had to engage and manage servants, pay all the housekeeping bills and arrange for the entertainment of my numerous guests.

He goes on to remark, perhaps inconsequently but certainly with some lack of proportion that 'I suppose it is the fate of mothers to suffer for their sons. Simeon prophesied that Our Lord would pierce the heart of His mother'. He must indeed have been made uneasy by his memories to have perpetrated such an analogy. The root of the trouble did not lie in expensive houses or what the neighbours might think, even about the then appalling stigma of tuberculosis. It was rather that he and his mother had next to nothing to say to each other.

Appointment to the College in 1926 did not improve his domestic circumstances. What celebrations there were, were arranged by his friends. Indeed within a few years after that, things were to go from bad to worse. The household was enlarged by the addition of

> . . . the last of my mother's numerous unmarried sisters who had constituted a problem for all their 'in-laws'. . . . Although I was a man of nearly forty years of age, my permission to introduce another person into our house was never asked. In this matter, as in many others, my mother acted with a curious insensitiveness, based partly on stupidity and partly on the failure to realise that I had grown up from a boy. This new arrival had become one of those chronic heart and asthma cases that cause constant alarm but live for years. . . . If I had known that, in fact, she would live nearly twenty years longer and survive my poor mother, whose whole life was plagued attending to her, I would have tried to shift her to some sort of nursing home. But any time I ventured to make a complaint, I was assured that 'she couldn't last much longer' and that all I needed was a little more patience and nature would solve the problem.

Over ten years later, when his mother was also in failing health, George finally revolted and insisted that either Auntie Nellie left the house or he would. She was placed in a nursing home, from which 'she was still able to keep a fairly close eye on what we did and she became a constant visitor'.

This relationship ended whatever possibility existed that George might have developed some kind of a home life. It was bad enough that the aunt was there: worse still, she was given (both in Northumberland Road and later in Burlington Road) attractive and well-lit rooms which he would have liked for himself. This, and the constant presence of nurses, for her or for his mother or for both of them at the same time, made his house intolerable.

The result of the constant presence of this unwanted old maid, watchful, dependent and delicate, was to deprive me of all privacy in my own house. I spent more and more time in clubs, which I came to regard as a refuge from the curiosity of this ceaselessly vigilant virgin. Moreover, when I was at home, there was no possibility of confidential conversation with my mother. Even if we had been alone together, confidences would not have been easy. We were both naturally shy, and had more than even the normal amount of embarrassment that exists between a mother and a grown-up son. My mother hated facing unpleasant realities or even unpleasant possibilities and had constant resort to euphemisms. Moreover, there was the ever present but seldom-mentioned conflict over religion which poisoned our relations. My mother was most unhappy about my laxity and neglect of the sacraments, but was afraid to mention the subject for fear of driving me into a temper. This was a chronic cause of irritation in our relations, a wound that might be bandaged over but never healed.

The concluding sentences of that quotation raise a matter which may be considered here; although it takes us out of the present sequence of events and into the future. At some stage in his years at the Bar he gradually abandoned the regular practice of religion.

My faith, though dormant, was not dead. It continued to colour my attitude on all important questions. Moreover, through all this period I prayed a good deal, paid visits to the Blessed Sacrament and lit innumerable votive candles. I never omitted any day to visit some church to light a candle for a certain petition of a purely temporal nature.

What worried his mother was that, however frequent the visits may have been (and she was hardly likely to be told about them), his attendance at Mass became irregular and eventually ceased altogether. This was due to something much more than indolence and much less than failure of belief.

I have attempted to reconstruct in my memory the sequence of events which led to my abandonment of the active practice of religion. I have come to the conclusion that there was, at no point, a deliberate decision. There was a gradual negligence, interrupted by a couple of repentances and periods of good resolutions which were again broken. My father and step-brothers did not take religion very seriously, and it was easier for me to slip into easy-going ways than it would have been if my whole family had been devout and practising. I was worldly and thoughtless, inclined to procrastinate. Some of my early experiences in the confessional had not been very encouraging. These were probably the reasons why I drifted into the habit of neglecting my annual Easter duty and its preliminary confession.

He may not have practised his religion; but he never thought that it was of no importance to his life. He never lost the will to believe. His position was not all that uncommon even at that time. Certainly, regular attendance at Mass, especially among the professional class, was then as much a social as a religious duty. The memory lingers of the doctors and the lawyers at half-eleven Mass in University Church every Sunday, the fifteen minutes of gossip outside the church afterwards, the hats doffed to the wives of the judges or senior members of the hospital staffs. That was one side of Catholic professional life; the other was composed of those who did not feel it necessary to discharge their religious and social obligations. The only set of professional people, although the Bishops never seemed to realise it, who were reasonably certain to be always on parade were those Catholics who had gone to Trinity.

There was another influence at work in George's case.

My reason for continuing this habit (of neglect) for so long can be more easily explained than its original adoption. It was a manifestation of the relations that had come to exist between

my mother and me. My refusal to resume practice became
almost a matter of pride, a test of the strength of our mutual
will-power. . . . I felt that here was one thing on which I had
had my own way. My mother exerted a great deal of gentle
pressure on me which really amounted to a subtle and insidious
form of bullying. On almost every matter on which we had a
difference of opinion she got her own way in the end. I knew
that there was nothing that would have given her greater
pleasure than my toeing the religious line. I knew she was
praying for it. I felt that if I gave in on this point she would
have experienced a sense of triumph. I could not bear the
thought of the quiet gloating that would go on between her
and my cousins behind my back. I do not think that I ever
abandoned the intention to resume practice, but I was determined to do nothing as long as she was alive.

This was indeed something less than the relationship, mentioned in the first chapter, between St Augustine and St Monica.
In the event he resumed practice about a year after his mother
died. It is doubtful if many friends ever noticed that there had
been any change: these were not matters that he discussed often,
and when he did it was quite impersonally.

He never doubted, however he may have neglected, the teaching of the Church. He did have his own, rather personal, views
on some matters. He firmly believed that the Faith had been
preserved in Ireland by the priests and the people, not by the
hierarchy and still less by Rome. He felt a great debt of gratitude
to those who had endured deprivation and suffering in the penal
days. He had no sympathy with the triumphalism which, he felt,
marked the pontificates of the Pian succession. It was characteristic of him that he should attend the great Mass in the Phoenix
Park to celebrate the centenary of Emancipation and that he
should keep well away from the Congress three years later. He
was in no way impressed with the proceedings of the Vatican
Council. He did not feel himself to be in any need of promptings
towards ecumenism; and in any case he felt that ecumenism had
limits which were being ignored. With other results of the Council
he was in violent disagreement. He resented the change from
Latin to trans-atlantic English in the Liturgy. His favourite (if
that is the word) example of the change was a new rendering of

a fundamental text : *Thou art Peter and upon this rock I will build My Church and the head of the underworld will not prevail against it*. More and most of all, because he was a rather special kind of Irish Catholic, was the abolition of the saying of the *De Profoundis* after each low Mass. He was not sure (and one understands that the matter is undecided) whether the psalm was said as a reminder of the penal days or in gratitude to Protestant benefactors of the time. One way or the other, to abandon it was a breach of faith and continuity with the past.

He retained an abiding sense of providential direction. The circumstances of his life may have contributed to this : he planned to go in one direction and found himself travelling easily and happily in quite another. He did not believe that that happened by chance : rather he believed that nothing ever happened by chance. Always in his life he noted coincidences and honoured anniversaries even when they concerned nothing that seemed to be of importance. He firmly believed that it did matter, perhaps to himself, perhaps to some other person, for some reason that he might never know, whether he did this or did that, whether he did it now or did it later, whether on going out he turned right or turned left. What might seem the merest chance to others had some element of providential design. There is a passage, from Newman of course, which seems to put the matter exactly.

> Let a person, who trusts that he is on the whole serving God acceptably, look back on his past life, and he will find how critical were moments and acts, which at the time seemed the most indifferent : as for instance the school he was sent to as a child, the occasion of his falling in with those persons who have most benefited him, the accidents which determined his calling or his prospects, whatever they were. God's hand is ever over His own, and He leads them forward by a way they know not of.[1]

To return to the life of the household in Northumberland Road : in 1932 the family sold their interest in the Wicklow Hotel. Since the death of Richard O'Brien in 1906 it had been most successfully managed by Mr Thomas Mahon. Now, the lease of the hotel was about to expire and would be renewed

1. Newman, *Parochial and Plain Sermons*. Vol. IV p. 261.

only on much revised terms involving a considerable capital expenditure. The family decided to sell to Mr Mahon who was willing to set up for himself. In later years George could never make up his mind whether or not the right decision had been taken : his conclusion on any occasion was determined by the then state of the tourist trade. What he remembered very vividly was that his opinion was not asked at the time. 'I was always treated as the small boy of the family. . . . My views, if expressed would have been ridiculed and ignored'.

The sale came when there seemed no reason why the depression should not go on for ever. Also, it coincided with the advent to power of a party that sharply increased taxation and was clearly opposed to the economic policies that George had espoused. From now on he would be dependent on an income from investments which, although ample even then, was unlikely to grow greatly, and on his salary from the College. At the same time he would clearly pay out more tax : the days of 3/6d. in the pound standard rate had gone for ever. This alteration of circumstances and fears for the future ushered in a new period of anxious strain during the middle and later years of the 1930s.

The second event was the move of house to 3 Burlington Road; 'a detached house with a small but sunny and secluded garden near the centre of the city'. Two points may be made about the decision to move. First, the immediate reason was to provide better accommodation for Auntie Nellie. Second, the house-hunting and the decision to purchase were both done by his mother.

The aunt remained in the house until 1942 when she left in circumstances already noted. George's mother, although long bed-ridden, survived until 1946 by which time he was well into his fifties and over half-way through his professorship. She may have been shy and unpractical. Perhaps an equally good case could be made for the proposition that she knew exactly what she wanted and was completely successful in getting it. Viewed in a certain light, she might have passed for one of those formidable matriarchs in which Ireland then abounded. 'My poor mother' ?

One is reminded of what George Moore wrote of Edward Martyn and his mother.

Life affords no more interesting drama than when the fate

of temperament irretrievably separates two people bound together by the closest mutual ties, and the charm is heightened
when each is sensitive to the duty which each bears the other,
when each is anxious to perform his or her side of the contract; and the drama is still further heightened when both
become aware that they must go through life together without
any hope that they will understand each other better.[1]

Wherever the responsibility lay, if it lay anywhere, the son
never felt at home in his mother's house. He became a club man.
He had to have company every evening. He had comparatively
few friends of his own age : it was natural that he should develop
the practice of inviting younger people as his older friends died
off. A great deal of his later reputation among students arose
from this amiable habit. It might be agreed that Mrs O'Brien,
through the strength or the weakness of her character, had a very
great deal to do with the fashioning of that reputation. It was
bought at a high price.

1. *Ave.* London, Heinemann, 1911, p. 239.

6

Plunkett House:
The Irish Statesman 1918-21

In spite of everything that has been said and quoted, the year 1918 was not far advanced before he had embarked on a completely new course of activity. For the moment it gave him an occupation; in the long run it was to give him a profession.

For reasons which will be set out later, he turned to a consideration of the College as a substitute for the Law Library. He took up the writing of economic history. His first major work was *The Economic History of Ireland in the Eighteenth Century* which was published before the end of 1918.

This seems almost incredible. At the end of the first week in January he was still thinking of going back to sessions. How he could have planned and written a book of some 150,000 words in so short a space of time must remain a cause for wonder. Some things stand out; the industry which achieved so much in so short a time and the resilience and the tenacity which inspired it. Further, as will shortly be seen, the publication of the book introduced him into new circles which were to be useful in shaping his career.

Even with the book in hand, he had to find a new way of living and to develop new interests. This was not the easiest thing in the world either for him or for anybody else.

It is only fair to my poor mother to acknowledge that she did attempt, at intervals, to induce me to do some of the more normal things that young men do. She persuaded me, for example, to go to dancing lessons. . . . These lessons, however, led to no result. I always hated evening dress and late hours and was not attracted by the partners whom I encountered. My mother also attempted to make me partake of normal youthful society at home. On a couple of occasions she invited parties of young people to tea or supper. I am afraid I was very unco-operative at these gatherings which, after a few very unsuccessful experiments, were discontinued.

That must have been a great mercy for everybody concerned. In any case, at that time fresh air and outdoor exercise were the accepted remedies for a nervous breakdown. For some years, until he reached a new balance, he took up a variety of interests which may surprise those who knew him only in later years. Where fresh air and exercise were to be found was a matter for consideration. 'I had been brought up mainly in the city and suburbs. I had none of the interests of the country child. I had no interest in farming, gardening, fishing or shooting'. Team games were out: he had always avoided them. Long walks in the country were marginally more acceptable: he had indulged in them at Belvedere and the College. But the countryside bored, when it did not repel, him.

Indeed I have never been much of an admirer of nature and natural beauty. My admiration has been directed to human beings and their creations. In this respect, as in many others, my tastes were akin to those of the Greeks, who regarded nature with indifference if not with fear and adversion. I have always been inclined to regard the country as an expanse of mud and farming as a combination of cruelty, indecency and dirt.

This outlook limited the choice of open-air activity. Eventually he settled for horse-riding and golf. Riding lessons started in the Phoenix Park where he put in an hour or two most days. He graduated to hunt with the Ward, the Meath hounds and the Fingal harriers. He never claimed any degree of expertise. Nevertheless, it used to come as a surprise to his students in later years to hear him discourse on Fairyhouse or Punchestown in the years just after the war.

When he was still at the Bar he had been brought to Portmarnock by Dan O'Brien. He soon became a member; even then, one imagines, he was a clubbable person. Many years afterwards students who had been brought out by him for a walk along the strand were surprised to be brought into the club-house for tea.

They were still more surprised to hear him greeted by members with affection and respect. That the Professor had got into so good a club, that he was so well received by golfers, came as a surprise. It did not fit into the mental picture which a student would have of his professor.

The pathetic thing about the riding and the golf was that, so far as one can guess, he never really liked them. He never had the joy of doing them because he did them well, or because he thought that some day he might do them well. They were purely therapeutic : they kept the demons at bay. Students could not be expected to realise the grim struggle in which he was engaged; but they did not make any particular joke about such incidents; they had an affection for him even if they could not guess how much he needed affection and support.

If I were to estimate the number of days I spent at golf and hunting in those years the total would be quite large. Both activities really led nowhere. I was never any good at either and was always a bit of a rabbit at outdoor games. I did not really care about country pursuits. I liked country houses but not the country. I have always been essentially a city man with a vague dislike and fear of rural solitude. I do not think that I made a single new friend in the hunting field or on the golf course as I was never at home with sporting people who, no doubt, regarded me as a highbrow. Both activities were really symptoms of anxiety. For years I thought I could not take enough exercise to 'keep fit'. I worried excessively about the duty to walk, play golf, ride and swim—all with the object of preventing another breakdown. I was still under the illusion that the cause of my illness at the Bar had been physical, whereas in fact it was 'a mind diseased'. However, if all this physical exercise did not do as much good as I believed, it did me no harm. It was a healthy pastime and kept me out of mischief. It kept me moving around within a fairly wide radius and probably prevented the distance phobia from growing worse. It helped to work off some of the alcohol which I was imbibing pretty freely. It redressed the balance from undue bookishness and prevented my developing into an aesthete or a highbrow. It played a part in my life during a period of transition. When the transition had finished it ceased

to be useful or relevant. Its function had been performed and
it came to a natural end.

There may have been one other advantage in riding and hunting. He was not likely to meet many of his late brethren of the
Law Library. Before the wounds of the Court of Appeal had
healed—if they ever did—he was shy of meeting people who
would have remembered him when he was at the Bar. In the
very early years it would have been intolerable. There was a lot
to be said for being in places where the immediate past was not
likely to reappear.

In the course of his outings on horse-back he met E. J. Riordan,
then Secretary of the Irish Industrial Development Association.
This was a fortunate meeting.

> He knew a great number of people, mainly because he was so
> interested in his fellow human beings. He was genuinely un-
> selfish, kind and hospitable. He seemed to like me particularly,
> I think, because I possessed two things, leisure and education,
> which he had missed in his own youth. Ted introduced me to
> many new friends at the time when I was particularly aban-
> doned. I had lost all my old legal contacts and had not begun
> to make new friends.

Another important and more immediately fruitful friendship
was that with Diarmuid Coffey. They had been at the Inns and
Leinster Bar together. Coffey had also abandoned practice. His
father, a distinguished archaeologist, had been Keeper of
Antiquities in the National Museum. The family was, as the
phrase then went, well-connected. It was no wonder that
Diarmuid had been involved in that highly exclusive enterprise,
the running of guns into Kilcoole in July 1914. 'The Coffey's
house in Harcourt Terrace was the centre of much literary
society. I used to go there to play bridge and I met there people
who, as a young barrister, I would not normally have met'. In
the early part of 1918 Coffey suggested that he should become
a member of the United Arts Club. This was to produce a long
and varied series of consequences.

At that time, the Arts Club occupied part of 44 St Stephen's
Green. It was a charming house, catching the setting sun in the
long evenings of summer. The story went that it was haunted,

that a ghost might be encountered at a certain turn of the staircase, while one member claimed that an apparition had entered
and left his bedroom through a solid wall. It will be understood
that such experiences were given a quite different explanation
by the members at large; but students of the occult may well
enquire whether ghostly visitors still frequent the site which, not
without a certain symbolism, is now occupied by the First
National Bank of Chicago.

The corporeal membership were a distinguished lot. 'Among
those who dined there frequently were W. B. Yeats, Dermod
O'Brien, Conor O'Brien, Cruise O'Brien, Hugh Law, Miss
Macnie and James and Eileen Duncan. . . .' The club was a port
of call on every evening, especially for those who, like George,
had no special impulse to go home. Its great feature was a
monthly dinner which, according to a custom then strong in
Dublin, was garnished with poems and songs written specially for
the occasion to praise, often with civil leer, some member who was
then in the public eye. There was an abundance of talent for
these diversions; 'Willie Dawson and Florence Marks in particular were very pretty wits at other people's expense'. So George
remembered the dinners; one feels that he remembered more
than he was willing to record. But, as will appear, he was well
able to look after himself. Few of those poems and songs appear
to have survived, which is a great loss to the understanding of a
part of Dublin's life at that time.

Life in the Arts Club did not simply centre around interesting
personalities.

> I found a new kind of nationalism unlike anything I had
> met before. I found myself for the first time among people
> whom I found socially agreeable and who had nationalist
> convictions. I had always previously thought, I imagine, that
> the upper classes in Ireland were all unionists and that
> nationalism was confined to the lower and middle classes. But
> now I discovered that people whom I could admire for their
> social ease and upper class attitude were nationalists.

Readers of *Adam and Caroline* will reflect that nationalist
views might have been heard in the Arts Club long before 1918.
But that year was climacteric. In the spring, the threat of conscrip-
tion had created a real, if temporary, unity of mind. In Decem-

ber the general election brought the end of the parliamentary party which had dominated life in Ireland for a generation. It was replaced by the Sinn Fein party which had pledged itself to remain aloof from Westminster. Suddenly, for the first time since the Union, the centre of gravity of Irish politics had shifted from Westminster back to Dublin. It was no reason for wonder that the Arts Club should have borne a faint resemblance to the drawing-rooms of Petrograd a couple of years before. The ending of a regime was in the air and was chattered about by many who had no thought then of what such an ending might imply.

I had become quite a romantic young rebel. The Arts Club, the Abbey Theatre, the Irish Bookshop, the Crock of Gold and the Sod of Turf were all full of rebels—rebels with genteel outlooks and upper-class accents. The real rebels were far away in the background.

Through his membership of the Arts Club, George made the acquaintance of Sir Horace Plunkett. Plunkett had played a great part in Irish life since his foundation of the co-operative movement thirty years before. He was still in harness, endeavouring to find the middle of the stream of opinions and thoughts. As things turned out, the stream was to run more fully and violently than ever before. It was to cut new channels for itself. That was not yet fully apparent as the year ended with confident hopes that 1919 would bring a peace that would justify, if justification were possible, the slaughter of a generation. There was a magical air abroad of old worlds crumbling into a new age. The hopes of 1919 have been so deeply buried under the greater horrors yet to come that it is hard to realise that for one moment in this century it seemed possible that the world could be recast in a more splendid mould.

> *The world's great age begins anew,*
> *The golden years return. . . .*

As Sir Horace saw it, a new world had to be built on the shell-torn foundations of the old. In the case of Ireland, this called for a body of patriotic men who would study the changes in Irish life that had been imposed by the war and its consequences. They should come from all parties, all religions, all strains of race. Ideally, they would form a new Recess Committee which then as now appeared to be the greatest achievement of Sir Horace's career. Early in 1919 therefore, he founded the Irish Reconstruction Association. In this body, he hoped, everybody would come together to study the post-war problems of Ireland. No one then realised that for Ireland the real war had yet to come.

Clearly, some one with a training in economics was needed to help in such work. Such people were few in Ireland just then. George, however, had just published his first book. He was known to be unemployed. Almost certainly Father Finlay was consulted and gave his approval; very likely the idea came from him. Accordingly, George was vetted over dinner in the Stephen's Green Club by Plunkett's henchman, R. A. Anderson. (How many times this was to be repeated in the decades ahead, with George doing the vetting). The dinner was a success. He was brought around to Plunkett House, 84 Merrion Square, to discuss terms. He was signed on in the IRA—such initials meant no more than any other combination of letters. He was back in business.

The IRA published some pamphlets but it never quite got off the ground. Many of those who joined it belonged to the Ireland that had already passed away. They did not speak the same language or share the same values as those who had grown to maturity since 1914. That apart, it was impossible to plan constructively while the future of political power in Ireland was still in doubt. Every consideration of a specific problem led back to the same questions : what would be the powers of government; what financial resources would it control? Sir Horace had often complained of the Irish habit of spelling Political Economy with a large 'P' and a small 'e'. In 1919 it was inevitable. The only way to make progress, he concluded, was to establish a political organisation—the Irish Dominion League.

Before embarking on that topic it may be useful to recall the way of life in Plunkett House at that time. It was a curious mixture of the older Ireland and the new. The co-operative movement was still an object of world-wide interest. Its library, presided over by Florence Marks assisted by Diarmuid Coffey, was a place of pilgrimage. 'One was never surprised to meet an Italian, an Egyptian or a Chinaman on the stairs leading to the library.'

Plunkett House also contained the editorial offices of the *Irish*

Homestead, the organ of the Irish Agricultural Organization Society. It was edited by AE (George Russell) and his secretary, Susan Mitchell.

> Their office was decorated by AE with mural paintings in which noble figures, of more than life-size, led geese and swans on daisy-chains against a background of sunny landscape. . . . One night in the middle of the 'troubles', Plunkett House was raided by the Military when I happened to be there. They were looking for seditious literature but, when they saw the heap of books, pamphlets and papers, they flinched from the task of looking for a needle in that haystack. The British Tommies were slightly taken aback by the mural paintings. One of them thought that he was 'seeing things' and that he was heading for the DTs. Matters went no better when the search-party reached the back drawing-room which contained a portrait of Sir Horace. I had difficulty in persuading the officer in charge that the portrait of Sir Horace was not of Count Plunkett. He was deceived by the similarity of the names and the beards. However, he took my word.

It is not much of a story but it has perhaps an old-world charm. It was not to be long before even regular troops would become less trusting and less well-behaved. Even at that, George and Plunkett House were fortunate that the search was conducted by the regular rather than by the irregular forces of the Crown. He has left a little sketch of life in Plunkett House.

> The interesting population with which (it) was inhabited was outwardly very united and friendly. There was an afternoon tea party every day in (Anderson's) room at which everybody —with the exception of AE and Susan Mitchell—attended. But I think there must have been a considerable amount of silent strain and tension. Plunkett House was in many ways like a Court in which Sir Horace was King. Courts as a rule contain courtiers and favourites, and Plunkett House was no different from other courts in this respect. Some of the members of the IAOS staff must have regarded us as interlopers. Especially among the different generations of typists, there must have been a good deal of jealousy. There were court intrigues with petticoat influences in the background. I did not quite realise

at the time the intensity of feeling that must have prevailed among my co-inhabitants.

The intrigues and the jealousies were not solely feminine. It was said of Sir Horace that he was singularly unfortunate in his choice of some of the young men whom he brought into Ireland to help in his work. A contemporary saying was that if Saint Patrick had banished snakes from Ireland, Sir Horace had brought some of them back. These things did not disturb George at the time.

I was blissfully unconscious of the fires which burned beneath the pleasant crust on which I was enjoying life. I danced joyfully on the slopes of Vesuvius.

I spent most of the day in Plunkett House and most of my evenings at the Arts Club. I also managed to do a great deal of historical research and to publish another book. Altogether I was happy in the feeling that I was earning some money again, was occupied and was laying the foundation of a pleasant academic career.

There is a reminiscence of him in that spring of 1919, the first spring of peace for five years (and, as it turned out, the last for another five). Grafton Street and the north side of Stephen's Green still provided a place to promenade, the Beaux Walk transplanted only slightly after a century and a half. There on sunny mornings he was to be seen with straw hat and cane like any pre-war masher, moving through the pretty girls and young officers on their way to lunch at Kidds in Nassau Street.

He was now invited to dinner parties at Kilteragh, the house which Sir Horace had constructed for himself at Foxrock. Everybody interested in co-operation or in the solution of the Irish Question ended up at Kilteragh, 'travellers, economists, poets, reformers, realists, all the pathetic or preposterous who dream for Ireland', as Shane Leslie put it in *Doomsland*. Sir Horace enjoyed an international reputation : every visitor to Ireland of any importance believed that to meet him would justify the journey.

This led to some difficulties on occasion. There was the case of the Cabinet Minister who came over to study Anglo-Irish relations in the months before the fighting started. He was not of the first rank in Cabinet, but it was necessary that he should be well informed before he went back on the mail-boat. Unfortunately, a crisis arose on the very morning of the day that he was due for dinner; the cook informed Sir Horace that she was leaving the house on the spot. This was no matter of a wage dispute. She had surprised Sir Horace's then secretary in the act of love with a youth who was deputising for the regular postman. She would not remain under the same roof. The crisis was solved by recourse to the one person in Ireland who could be trusted to handle delicate affairs of high or low degree. Father Finlay was rung up at 35 Lower Leeson Street. He walked around to Harcourt Street station and caught one of the then frequent trains. He pointed out to the cook that the Minister's visit might turn out to be of enormous benefit to Ireland and that her well-justified anger should not be pressed to the point of hazarding the future of the country. The cook was mollified and discharged her duties like a culinary Joan of Arc. The dinner was a great success, though the Irish Question remained unsolved.

Another story illustrates another side of the Question. George mentioned Arthur Cox to Sir Horace. An invitation to Kilteragh followed at once. This was very awkward. Arthur's father was a close friend of John Dillon who had been a life-long opponent of Sir Horace and the co-operative movement. Arthur could visit Kilteragh only on condition of the strictest secrecy. Such were the smaller tensions of Irish life in those days.

It has been said that Sir Horace had come to believe that the Irish Reconstruction Association had no future. There was more immediate work to be done. The fighting had been ended by the Armistice in November 1918; the Peace Conference met in January 1919. This, it seemed at the time, meant that the Home Rule Act of 1914 must soon be brought into operation. It was on the Statute Book; its operation had been suspended for the duration of the war. That proviso would cease to have effect once the Peace Treaty had been signed, as it was in June 1919. But was it possible to implement the Act as it stood after so much had happened in Ireland and in the world? Above all, as it seemed to a generation that believed partition to be impossible or, if possible, nothing more than a hateful and temporary makeshift, what was to be done about Ulster?

Sir Horace had been reared as an Irish unionist. He never pretended to be anything else even when he aspired to spread co-operation throughout the country. Equally, he believed that Ireland had suffered many injustices through the Act of Union. This, to his mind, was bad in itself. It was still worse in its wider consequences because good Anglo-American relations would never be on a secure basis as long as the Irish Question remained unsolved. Ahead of his generation in many ways, he was deeply conscious of the importance to Great Britain of such good relations long before 1914. No small part of the inspiration of his work in Ireland before the war was to promote good relations between Great Britain and Ireland and, once they were achieved, between the United Kingdom and the United States.

He had believed that this could be achieved by remedial legislation, by the policy of 'killing Home Rule by kindness'. The calculation was that if economic grievances were once removed, the Irish people would settle down as the Scots had settled down over a century before. More than that, they would have a greater future and more opportunities as partners in the government of a secure and stable Empire than they could ever hope for in any form of isolation. (Things, of course, did not turn out in that way; but at least some members of the Home Rule party clearly feared that he was on the right track). By 1919, however, he was convinced that he had been mistaken. There had been thirty years of remedial legislation. The war had brought a prosperity to the country unknown in living memory. In spite of all these things, the people were as tenacious as ever in their demand for self-government.

Accordingly, in the early summer of 1919, Plunkett founded the Irish Dominion League. This was not a promising venture. Its supporters were largely drawn from what had been, before 1903, the land-owning class. They were largely unionist in their instincts. Some of them had been associated with the first suggestions of devolution fifteen years before : others had come to believe that a new initiative was necessary. Their weakness was that they were out-dated; they belonged to an era that had ended in 1914. They could not have won a constituency anywhere in the country, north or south. At home, they would get no support from the survivors of the parliamentary party who were still resentful at their rejection in the general election. They would get still less from Sinn Fein. In Great Britain there were many, some of them influential in the cabinet, who were determined to limit still further the already restricted provisions of the Home Rule Act if, indeed, they could not somehow get rid of it altogether.

Plunkett's answer might have been something as follows. It was not yet known what the British government thought about Ireland. (It did not become known until long afterwards that the British government wasn't thinking about Ireland at all.) But it was possible to believe, if one was very optimistic, that White-hall would have learned from its war-time experience in which representatives of the Dominions had sat in the War Cabinet and had signed the Treaty of Versailles. Moreover, the influence of at least some of the Dominions was known to favour a gener-ous Irish settlement, even if none of the overseas premiers wished to have that contentious subject dragged into his own politics. Over all this lay the imponderable issues of Anglo-American relations. The Fourteen Points had been published to the world. They spoke of self-determination. It was not then apparent that President Wilson had aroused hopes that he could not hope to satisfy. But, Wilson or no Wilson, opinion in the United States had to be placated. The issues at that time were very open. Dail Eireann had declared the Republic. It was not at all clear whether the people were willing to fight for it or whether they would accept what more than Home Rule they could get without fighting. The merit of Dominion status, as it then appeared, was that it provided a solution which a British government might accept without loss of face and, above all, which the Ulster Unionists could not easily reject. They could not insist on separa-tion from a self-governing Dominion. Partition would be impos-sible; and to all that generation, unionists, nationalists or separ-atists, partition appeared as the ultimate disaster. All this may have appeared only too clear to the older generation in Ireland in the early months of 1919. The trouble was that the gap be-tween generations in Ireland has possibly never been greater than it was at that moment.

The Irish Dominion League needed an organ through which it might diffuse its views. Plunkett opened negotiations with some members of the League with the object of founding a weekly journal. What George in reminiscence called 'a gentleman's agreement' was reached whereby one member would put up sufficient capital. This was not a happy description of what was intended. The capital to be subscribed did not belong to the member but to his wife. The *quid pro quo* was a knighthood (or a baronetcy, George was not always consistent on that. Granted the ease with which honours were obtained in 1918 neither would have presented much difficulty). Unfortunately the lady would not provide the money to her husband for transference to Plunkett. The news was broken at a table in the Stephen's Green : 'Boys, she won't part'. As had happened so often in the co-operative movement, Plunkett was left to find the money himself.[1]

Nevertheless, the *Irish Statesman* appeared on 28 June, 1919. The editor was Warre B. Wells, an Englishman who had edited the wartime Sunday edition of the *Irish Times*. He wrote the first book on the Irish Convention and later published two books of recollections of the Dublin scene. The assistant editors were Cruise O'Brien and George. One has a feeling that, while they got on reasonably well together, they did not like each other very much.

The editorial offices were on the third floor of 13 St Stephen's Green, at the corner of the Green with Dawson Street, above Grandy's 'the colonial outfitters'. They were not comfortable. They were reached by steep stairs. Below them the trams screeched over the points that bore them on their journeys to Donnybrook and Clonskea, Terenure and Dartry Road. The rooms had, however, two off-setting advantages. They looked over the Green and had all the afternoon sun. Also, they were convenient to the clubs. In the Stephen's Green, a few doors away to the right Sir Horace held court. He had resigned from the Kildare Street after a particularly savage row with its unionist members. To the left, the Arts Club was only a couple of minutes walk away. The editorial staff turned left more often than right.

We were a very happy family. I am afraid that we were all rather cynical over the lofty cause we were supposed to be

1. Readers of Miss Digby's *Horace Plunkett* (Basil Blackwood, Oxford, 1949) will observe that her account of the financing of the paper is incomplete.

The would-be purveyor of the capital, whom she names, was never forgiven for what was considered to be his perfidy; and the misfortunes of his later life were felt to be some form of delayed retribution. It does not seem that he did anything worse than to over-estimate his influence with his wife in the spending of her money.

serving. We wrote about half the paper ourselves and enlisted the services of many distinguished contributors. . . . The following list of contributors, taken almost at random from the index gives some idea of the literary quality of the paper : AE, George Birmingham, Thomas Bodkin, Ernest Boyd, Erskine Childers, John Eglinton, Darrell Figgis, Douglas Goulding, J. W. Good, Stephen Gwynn, Paul Henry, J. M. Hone, Shane Leslie, Brinsley MacNamara, Susan Mitchell, Eimar O'Duffy, P. S. O'Hegarty, Forrest Reid, Lennox Robinson, G. B. Shaw, E. O. E. Somerville, James Stephens, J. B. Yeats. . . .

Clifford Sharp, the editor of the *New Statesman*, of which we aimed at being an Irish counterpart, in format though not in fabianism, came to help us to produce the first number. The printer was George Roberts who was a superb craftsman. Between the army of talent which we succeeded in getting as contributors and the excellent typography, the paper was equally agreeable to the mind and to the eye. No periodical of the same standard has since appeared in Ireland.

The one weakness, as it was thought, which led to its disappearance after fifty-two issues, was its high price of six pence.

The whole atmosphere of the office was bohemian. All sorts of authors and poets used to drop in when they came to Dublin, and the office was a very merry place. The Arts Club was not far away in Stephen's Green and the activities of the office were frequently adjourned to the Club after business hours. Indeed many leading articles and book reviews were written in the Club. . . . Behind the scenes we treated it as a huge joke. We were like a party of schoolboys who had got hold of a rich uncle.

Cruise O'Brien was more succinct. He described it as 'milking the cow.' In fact the rich uncle spent most of his time in the United States during the life-time of the first *Irish Statesman*. He kept a close watch on what was published. Around this time, the United States was moving towards 'the experiment noble in purpose' known as Prohibition. Mr W. E. Johnson, a leader of that campaign, popularly known as 'Pussyfoot', announced his intention of visiting Dublin. In a leading article (unsigned, as were all leading articles and most of the reviews), George suggested that the visitor should be thrown into the Liffey. Sir Horace did not take kindly to this light-hearted suggestion and a long correspendence followed in which George's offer of resignation was firmly rejected. Plunkett's point was not the rights or wrongs of Prohibition but the over-riding necessity of not alienating any section (and at that time the prohibitionist section was dominant) of American opinion. George's attitude was not based on such global considerations.

My views in this article reflected the characteristic attitude of my Arts Club companions. As an undergraduate I had been a great 'Chester-Belloc' and had come to believe in the myth of a Merry England composed of hearty, alcohol-loving craftsmen and peasants. It was part of my creed that the good Catholic was always half intoxicated. This was about the only article of my faith that I practised assiduously. These ideological beliefs were enthusiastically held in the Arts Club. Pussyfoot represented the enemy, the kill-joy puritan devil whom we all agreed to spurn and revile.

The *Statesman* lasted for just one year : its last issue was in June 1920. In those twelve months, affairs in Ireland had gone from bad to worse. In the summer of 1919 it was still possible to believe that the situation might be resolved without extensive violence; twelve months later both sides had settled down to fight it out. Neither of them was interested in Dominion status : for the Dail it was too little, for the British government it was far too much. In later years George made no claim that the *Statesman* had influenced the course of events. He did assert, and with some justice, that it had some influence on the section of British public opinion, then still powerful, which was instinctively in favour of a solution along liberal lines and was increasingly restive at the methods used by the government to fight the IRA.[1]

1. The reader may be referred to Chapter Thirteen (Ireland, 1913–21) in Part Two of *The History of the Times: The 150th Anniversary and Beyond 1912–48*, published by *The Times* in 1952.
    It describes the efforts of the then Editor, Wickham Steed, to press the British Government into declaring its policy towards Ireland. Its own proposals, set out in this chapter, were largely inspired by an interesting and rather enigmatic figure of the time—R. J. Herbert Shaw, formerly Secretary of the Irish Unionist Alliance and later concerned in the foundation of the Unionist Anti-Partition League. This move, in June and July 1919, owed much to reports of American interest in Irish affairs.

If one reads through the files of the *Statesman* one may note how the tone of comment becomes, if not increasingly favourable to republicanism, at least increasingly convinced that nothing less than a radical settlement could be of any use. This must have had an effect on readers in Great Britain whose minds would already have been made receptive by the remarkably high literary achievement of the journal.

For George himself the connection with Plunkett and the *Statesman* was invaluable. He was taken up and given a sense of purpose and belonging when such encouragement was desperately needed. In later years he never forgot his debt to Plunkett. It was a happy time after much unhappiness.

> The days passed very pleasantly. The office did not make much demands on my time, but I always had it to go to if I wanted. I did a good deal of research in the Royal Irish Academy and the National Library. We spent our evenings in the Arts Club where we had occasional 'jamborees' at which new 'sagas' were performed. Looking back on it from a distance I see that my life was a pleasant blend of the academic and the bohemian. The war had ended; the serious Irish violence had not yet begun; my business was flourishing and I was completely free of financial worries. I could not be reproached with idleness. I was earning a small salary at perfectly respectable journalism, and at the same time making more secure the foundations on which the, now assumed inevitable, academic career would be built.

All this was a great deal better than catching early trains to country sessions. It was good while it lasted. But when the *Statesman* ceased publication, he lost his small salary and, what was a great deal more important, a great deal of his purpose in life. Fortunately, writing took up a good deal of his time in the next eighteen months to two years. The fact remained that a second career seemed to have ended and the habits that had been acquired could not be easily shaken off. The period from the middle of 1920 to the middle of 1923 was one of strain.

The Irish Dominion League survived the *Statesman* but its relevance to public affairs, never perhaps very great, had almost disappeared by the spring of 1921. The situation was changed out of recognition by the Truce in July 1921. However the fact might be hedged around, Dail Eireann had been recognised. It had won the battle of wills. What remained uncertain, and was so to remain for months, was whether any settlement could be negotiated. The question necessarily arose whether the League could serve any useful purpose. George thought it could. He addressed a letter to Sir Horace which deserves quotation in full, not so much for its historical value but because it shows how clearly his mind worked and how he could impress his point of view on others. Those who knew him in much later years will recognise the technique at once.

I happened to be in the office today when the future of the IDL was being discussed; and I know you will not consider it an impertinence if I write to tell you my own view of the matter. My only excuse of offering an opinion unasked on the subject is that I am profoundly anxious that the IDL—and its President—should cut as good a figure as possible before the public.

While I was doubtful about the wisdom of the foundation of the League, and have been at all times pessimistic about its success, I am quite clear that its existence should not be discontinued at the present moment. The political situation is moving with such kaleidoscopic rapidity that it is quite impossible to foretell what the next week or the next day will bring; but I think it is reasonably safe to say that we should know definitely within a month whether the present peace negotiations are going to result in success or failure. It seems to me that once that is known the proper action for the League to take will emerge quite clearly. If the negotiations end in a settlement, the basis of that settlement will necessarily be something resembling the dominion status; and in that case the League will be able to close its doors with a flourish, having achieved the ends it set out to attain. If, on the other hand, the negotiations break down, it will be the most natural thing in the world for the League to dissolve on the plea of the general hopelessness of any good being done by anybody. Thus, in either case the League will be in a position to go out of business without any confession of failure. On the other hand, to go out of business at the present moment would, in my opinion, amount to the clearest confession of failure. It would be open to the comment that the Dominion League broke down through lack of support at the precise moment when politicians of all parties were, for the first time, seriously discussing the possibility of a dominion settlement and it would create the—totally wrong—impression that the number of people in Ireland who favour a dominion settlement was negligible, and thus diminish the possibility of such a status being conceded by the Government.

If the above analysis of the situation be correct, it follows that everything points to the wisdom of the League's continuing to beat time for at least a few weeks more. I cannot help feeling that, if there were a settlement, the fact that the League was not 'in at the finish' would seriously injure the political reputation of its founders and supporters.

Plunkett's reply does not survive but the League was not dissolved before the Treaty was signed. George's letter was hardly necessary : throughout his long and active life Plunkett never despaired. The interest of the letter lies elsewhere than in the periphery of Irish political history. In the first place, it is a remarkable letter from a man not yet out of his twenties. In the second place, it shows the genuine care that he had then and later for Plunkett's reputation; personally, he had next to nothing to gain, financially or politically, from a continuation of the League. In the third place, the texture of the letter, now based on principle, now on an *argumentum ad hominem,* is exactly in line with the approach to issues which he was to use decades later. His colleagues in the College would recognise the style at once. He was always superb at defining issues and choices and, after that, keeping all possible options open.

The Treaty was signed on 6 December 1921. It was ratified by a narrow majority on 7 January 1922. The Dominion League was dissolved shortly afterwards. A new chapter in his life was about to begin.

7

After the Treaty 1921-26

HOLDING the views that he did, his attitude to the Treaty was predictable. It was

one of relief that at last we would have some peace and that there would be no more ambushes and shootings. . . . I regarded the Treaty as a great victory for the cause of Irish nationalism. It went further in the direction of complete independence than anybody had believed possible. . . . The retention of the Crown and the oath of allegiance did not take away from the magnitude of the achievement. Those institutions did not fetter the independence of the other Dominions, and, if they were found oppressive in practice, could be removed by diplomatic action at a later date. Partition was, of course, the great blot. But, here again, true statesmanship would have aimed at making the best of a very bad situation and at seeking to repair the damage to national unity before it became irreparable. . . . I felt then, as I still do, that the refusal to accept such a far-reaching instrument was political madness, based on personal jealousy rather than on any reasoned conviction. . . .

In his later years he might have worded these opinions rather differently but he certainly held them strongly at the time of the split and for long afterwards. At the time he had no hesitations. Apart from his own feelings, all his friends, those whom he had met in College or at the Bar as well as those whom he had met later in the Arts Club or Plunkett House, were for the Treaty. The fact that Arthur Clery was against it seemed to clinch the matter.

More deeply, his feeling was that a great opportunity to make a new start and to refashion the country had been needlessly thrown away.

As long as Home Rule was denied, the greater part of the national energy was dissipated in the movement for independence. Elections were decided on the national issue without regard to the personal ability of candidates to sit as members of parliament. Whoever was elected, the public services were still carried on. The postman delivered his letters and the policeman tramped his beat. The real case for Home Rule was that the people would never again settle down under the Union. They were discontented and irresponsible. This was bad for them morally. I think that it was considerations of this nature that made Father Finlay a nationalist. He believed that self-government would have the same tonic effect politically that agricultural co-operation would have economically.

His College friendships were now to bear much fruit. Throughout the period of the first government he was in constant demand to sit on committees of enquiry and the like. These assignments kept him busy at a time when he had not much else to do. They were not remunerated, but they brought him in touch with the economic issues of the day. They also entangled him in controversies arising out of the political implications of those issues. The results were to affect all his later career. It seems best to deal with these matters in a separate chapter. We will now turn to his remarkably varied life in the decade between the Treaty and the change of government in 1932.

The memory of what had been regarded as normal life had grown faint when hostilities ended in 1923. There had been the European war, the rising, the Black and Tans and the civil war. It was ten years out of one's life. The return to normality went slowly. The Custom House and the Four Courts still lay in ruins : Upper O'Connell Street was a pile of rubble. Every street in the city was full of pot-holes and craters. These marks of the struggle were tacitly ignored as peaceful life returned. For a few indeed, it may have seemed as if it had hardly been interrupted. The clubs and learned societies emerged in the twenties much as they had been ten years before though the members were fewer and that much older. (This was to have much relevance to George's career.) It was symbolic of the limits of change that the tricolour did not fly at international matches, such as at Fitzwilliam or Lansdowne Road, until the next decade. The King was still saved with heart and voice at every Horse Show until 1939. Anglo-Ireland might have lost the Castle, but it survived barely touched in its cantonments.

A stage had been reached at which one could not go on fighting. There was a truce of exhaustion, tinged with a feeling that, one way or another, some things had been settled at least for a while. This, of course, did not apply to those who opposed the Treaty—a large exception seeing that they were to come into government in ten years. It did apply to the then much larger number of people who desired a patch of peace. The normal avenues of human intercourse were reopened though some street-signs had been changed and no-go areas still abounded. There was a better, though still uneasily better, feeling than there had been for years.

An example, ridiculous in itself, may be dredged up from the memory of those years. Barrel-organs were still part of the furniture of the streets. Around the middle or later years of the decade, a group of ex-servicemen invested in one of them. Physically they bore some resemblance to Captain Bairnsfather's creation of Ole Bill, but they showed themselves to be acute observers of the social and political scene. They did not play the popular tunes of the day. They played national anthems. They did not appear in Grafton Street; they confined themselves to Merrion and Fitz-william Squares where the doctors now held undisputed sway after the exodus of Castle officials in 1922. They would start on a side of one or other of the squares. The doctors' plates on the hall-doors were a fairly (though not completely) reliable guide to the politics of the household within. At the first house, it might be, King George would be sent happy and glorious. A parlour-maid—there were still such in those days—would open the door, go down the steps and present the musicians with sixpence or maybe even a shilling. They moved on to the next house, whose occupant was clearly one of the risen people. The lighter strains of *A Soldier's Song* would ring out. Again, a parlour-maid would emerge and tribute be paid. At times, it might be neces-sary to play one anthem or the other five or six times in succession. That didn't matter to anybody, least of all to the crew of the barrel-organ which, at the end of a morning's work, would be seen derelict outside Higgins's public-house in Lower Pembroke Street while the offerings of loyalties were washed down inside at seven pence a pint. This was quite ridiculous. But the passers-by took it as a good joke. That would not have happened in the Warsaw or the Prague of the 1920s.

George's life flowered in this relaxed atmosphere. Those years of the early and middle twenties were a time of making new friends and, through them, becoming a member of some institutions which were to be important to him in later years. In 1920 he was elected to the Royal Irish Academy on the proposal of Father Finlay. He was unusually young to be elected but he had already published books that had been well received. As will be seen later, he was elected just in time to be involved in matters which might have seriously injured its work. He was elected to the Council of the Academy in 1924 and served on several occasions. He was a Vice-President in 1944–45 and again in 1949–50. The Academy was a meeting place for members of the College staff, of whom he knew few in those days, and for the staff of Trinity, of whom he knew even fewer. It was through their common membership of the Academy that he met William Fearon who was perhaps his closest friend in later years and certainly one of the very few of his friends who was a contemporary. Fearon became Professor of Biochemistry in Trinity and later still represented the University in Seanad Eireann. They had much in common.

> We were the same age, were the only sons of widowed mothers and had been brought up against the same background of pre-war Kingstown. We knew so many of the same places and people in our youth that we spoke the same language and could take a lot for granted in our conversation. Our careers were destined to run on very parallel lines, both bachelors, doctors, professors and senators.

In 1925 he became a member of the Royal Dublin Society. That institution was, just then, engaged in an anxious and cautious transformation. It had not been, any more than the Academy, involved in politics directly. It had, undoubtedly, acquired (or deepened) a unionist tinge under the long presidency of Lord Ardilaun before 1914. It was only a few years since its members had been so unwise as to attempt to expel Count Plunkett from membership because he was the father of an executed rebel. Its membership was still small, rather more than three thousand, and tended to be exclusive. When George joined it, it had just been displaced from its premises in Leinster House so that the Oireachtas might have a safe meeting place.

The particular importance of the RDS to George was quite practical.

> Its library was exceptionally well-stocked. I can date my second period of general education to this period. My first had been in Glasgow eight years earlier. I now read widely in all kinds of subjects and added greatly to my knowledge and culture. It was about a year later that I began to lecture in the College. I suddenly found myself called on to teach a subject in which I had no regular discipline. I taught myself a good deal about economics and economic history in the RDS. I read section 330 of the library from end to end. . . . I owe a very great part of whatever professional proficiency I possess to my hard study in the library.

It was almost inevitable that he should rise high in whatever society he joined. As a constant reader in the library, he was soon made a member of the book-buying committee. This was one of the first steps in the *cursus honorum* by which the Society recruits its officers: the equivalent on the agricultural side was the stewarding of butter exhibits at the Spring Show. He rose to the Committee for General Purposes, then after several years and many deaths to the Council and later still to a vice-presidency.

In some moods he was very proud of membership of the Council: one remembers that about 1939, soon after he had been elevated to it, he argued that *en bloc* it would admirably provide the nucleus of the new Seanad which Mr de Valera had just established. In other moods he would complain that the Council was allowed too little freedom of discussion. It does not seem that the RDS has changed much over a generation. One other consequence of membership which he deeply appreciated was to be made a Trustee of the National Library in 1934. Eventually he became chairman of the Trustees, acting in that capacity from 1967 until just before his death.

There was one other institution which he joined at this time which was to play a great part in his life. In 1922 he became a member of the Royal Irish Yacht Club in Dun Laoghaire or, as a clear majority of its then members would have had it, Kings-

D*

town. (For many years, until note-paper became hard to get in war-time, the members of the club could write their letters under the heading of the English or the Irish name of the borough. Not all that far removed from the barrel-organ.)

It need hardly be said that he was no sailor. He knew nothing, and cared less, about sailing. In his later years he grew testy when sailing members and their guests came late into the dining-room. So far as he was concerned, they were improperly dressed, they were noisy and there were too many of them. For him, the Irish was a dining club. It became for him something more : in all too literal a sense a home from home. His membership did not, perhaps, begin too well. He gave parties which included Kevin O'Higgins and Paddy Hogan and, later, the delightful German Minister-Plenipotentiary, Dr von Dehn, who was later recalled and disgraced by the Nazis. It did not occur to him at the time that the older members, glowering down at his party from the round table, would have disliked Sinn Feiners perhaps rather more than they disliked Germans. But he became an institution as he grew more senior. He met his friends there and he introduced new members in their turn. He was delighted when he was made an honorary member. In his last illness, his test of his prospects was whether he would be let out to lunch there, and so he was; a token of recovery which was soon belied. Probably he liked the Irish more than anything else in his later life.

In this way he acquired a variety of new interests within a comparatively short time. This was an extension rather than a change in his life. In making new friends he did not sacrifice the old. He had few friends to lose; after the collapse at the Bar and the end of the first *Statesman* he had no position in life. It was natural that he should respond to any invitation into new circles. It was equally natural that he should receive such invitations from the members of institutions whose numbers and activities had been run down in the years after 1914. He was already a good and tactful conversationalist : what a later generation would call 'a good mixer'. Further, if his distinction was very different from what he had hoped, it was still real. He had published serious books; he had helped to edit the *Statesman*; he had been taken up by Horace Plunkett. There were many reasons why he should be asked to join this or that : there was no reason why he should refuse.

Personal acquaintanceships led him further afield. His meeting with Ted Riordan had many consequences. Riordan was passionately interested in the possibilities of economic regeneration. He was instrumental in placing George on the committees of enquiry which will be mentioned later. Through Riordan, George met Timothy Smiddy for the first time. Smiddy was then professor of Economics in University College, Cork. Later he was to become a diplomatic representative of the Irish Free State (a landmark in the development of Commonwealth relations) when he became Irish minister to Washington. Later still, he became a director of the Central Bank. In the 1930s and the two succeeding decades he was close to Mr de Valera and advised him on economic affairs. In these ways he was a person of considerable influence in the first thirty years of the Irish state which owes him a debt of gratitude that has never been fully recognised. He was the kindest of men and a great encourager of the young. It was always a joyful occasion and an uplift to the spirit to meet that dapper, friendly figure in the street.

Another in the same circle was Father Connolly, the editor of *Studies* from 1914 to 1950. He was an influential figure in the three decades after the Treaty. He made *Studies* into a forum where the economic and social issues of the day might be defined and discussed. By the standards of today, these discussions may not seem to have gone very deep, but it was a conservative time. Nowhere else, if one excludes the comparatively short-lived *Statesman*, were such issues discussed; politics still revolved around the oath of allegiance and the annuities. *Studies* discussed the issues of what might be done in Ireland, more important, what kind of country Ireland should be, what philosophy should guide its policies. George became one of its most regular contributors. It was a connection of which he was very proud and which he valued greatly until 'Mops' Connolly retired.

These connections related to George as an economist and a professor. There were many others of a more general nature. They will now be listed with what may seem copious quotations from the recollections. They will, however, illustrate the curious subdivisions of Irish life at that time.

A venture that provided some interest during these rather barren years was the Irish Book Shop. The first begetter of this enterprise was, I think, Mrs Coffey. There was an idea that there was room in Dublin for a first-class bookshop that would specialise in Irish literature. A group of twelve people was collected, each of whom contributed £50. The influence of Plunkett House was so pervasive in our circle that we founded, not as one would have supposed, a private company but a co-operative society. With this small capital, reinforced by a loan from the National Land Bank, we opened a shop in Dawson Street. . . . Mrs Stopford Green, who was one of the partners, suggested that P. S. O'Hegarty should be appointed manager. 'P.S.' had given up his excellent position in the Post Office because he could not conscientiously take the oath of allegiance then being administered to Irish civil servants, and was unemployed. . . . 'P.S.' was a great bibliophile and collector as well as being a voracious reader. Never was there a man more suited for book-selling. He could discuss the technicalities of first editions and criticize their literary content with the same degree of expert knowledge and good taste. After the Treaty 'P.S.' was suitably rewarded for his patriotic record by being appointed Secretary of the Department of Posts and Telegraphs and we lost his services, though not, I am glad to say, his friendship. . . . During the couple of years that 'P.S.' was manager, the Bookshop was the centre of literary Dublin. Authors and critics were constant customers and one was always sure of good talk if one dropped in. If there were no customers there was 'P.S.' himself who was always good company. In the basement below the shop Mrs Coffey opened a little teashop called *The Sod of Turf* where potato cakes and other native delicacies were served in surroundings suitably dismal for the superior spirits of the Gaelic renaissance. Further along the street, Mrs Kennedy Cahill ran *The Crock of Gold* whose windows were always full of gaily coloured tweeds and homespuns. There was a pleasant atmosphere about all these enterprises, which were in the Ruskin-Morris traditions of arts and crafts, of the intelligentsia redeeming the vulgarity of trade.

A very different friendship was that which developed with the Marquis MacSwiney of Mashanaglass. The title was papal; various stories, all of them malicious, circulated in Dublin about its origin. In full fig the Marquis was an arresting sight, 'bedizened', as Jack Fitzgerald said in a memorable after-dinner speech, 'back, belly and sides with the stars and orders won on many a hard-fought battlefield'. Titles of all descriptions were suspect just then, and the concept that there could be titles other than British had not yet been accepted.

George retained an unusual degree of affection for the Marquis. They had become known to each other while the Marquis was still in Rome, a point in one of George's books having started a correspondence. Later the Marquis moved to Dublin where

he attempted the social education of nationalist circles in Dublin but he overrated the aptness and enthusiasm of his pupils and slowly gave up the attempt. He was, in any event, not ideally suited for this very delicate experiment owing to his own peculiar temperament. He had the unfortunate habit of quarrelling with his friends. The slightest real or imaginary affront converted enthusiastic friendship into inveterate enmity. I succeeded in avoiding a quarrel, rather by dint of not seeing him too often.

This was the more easily done because as time went on the Marquis turned increasingly to the organisation of the Knights of Malta. On the other hand, they met often at one of his most fruitful initiatives, the foundation of a dining club among the members of the Academy. This was one area in which he brooked no rival : he was the unquestioned *arbiter elegantiarum*.

These were years, it is necessary to remember, that were not all that happy for George. He was taken up all round, he moved in many circles, his advice was sought by the new government. But none of these activities brought him any money. That did not matter in one sense : the hotel was still doing well. But he was still without a recognised occupation and there seemed to be no sign of anything happening in the College. This may explain the unusually grateful tone of his reference to the Marquis.

The Marquis was always kind and friendly to me even in this later stage of his career. If I did not see very much of him it was my fault as much as his, because I deliberately kept at a fairly safe distance in order to avoid a row. . . . But at the time of which I am writing, when I was a young scholar attempting to make a reputation as a historian, I saw him a great deal and received from him encouragement and recognition. . . . (He) was kind to me at a time when I needed kindness.

In these years also he made contact with two very different sectors of life in Dublin. What he wrote about them may be of interest, if only because it depicts some ways of life and thought which have long passed out of memory.

Through membership of the Irish he made the acquaintance of William Butler, historian and at one time a Commissioner of Secondary Education.

William was a nephew of his famous name-sake, Sir William Butler. He came from a family of Catholic landlords who had held on to their property in Tipperary all through the penal times. . . . I had always thought, or rather, I should say, had held the view without giving the matter any thought, that Catholics in Ireland, apart from a few notable exceptions such as the Fingalls, were socially inferior. Of course, it was true; it was the inevitable result of the course of Irish history, that the great majority of the landed gentry were Protestants, and that of the working class, Catholics. My fellow students at Belvedere and University College and all my Catholic barrister friends came from the middle class, either professional or business. Most of them were not more than a generation or two removed from poor family surroundings. I discovered from my association with William Butler that there was a class of Catholic gentry with a very good conceit of their own position in the world. . . . Their ancestors had suffered so much from protestant domination and privilege up to recent times that they were rather bigoted. They mixed freely with Protestants but they were very conscious of the religious division. Although they had mostly been at school in England and were more like English than Irish Catholics, they were slightly anti-English because they regarded England as the bulwark of protestantism in Europe. . . . In so far as they were nationalists, they were nationalist in the O'Connell rather than the Parnell tradition. That is to say, they put the interest of the Church first, and wished for Home Rule mainly as the instrument for ending Protestant ascendancy. They blamed Parnell for having linked together Home Rule and Land Reform, as a result of

which, they said, nationalism had become a lower class movement. The richer and more cultivated sections of society had
been driven into opposition to Irish self-government in order
to preserve their landlord interest. They had no sympathy
with the later developments of Irish nationalism, such as the
Sinn Fein movement or the language revival. They were very
conservative and had little or no interest in labour problems.
The 'condition of the people' left them unmoved.

The political and social outlook of this circle appealed to all
my own sympathies and prejudices, and I fitted into their
society very well. Although I came from a lower social class, I
was accepted and made welcome by many of Butler's friends.
. . . I think that this class represents my true spiritual home.
Its valuations, its outlook is my outlook, and its standards are
my standards. It satisfies my ideal of the Catholic gentleman
who possesses a poise based on an assured equilibrium with
the outer world of society and the inner world of ethics and
religion.

He was introduced to a very different section of life in Dublin
by William Fearon. In the 1930s E. G. Peake was one of the
brewers in St James's Gate and lived in 98 James's Street. Peake,
a friend of Fearon's, was deeply interested in economics and
finance: a reference to him and an acknowledgement of his
suggestions will be found in Keynes's *Treatise on Money*. He
and George took to each other at once. So began another circle
of bachelor dinner parties. Into his very last year of life he was
always at pains to organise things so that he had someone to
dine with every evening. In the 1920s this cannot have been
any problem.

His new acquaintances were the brewers who, in those days
at least, held themselves aloof from Dublin life. Their roots were
not in Dublin, they were temporarily on service in a strange
country.

They were old-fashioned individualists in politics, believers in
free trade and competition. They were the products of what
Roy Harrod has described as 'Cambridge civilization both
in its stability and self-confidence and in its progressiveness'.
They were not interested in Irish politics: they were still
less interested in religion; so that the two principal causes

of argument at that time were eliminated from the start.

Instinctively he shared many of their views about society. On quite another plane they excited his curiosity. There was in him a strong strain of Proust. He must speak for himself on this matter.

There was an assured attitude towards life based on a secure position in society and an ample income. Fundamentally, I suppose I agreed with the people in this circle on most of the important valuations, and that is why we got on so well together in spite of the difference in our background. I agreed with their liberal, individualistic outlook which was consistent with the atmosphere of my Victorian childhood. Success and failure in life were regarded as the normal rewards and punishments of business enterprise or the reverse. It was tacitly assumed that the best way of helping the working class to better their lot was to let businessmen scramble for profits. Increasing production would raise wages and competition would lower prices. This was the creed of the great classical economists and I was glad to find it enthroned in such an intellectual and successful circle. I have little doubt that these friendships coloured my teaching of economics.

The time was the middle twenties, when it was still believed that the post-war world would be the pre-war world restored and improved. Businessmen could still be confident—perhaps all the more so if they belonged to the Brewery or the Bank. In later years George was to revise his socio-economic values, but that did not happen until he had been many years in his chair. All this scene seems a world away from the Dublin of the second and third decades of the century as it has been portrayed by novelists and dramatists. But it is the same city.

To return to George.

When I reflect on the qualities that attracted me in many of these new friends and acquaintanceships, I can reach certain conclusions which cast light upon my own character. I was attracted to most of my friends more by their good manners than by their deeper intellectual or moral qualities. I am afraid that I am more attracted by good manners than by good morals or, perhaps I should say, I am more repelled by bad

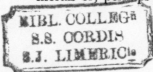

manners than by bad morals. . . . Some of my friendships were based on social curiosity, which may be labelled snobbery by hostile observers. But it was not really snobbery, which consists in looking down on one's inferiors, a fault of which I was never guilty. My desire to be friendly with some of my more highly placed acquaintances was analogous to my desire to see the interior of a fine Georgian mansion. It was an artistic curiosity, an anxiety to investigate at close quarters something that I had admired from afar. It was a tribute to a way of life which embodied my notion of an elegant and civilized mode of existence, based on the possession of leisure and culture. That the reality was not always as good as the expectation did not matter. The point was that I had made the investigation in person and had satisfied my curiosity at first hand. There was another motive in operation, namely my desire to satisfy myself that I was accepted on equal terms by people whose position could not be questioned. It was part of my desire for security, or my anxiety to gain support. During my childhood, I had been impressed with the inferior position of people who earned their living in business. I suppose I must have suffered from an inferiority complex on this subject.

All these activities, it might be thought, were quite sufficient to fill his days. But there were other things to do. One in particular became important in the closing years of the decade, the responsibility of acting as escort to the wife of the King's representative in Ireland. James MacNeill had become Governor-General in 1928. He was thoroughly hospitable but had little taste for social activity. His wife, Josephine, was handsome and highly intelligent. She felt it her duty to be seen around the city. It was a long time since any vice-regal consort had been active in this way, if one excepts Lady Aberdeen. Gradually George drifted into the position of being one of her more usual escorts. He was already acting in much the same capacity for Mrs Kevin O'Higgins. This made demands both on his time and on his tact because, it was understood, the two ladies did not get on well together.

The precise status of the Viceregal Lodge was a matter of some discussion. Clearly, it was much too royal for many; as Mr de Valera was to emphasise when he came into office. It was not nearly royal enough for those who remembered the glittering days of Lord Dudley but forgot that much had happened in Ireland and the world since 1905. At one function there Gogarty remarked to George that he was not sure whether he had come up in the world or whether the Lodge was going down. George replied that it was a matter of meeting on the staircase.

There were the salons; AE on Sunday evenings, Con Curran on Wednesday evenings and Sarah Purser every second Tuesday. The hospitality available was unequal. Miss Purser was notoriously economical. This did not deter her from criticism of AE's 'sloppy tea and stale cakes' or wonder at the lovely cakes at Con Curran's. ('How do they do it on his salary'?)

These meeting places could be distinctly mixed. There was, for example, the unconstructed survivor of the older regime who invariably referred to the President of the Executive Council of the Irish Free State as 'that murderous pot-boy'.

At the end of 1922 I became a member of a very interesting dining club which met one night each week in the old Moira restaurant. W. B. Yeats had requested Lennox Robinson to collect a number of people, each expert in a different subject, who would meet and conduct an informal discussion on public affairs. Yeats had become a senator and was beginning to take himself very seriously. I think his idea was to have somebody to brief him for debates in the Senate. On November 15th Lennox Robinson gave a small dinner party in the Moira 'to meet Mr Yeats. . . . to discuss matters of interest to all of us'. It was arising out of this dinner party that the dinner club was formed. The original members included, in addition to Yeats, Lennox Robinson and myself, Desmond Fitzgerald, Tom McGreevey, Brinsley MacNamara, P. S. O'Hegarty and L. Smith-Gordon. Others were co-opted from time to time, amongst whom I particularly remember J. W. Good, Bryan Cooper and Henry Clarke. We were, I believe, known as the Twelve Apostles. As is usual in gatherings of this kind the original purpose of regular conversation soon faded out and we indulged in general conversation. Yeats used to talk with great effect even when he talked nonsense. I think he resented my habit of puncturing some of his finer flights of fancy by the introduction of a designedly inconvenient fact. . . . We occasionally had visitors and I remember one evening we had James Larkin who impressed me very favourably. He had a much greater knowledge of literature than I would have expected, having lived in London in the nineties. He and Yeats exchanged recollections of the Yellow Book circle. Larkin also pleased me by his generosity towards his opponents. He said that he admired W. M. Murphy because he was a hard but clean fighter for his own side. Ultimately our dining club came to an end because, in a weak moment, we admitted as a member, against our own better judgement and under the pressure of his importunity, a bore. Our new member was such a capital example of his kind that the other members gradually fell off in attendance and the club quietly died. . . . We attempted a resurrection later in Jammets, with the bore omitted, but, like other attempts to repeat successes, the effort failed; the original impetus had departed. My most permanent benefit from the dinner club was the friendship of Bryan Cooper, who ran a most opulent and hospitable house in Dalkey and of J.W.—'Jimmie'—Good, whom I afterwards got to know very well indeed. Alas, those two good friends died young—both under fifty. It was I who suggested that Bryan's life should be remembered in a short biography. This suggestion led to Lennox Robinson's little masterpiece.

There were plenty of other dinners as the decade went on. They were part of an almost self-conscious revival of pre-war habits. There had been a long tradition of private entertaining in Dublin before the war. The doctors were pre-eminent in the revival. They had more time, and perhaps more money, than the other professions. They feared no competition from those engaged in manufacturing and trade who tended to keep themselves to themselves. Prominent among them was Kennedy Cahill who entertained lavishly and, in keeping with another tradition, regaled his guests with music after dinner. Joseph O'Mara, or in his absence Joseph O'Reilly, was a regular contributor at these evenings. George was inconsolable when Kennedy Cahill died suddenly, and spoke as if it were the end of an era. In that he was more correct than he could possibly have foreseen. The date was January 1930, soon after the Wall Street crash which ushered in the Depression and the end of the attempt to recreate a world that had ended in 1914. The later 1920s were an interlude that had singularly little to do with what had gone before or was to come after. But it was about the only period in this century that knew that it was post-war and never had to worry whether it might not be pre-war also.

8

The Second *Statesman:*
The Abbey Theatre 1923-30

In 1923 Horace Plunkett decided to revive the *Irish Statesman*. The first series had promoted the cause of Dominion Home Rule; the second proposed to defend the Treaty and to explain its potentialities not only in Ireland but also in the United States.

The Treaty was being represented in the United States, not as a measure of liberation but as a measure of oppression. It was with the object of educating American opinion and, in particular, Irish-American opinion, that Plunkett decided to revive the *Irish Statesman*. By putting things in their right perspective in the United States, the paper would save the Irish government from ill-informed and ignorant criticism. This argument impressed Plunkett's American friends, who contributed a considerable amount of money to put the paper on its feet. The revived *Irish Statesman* was designed, therefore, primarily to appeal to Irish-American readers.

The money came from the United States or, more exactly, from Irish-Americans such as Senator Cullinan and Judge Campbell. They represented a group that had already brought pressure to bear on the Wilson administration to interest itself in the Anglo-Irish situation some years before. Several of them were to support Al Smith in his presidential campaign in 1928. The Irish-Americans gave their subscriptions without any strings: 'they regarded them in the light of donations to a political cause of which they approved rather than as a serious business investment'. Plunkett gave one share each to James Douglas, Lionel Smith-Gordon, Yeats and George to qualify them to act as directors.

Although on any difference of opinion, we could always outvote Plunkett, we always, in fact, deferred to his views, sometimes against our better judgement. The money invested was his, not ours, and he was getting to an age when a man likes his little fancies indulged.

Two matters arose on which there was a difference of opinion : the importance of the American circulation and the editorial staffing. Together, the decisions taken may have affected—in George's view they did affect—the survival of the paper.

It is indubitable that the Irish-American public was the audience which Plunkett had mainly in mind when he decided to revive the paper, and it was on account of its probable appeal to that audience that the American subscribers had been willing to support it. In spite of a good deal of publicity, the American sales remained very small, and, indeed, the paper in the form which it assumed was scarcely designed to appeal to American tastes. Nothing would persuade Plunkett that there was not a large untapped market in the United States. He exaggerated the degree of interest that the average Irish-American takes in the affairs of his native land or the native soil of his ancestors. He believed that a gigantic advertising campaign would result in a large number of new subscribers.

Accordingly, a substantial part of the capital was sunk in an unrewarded advertising campaign in the United States.

The wise thing to have done would have been to budget for an annual loss and to eat slowly into our capital. Our expenses of production were high owing to the extravagant editorial arrangements, and it was unreasonable to expect a large circulation even in Ireland for a paper which catered for popular appeal so little and made so few concessions to political passions or prejudices. Our principal purpose, after all, was not to make a profit but to educate public opinion, to represent a point of view not otherwise represented, and to provide the country with a weekly organ on a high cultural level. . . . If we had invested what we wasted on the American publicity at five per cent and dissipated a small part of our capital every year we could have prolonged the life of the paper for many years.

A reading of the files of the second series does not suggest that Plunkett's intention was consistently pursued. Many of those who remember the paper seem to be altogether unaware of its intended mission to Irish-Americans. It performed immensely valuable services to Ireland : its interest in Irish-America seems to have been remarkably faint. As things turned out, Plunkett was seldom resident in Dublin during the seven years of publication. Moreover, he was now an ageing man, unwilling or unable to keep as firm a hand on the reins as had been the case with the first series. The direction of the paper passed into the hands of the editorial staff who had interests other than his.

The staffing of the paper presented difficulties. For one reason or another it was not possible or thought desirable to recall those who had produced the first *Statesman*. The first invitation to act as editor was sent to Robert Lynd 'an Irishman, born in Belfast, of nationalist sympathies and an absolutely first-class professional journalist'. He was willing enough to accept and thus sacrifice his London connections but the terms that he asked (£1500 p.a.) were more than Plunkett would grant. J. W. Good was then approached. 'Good was willing to work on the new paper and in fact became assistant editor and a most invaluable member of the staff. But he was unwilling to assume the responsibility of the editorial chair. He told me afterwards that he had made a resolution never to edit a paper'.

Plunkett then proposed a solution which was accepted. In George's view it had been the solution most attractive to Plunkett all along. The new *Statesman* should be amalgamated with the *Irish Homestead*, the weekly journal of the co-operative movement which AE had edited since 1905. It followed that AE would become editor of the amalgamated paper at a salary which, though low enough even by the standards of that day, would do something to compensate him for the many years spent in the service of the *Homestead*. This was done. AE became the editor of 'the revived *Irish Statesman,* incorporating the *Irish Homestead*'. His editorial staff was J. W. Good and Susan Mitchell.

A paper edited by such a team could not fail to be a remarkable publication. AE was one of the most gifted men of his generation, equally talented with brush and with pen. He was

known all over the world as a poet of the first order. His controversial pamphlets at the time of the Larkin strike and during
the 'troubles' had exercised considerable influence on public
opinion. He knew all about the co-operative movement and
had written weekly articles on Irish agriculture for over thirty
years. AE wrote to me privately that : 'I want to get good
manners into the Irish treatment of political problems, likewise
good sense. I am afraid it is like offering cold water to people
poisoned by wood alcohol.' J. W. Good. . . . possessed a thor-
ough knowledge of modern Irish politics on which he had
written a couple of authoritative books. He had served on
many newspapers of different political colours and was a
past master of the art of writing a leading article on any
subject at short notice. . . . He was very widely read in general
literature and his critical judgements were always worth attention. Susan Mitchell was the wittiest woman in Dublin. Her
caustic tongue had put George Moore to flight. She was
capable of writing delicious songs and short poems.

The first number appeared on 15 September 1923. The aims
of the paper were set out as follows : 'It is our conviction that
our great need for a generation is not so much modification of
our political status as that cultural and economic development
for which we have ample power'. The same point was made
elsewhere in the issue by Bernard Shaw who claimed that 'Ireland
is at this moment a regular rag and bottle shop of superseded
ideas, or superstitions'.

The contributors were as distinguished as in the first series.
The first volume, to go no further, contained Thomas Bodkin,
Austin Clarke, Padraic Colum, Edmund Curtis, J. Lyle Donaghy,
Robin Flower, Monk Gibbon, Alice Stopford Green, Oliver
Gogarty, Denis Gwynn, F. R. Higgins, Douglas Hyde, Michael
MacLiammoir, Sean O'Casey, Liam O'Flaherty, Horace
Plunkett, Forrest Reid, Lennox Robinson, G. B. Shaw, Walter
Starkie, James Stephens. It was no wonder that to get published
in the *Statesman* became the ambition of every young Irish
writer.

George's association with the second *Statesman* was much
more distant than with the first. He contributed book reviews
from time to time. Otherwise he attended the monthly board

meetings and the weekly tea parties which were held every Friday afternoon in AE's room. The intention was that the next week's issue should be discussed

or, rather I should say, was meant to be discussed because, in practice, the meeting drifted into general conversation, which, in its turn, had a way of turning into a monologue by AE. On many occasions we had distinguished English and foreign visitors who were brought to see AE as one of the celebrities that every sightseer in Dublin should see. . . . I remember in the middle of the general strike in 1926 we had an English colliery proprietor to tea. He was most anxious to tell us all about the strike, and we were anxious to know what he had to say. Good was particularly anxious because he was preparing a leading article on the subject for the following week's paper. Before long AE was in full sail and the coal magnate had the unusual experience of being lectured on his own business by a philosopher who treated the issues at stake *sub specie aeternitatis.*

Comparisons between the first *Statesman* and the second were inevitable. George had never any doubt about which was the better.

In the first place the appearance of the paper had disimproved. The original *Irish Statesman* had closely followed the *New Statesman* in respect of format and type. . . . Roberts (the printer) was a master of the art of typography. He took a great pride in his work, and would always subordinate economy to artistic excellence. . . . The new paper adhered closely to the format of the *Irish Homestead* which had always been a plain, not to say ugly, publication. . . . The old paper had been a thing of beauty which would have been worth looking at even by a person who knew no English—like Yeats's monologues that would have been worth listening to by a person who didn't understand what he was saying.

Another defect, in his opinion, was that what the paper had to say (apart from the literary contributions and the reviews) was not always worth reading. A great deal of each week's issue was written by the editor.

Various initials of imaginary contributors were appended to the articles and reviews. But no initials could deceive the habitual reader as to the origin of the articles, all of which clearly and obviously were drawn from the bottomless well of AE's abundant personality. . . . This outpouring of energy was done with the best possible intentions. It was designed to save contributors' fees in the interests of economy. But the result was a certain monotony.

Worse still, the paper was not always up to date. 'AE seemed to be almost possessed of an anxiety neurosis about being caught short of material'. The result was that next week's leader was ready before this week's paper had appeared. When it did appear it was often philosophical and abstract. Such an approach may have been a great improvement on the level on which Irish politics were discussed in the 1920s; but it seems a fair criticism that a journal of political comment should be both up to date and to the point.

Whenever in later years George launched his table-talk on the history of the two papers, he always made two points. The first was the superiority of one over the other. The second was that the later *Statesman* was not killed by a libel action; rather, the action prolonged its life. He recalls.

I can well remember the unpleasant shock which I received one Friday morning when I read a book review that was, to say the least, unusually harsh. This review was by one Gaelic scholar of the work of two other scholars in the same field. One expects bitterness and lack of charity among the students of celtic subjects, but, even by their standards, this particular effort went rather far. Among other things it accused the publishers of the book of obtaining money under false pretences from the Oxford University Press. My legal training had taught me to beware of defamation in anything which I wrote or published, and my immediate reaction to the review was that a writ for libel might be expected to arrive at the *Statesman* office.

It did. In the Michaelmas term of 1929 the case of *Clandillon v the Irish Statesman and O'Sullivan* was heard before Mr Justice Hanna and a jury.

After a long and not very well conducted trial, the jury disagreed. The plaintiffs let the matter drop at that stage. We
found ourselves saddled with heavy costs which would have
crippled us if we had not received generous support from our
friends and admirers. A fund was opened to help us to pay
our costs. In spite of the fact that we shared it, very unwillingly, with our co-defendant. . . . the fund proved more than
sufficient for its original object. The surplus was given by the
subscribers to the paper for its general purposes. At that time
our resources had run very low and it was obvious that we
could not continue much longer. . . . The proceeds of the
costs fund enabled the paper to carry on a little longer than it
might otherwise have done. The truth is that the libel action,
instead of being responsible for its downfall actually prolonged
its life. However, it gave comfort and satisfaction to its enemies
to believe that the unsuccessful plaintiffs, even if they got no
damages, were the architects of its destruction. The death of
the *Statesman* was a severe blow to Irish journalism.

The second *Statesman* was the last occasion on which George
had much to do with Horace Plunkett. Plunkett had come into
his life at a highly critical juncture and had given him a fresh
opportunity and a new sense of purpose. He was grateful for
that for the rest of his life : he never forgot any kindness that he
had received. This feeling was intensified by the thought that
Plunkett had been extraordinarily badly treated by the country
which he had tried to serve for so long. The burning of his house
at Kilteragh by irregulars in 1923 had a dreadful symbolism. It
seems right at this point to quote from the recollections, first on
the burning of the house, which is a footnote to the history of
the civil war; second, George's views on Plunkett; and third, his
views on the class from which Plunkett came.

One tactic used in the civil war was the attempt to intimidate
members of the Oireachtas. A member of the Dail was shot
dead in December 1922. Members of the Senate were attacked
through their property; their houses, many of which were of
considerable historical and artistic value, were burned. Plunkett's
house at Kilteragh at Foxrock near Dublin, suffered the common
fate in January 1923.

The maddening thing was that the most precious of the

contents of the house could have been saved even after the attack but for the stupidity of the soldiers who came to protect the mansion after it had first been attacked. Plunkett had for many years conducted a voluminous correspondence with all sorts of people in England and the United States. The library at Kilteragh contained boxes and drawers full of letters on the affairs of the day from many famous people—amongst others, Arthur Balfour, Bernard Shaw, President T. R. Roosevelt, Colonel House, and very many other equally notable personalities. The first night that Kilteragh was attacked, some sort of infernal machine was exploded in the hall. All the furniture and pictures were destroyed but the house did not go on fire. Plunkett was away at the time but his secretary, who was living in one of the gate lodges, attempted to rescue the precious correspondence from the library on the following day. By that time, the military had taken over, on the principle of shutting the stable door after the horse had been stolen. They refused admission to the house, even to Plunkett's own secretary, who, one would have thought, had the right to enter. However, it was comforting to know that the letters were now safely guarded against further danger. Unfortunately, the military guard were only on day duty. They departed at nightfall and no guard replaced them. Later in the night the patriots returned, this time armed with petrol. The house was quickly set on fire and thus perished one of the most notable collections of modern times. If it had been saved, the *Life and Letters of Sir Horace Plunkett* would have been a work of value to the historian, not only of Ireland but of Anglo-American relations in the early years of the twentieth century.

This narration led George to reflect further both on the personality of Plunkett and, more widely, on the class from which he came.

All this insult and ingratitude did not damp Plunkett's interest in the welfare of the country. Most rich men, who had been treated as he had been, would have cast the dust of Ireland off their feet forever and would have sought a peaceful old age in a more appreciative environment. This would have been unusually easy for Plunkett, as he had numerous friends in England and the United States who would have welcomed him in their midst and would have accorded him an appreciation which, as a prophet, he did not receive in his own country. His love of Ireland, however, remained unshaken. He was a very good example of the pathetic unrequited loyalty which the Irish aristocracy have—or perhaps I should say, had—for Ireland. They adored the country that hated them in return : they idolized the people who ridiculed them. They never could understand why they were unpopular. They were willing to give devoted service when it was not wanted. They simply could not understand that their neighbours despised the idols that they held sacred. Their own dual loyalty to England and Ireland was incomprehensible to the people by whom they were surrounded. They were nationalists in a fashion of their own. Their nationalism was set in a wider imperial loyalty. The Irish Catholics should have understood them better than they did because their own nationalism was set in a wider religious loyalty. Both were nationalists and citizens of the world at the same time. Both recognised something outside Ireland as being worthy of their respect and their service. And yet they never understood each other. Ireland would have been a very different and a vastly poorer country if it had not experienced the impact of these two great imperial civilizations. . . Each party contributed something of value to Irish life, but each failed to understand the value of the other's contribution. Horace Plunkett not only failed to understand but positively misunderstood the real values of his Irish fellow countrymen. But he persisted in serving their interests according to his lights.

There was one person in George's circle who would have agreed with his assessment of the Anglo-Irish; but his relations with Yeats were always uneasy. They met frequently in the small dining club set up at the end of 1922 which has been already mentioned. It has also been mentioned that the main purpose of the club was to introduce Yeats to the political issues of the day. Conversation, however, ranged more widely and covered literature and art, subjects on which Yeats might be thought to speak with more authority than his companions. There was, however, one awkward night when Yeats developed a lengthy argument on the importance of freedom of conscience to the freedom of writers. It became apparent that the argument was based on the premise that the Reformation preceded the Renaissance. George did not let this pass; and relations were strained for some time.

The two men fell out further in the context of the *Irish Statesman*. In 1925 Yeats delivered his memorable speech on divorce in the Senate. He asked that the *Statesman* should publish a letter from him on the controversy that followed. This, according to George, led to what almost became literally a stand-up fight at one of the Friday teas.

> Yeats was a born mischief-maker. He loved a row himself and did not care how much his friends got involved. It was he who encouraged Lennox Robinson to publish the article in *To-Morrow* that cost him his position in the Carnegie Trust. I had ineffectually intervened in this sad controversy but failed to melt Father Finlay's heart. Yeats had had the satisfaction of shocking the *bourgeoisie* at poor Lennox's expense. AE had no intention of sacrificing himself on the same altar. He was a pawky northerner who liked to keep out of unnecessary trouble. On this occasion, Yeats called AE a coward and said that he had always been one. AE drew himself up to his full height and said : 'By God ! he would never stand being insulted in this way'. For a moment it looked as if the two great men would come to blows, but Yeats apologized and all was well.

This passage was continued with the following story.

> Yeats fancied himself as a great scholar, whereas, in fact, his genius was in no way matched by his learning. The title page of his book *A Vision* contained a frontispiece entitled 'Portrait of Giraldus from the Speculum Angelorum et Hominorum'. This adventure into Latin had been adversely criticized by the *Irish Times*. One of the regular attendants at our tea parties was Michael Tierney. He was, in fact, the sole person connected with University College, except myself, who wrote for the *Statesman*. One Friday Yeats showed Tierney the offending frontispiece in an attempt to find some answer to the *Irish Times*. Tierney, as a professor of classics, was obviously shocked at what he saw. If Yeats had been a first-year student, he would have come in for a wigging. Yeats, however, was insistent that some way out of his trouble could be found. 'Can't you write to

the *Irish Times*', he begged Tierney 'to say that I used an archaic form?' Tierney's blunt reply was devastating. 'There is nothing archaic about it. It is just pure bad Latin based on an ignorance of the language.'

The reader will perhaps reflect that the poet's knowledge of Latin was hardly a matter of much importance but that clearly George did not get on too well with him. This was a pity because George was now to become much more closely associated with him in the unlikely role of a director of the Abbey Theatre.

During 1924 the Abbey directors (Yeats, Lady Gregory and Lennox Robinson) discussed the possibility of obtaining a subsidy from the government for the theatre. In June of that year an offer was made to the government of 'the Abbey Theatre, its entire contents, scenery and wardrobes and the property it owns to the Irish nation'. The letter continued : 'We offer the Theatre without conditions or restrictions. We resign our directorships. It is for the Irish government, should they accept our offer, to determine the method of carrying on our work—whether they would wish us to go on for a little longer or whether they would at once accept complete control'. This was indeed a sweeping offer, if it were to be taken literally.

At this stage of his life, Mr Cosgrave claimed that he had never been inside the Abbey. He sent the letter to Ernest Blythe, then Minister for Finance. Mr Blythe thought that 'the offer to give the Theatre to the government was more tactical than serious and that in fact it was only an emphatic way of looking for a subsidy'. Certainly a take-over was not on. There were visions of parliamentary questions asking why Mr X or Miss Y had not been given such and such a part. Worse still, an inexhaustible issue would be presented on a plate to all shades of the republican opposition outside the Dail. Even within the restrictions imposed by a budget that balanced at £25 millions for the fiscal year 1924–25, it was much easier to grant a subsidy. The budget of 1925 provided a grant of £800 a year. Mr Yeats expressed his gratitude in the Senate; and in August 1925 Mr Blythe was fêted at a supper on the Abbey stage. The euphoria ended there.

The government, it seems, suggested that another director, a Catholic, should be appointed. This was where George came in, or was brought in.

In 1925 I was invited by Lady Gregory and W. B. Yeats to take a seat on the Board of the Abbey Theatre. The Government had granted the Theatre a subsidy and naturally wanted some representative on the Board. It must have been difficult to find somebody equally agreeable to the Government and to the existing directors. I was suggested by Ernest Blythe who was then Minister for Finance. I possessed no obvious qualifications, beyond being a Catholic which was apparently considered desirable. I imagine that the Board agreed to my name to avoid having somebody worse imposed on them. It was foolish of me to accept the invitation. I knew nothing about the theatre and received no director's fees. However, I was very much at a loose end and did not like to offend Blythe who was always friendly and kind. I do not look back on my directorship with any pleasure.

It is likely enough that the appointment would not have been successful even under the most favourable circumstances. It does seem as if whatever chances of harmony might have existed were lost through the failure to define why the appointment was made at all. Was George a financial watch-dog, to see that the subsidy was not squandered? If so, his religion was hardly relevant. Or was he there to see that plays did not offend public morality— which, in the Ireland of the 1920s had a very special meaning indeed? Clearly, no one, neither George nor Lady Gregory, ever knew for sure. It is notable that there is no contradiction on matters of fact between Lady Gregory's *Journals* and his own, much briefer, recollections. The issue was rather a result of misapprehension of respective roles.

In more favourable circumstances, this might not have mattered greatly : but the Theatre was headed for stormier weather than could have been foreseen. The mood of the middle 1920s was a post-war mood composed of weariness of the fighting, of disillusionment with its results, and of revulsion against many of the changes in the general way of life that the decade had brought. At one extreme were those who believed, and their beliefs were sharpened by defeat in the civil war, that not only was the republican cause holy but that those who had persevered in it were beyond reproach. The IRA man going to confession before an ambush was their ideal. There were many who had been brought up before the war in the rigorous piety and virtues that were then accepted. To many of them, whatever freedom had been achieved had been won by means that left them uneasy, being so far removed from the romantic idealism of Emmet and Davis. The achievement was not justified by what they saw around them. It was often the smaller things that vexed them most—not the rule of the gun and the armed robberies but things like short skirts and the threat to purity represented by what was comprehensively dismissed as jazz. Such things must be ended as the first step in the return to a simpler and safer age. Many of those who felt in this manner would not have been seen dead with the extreme republicans; but they shared with them a suspicious hostility to post-1922 manners.

Another factor, important because it was organised, was a sharp growth in polemical Catholicism, though the adjective is more appropriate than the noun. By 1925 the Catholic Truth Society had begun the first of a series of annual meetings in which those who were then known as 'prominent Catholic laymen' accused Mr Cosgrave's government of being too close to the Freemasons and deplored, with some confusion of proportion, the fact that girls were now being left home from dances in motor cars instead of, as in those days of greater physical and moral health, being walked home. The *Catholic Bulletin*, a monthly publication which will be mentioned more fully later, expressed these reactions and resentments in print. It was echoed by the magazines of some religious orders. The great success of this movement was the enactment of the Censorship of Publications Act in 1929. Long before that, however, it had many ways of making itself felt.

The Theatre was dangerously exposed in this situation. In the past, its plays had aroused hostility in some quarters, notably with *The Playboy* in 1907. Since then, there had been no rioting, but the distrust remained and had been sharpened by the curious episode of *To-Morrow*. This was a periodical (or rather it was planned as a periodical) to which two of the three directors of the Abbey contributed; a poem by Yeats on Leda and the Swan and a short story by Lennox Robinson on the theme of an Irish farm-girl who, having been raped, imagined herself to be the Madonna.

The effect may be imagined. Pressure was brought on the

E

government to institute a prosecution but Kevin O'Higgins refused to take any action, just as he was slow to entertain the project of a literary censorship. An easier success was secured. Robinson was secretary of the Carnegie Library Trust. His dismissal was obtained. George, as was mentioned earlier, interceded unsuccessfully with Father Finlay. Nothing happened or could happen to Yeats. This may well have been the cause of George's reservations about him, as a man who led other people into rows from which he escaped scot-free.

All this happened not twelve months before the decision to give the Abbey a subsidy and to bring George on the Board. Up to this time he had had no contact with the Abbey except as a play goer. Some years before, in his Arts Club days, he had helped to organise Sunday lectures there.

This project originated in the Arts Club, probably, I think, in the brain of Mrs Duncan who was an adept at getting other people to give free performances. Yeats must have been in the scheme in its early days because we obtained the Theatre free for the evening, apart from the payment of overtime wages to the attendants. The lectures were either free or open to the public for a minimum charge. We had some remarkable evenings. Possibly the most spectacular was the lecture by Professor Crawford of Belfast on the physical measurements of psychic phenomena, illustrated by slides showing materialization composed of ectoplasm. The illustrations were so gruesome that women fainted in the audience. There was a debate on another Sunday between G. K. Chesterton and Tom Johnson, the Dublin labour leader, on private property. I was not impressed by G.K.C., who seemed childish and dilettante. G. B. Shaw was staying at Kilteragh at the time and was present in the front row of the stalls with Sir Horace. When questions were being addressed to the speakers after the debate, Shaw was recognized by the audience who called on him to speak. He rose and said this was not his show and that he would not take the floor. Next Sunday, he said, he would take the floor and, if necessary, sweep the floor. On the following Sunday he gave his lecture on 'Equality'. He was most brilliant in answering questions from the audience after the lecture. His beautiful voice, his readiness, his wit and humour all contributed to a notable occasion. The following day he was at lunch at Kilteragh.

A lady in the party dared to doubt his sincerity in advocating socialism. When he had replied protesting his belief in what he had said the previous evening, Father Finlay surprised the table by saying that he agreed with Shaw about the virtues of communism, adding that the only difference between them was that Shaw talked about it while he himself practised it. He then explained the difference between the socialist contention for universal compulsory communism and the Catholic position that communism, like celibacy, could only be practised by a select few.

This excellent series of Sunday lectures did not extend beyond a single winter. There was some talk of arranging another series in the following winter but it never came to anything. I understood at the time that the reason was that Lady Gregory refused to give the Theatre without a fee. In the light of what I afterwards learned by experience I can well believe that this story was true.

In August 1925, almost immediately after George's appointment, Sean O'Casey submitted the script of *The Plough and The Stars*. Towards the end of that month George wrote to Lady Gregory saying: 'I feel quite safe in saying that I think it is excellent'. The trouble then began, starting with Michael Dolan who, as one of the projected cast, objected to the language. This point had already impressed Lady Gregory. Dolan approached George who said that he had already sent 'a general benediction' but agreed that 'there was a huge difference between reading a play at home and hearing it from a stage'. Accordingly, George then wrote again to Lady Gregory objecting to the love scene in Act One and to the introduction of a prostitute (and her song) in Act Two. Yeats, writing as it seems with the approval of Lady Gregory, replied agreeing as regards the love scene but defending the introduction of Rosie Redmond. George replied on 13 September 1925. The text of his letter is given in *Lady Gregory's Journals*. No copy survives in his own papers; but he was never known to dispute the facts. It was the closing part of the letter which gave deep offence.

He wrote:

I feel that there are certain other considerations affecting the production to which it is my duty, in a peculiar way, to have regard. One of them is the possibility that the play might offend any section of public opinion so seriously as to provoke an attack on the Theatre of a kind that would endanger the continuance of the subsidy. . . . Not being a dramatic author or critic, I feel that the only assistance of value I can render is by attempting to prevent the outbreak of a movement of hostility that would make it difficult or impossible for the government to continue or increase its subsidy.

Lady Gregory's reaction was, first, that George had not been appointed as a censor of plays but as a man of financial affairs. (In fact it does not seem that his precise responsibilities were ever spelled out but he was certainly regarded, and regarded himself, as some kind of representative of the government. Whether the government saw him in that light is another matter again). The second reaction was that if the Theatre had to choose between freedom and the subsidy, the subsidy should be sacrificed at once. This was very understandable; though it might be hard to reconcile with the terms of the original letter to the government. At any rate, George found himself isolated on the board.[1]

It seems fair to suggest that the clash was on two quite different levels. The first, and much the greater issue, was that George had no right to threaten the loss of the subsidy. On that point it seems, and a quotation from Joseph Holloway's *Recollections* will be given later in support, he did not mean more than he said. He did fear that the government would come under pressure from those who were hostile to the subsidy. He did not mean that he himself would recommend its termination nor was there any suggestion from anybody at the time or later that he had been in contact with any Minister on the matter. That being said, it may be added that a different wording of his letter would have avoided any misunderstanding. The version that we have from the Abbey side is that of Lady Gregory: she and George did not know each other very well. The second issue, on the text of the

1. All the more so, because he had brought the script of Robinson's *The White Blackbird* to the unlikely surroundings of the Royal Irish Yacht Club to get legal advice from his friends on the hint of incest which that play contained.

play, was comparatively minor. All the directors agreed in general about 'the bad language'. They agreed about the love-scene : they did not agree about the prostitute but did agree about her song, which did come out. There was no great clash of principle there.

In the event, *The Plough* opened in February 1926 and pro-voked scenes of protest which fortunately or unfortunately the Abbey has never witnessed since. In her life of Lady Gregory, Elizabeth Coxhead wrote : '. . . it is a great deal easier to sym-pathize with Dr O'Brien and his fellow-directors than with the rioters. *The Plough and The Stars* was tough going for 1926 and it is not a play for the squeamish even today'. The case against the rioters was their refusal to face facts. They objected to the bringing of the Tricolour into a public-house because it seemed to suggest that the men of Easter week might sometimes have taken a drink which was untrue. They objected to the prostitute because, they said, all the prostitutes had left Dublin with the British Army. As it happened, in the very week before *The Plough* opened, the most celebrated murder case of the decade had ended in Green Street Courthouse. It concerned the murder in the Dublin Mountains of a prostitute well known in the city as Honor Bright.

> Everything went quietly until Thursday night when there was a riot in the theatre caused by the alleged insult to the Repub-lican tricolour which was shown on the stage in a drinking scene in a low Dublin 'pub '. This was a danger that none of us had foreseen. Apparently the tender Dublin conscience was more offended by attacks on its sobriety than upon its chastity. I must say Yeats was splendid that night. He came before the curtain and told the audience precisely what he thought of them and of their forerunners who had made similar scenes at the *Countess Cathleen* and the *Playboy*. On the following nights we played with the lights up. A body of policemen lined the passages at the side of the pit to keep order. One evening a student began to sneeze and was hit over the head by a policeman who thought that his sneezing was the begin-ning of organized disorder. The play ran for two weeks in these conditions with no further serious disorder.

It does not seem from the foregoing that he realised that the objections to the *Plough* were not primarily based on moral issues.

The last word may be left with Joseph Holloway, whose recollections of the Abbey spanned the period from 1899 to 1926. Part of his diary entry for 12 October 1925 (when the dissension in the board was at its height) runs as follows :

> I was home with George O'Brien, the Director of the theatre appointed by the directors to see that the grant is properly spent. He has to read and approve of the theatre's new plays, and has just got one of O'Casey's pieces to pass judgement upon and did so by deleting many mentions of Christ and bad women. He thinks it is a fine play and likely to be very popular. . . . (He didn't like to turn down *The White Blackbird* in spite of the undercurrent, for fear it might be said that the government was interfering unduly with the liberty of the theatre, and so let it pass. Though in fear and trembling about what might be the result). He wouldn't like a row or, for instance, the Catholic Truth Society to march with banners up and down outside the theatre, or rows like *The Playboy* to occur inside. . . . I assured him that none of these things would occur. . . . That the days for rows at the Abbey were over. That the audience knew better than to make another *Playboy*. This very much relieved O'Brien's mind.

The end of this curious episode was that George decided on resignation but deferred action until *The Plough* had been put on again and received without hostility. Earlier action might be interpreted as running away. Accordingly he resigned later in 1926. He resumed his relations of guarded but peaceful co-existence with Yeats. His friendship with Lennox Robinson had never been strained even at the height of the controversy. Years later Robinson wrote to him saying that his attitude to the O'Casey play had been 'sincere, consistent and sympathetic'. It does not appear that he met Lady Gregory often afterwards.

9

Commissions and Controversies 1922-39

IN a strict sequence of events it might be expected that this chapter would deal with the manner in which George prepared himself for an academic career and with the circumstances in which he became a professor in 1926. It seems best to order matters rather differently. He did not enter the College after years of lecturing and research. He came in without having done any lecturing but after a considerable amount of publication. He had also been deeply involved in committees of enquiry on matters of economic policy. This involved him in much controversy : indeed he was never to shake himself free of some of the antagonisms that sprang from the years before he entered the College. It seems best to deal with these matters at this stage; and then to turn to his academic career.

The Provisional Government was established in January 1922 after the ratification of the Treaty. Its immediate task was to draft a constitution for the Irish Free State. It appointed a committee for this purpose which was unable to reach agreement and submitted three separate reports. Ministers decided to seek further advice. They consulted Tim Healy and George.

This was casting the net widely indeed. At this time Healy (who became Governor-General in the following December) was unattached in politics. He had survived the parliamentary party with which he had nursed so many feuds. His great legal and parliamentary experience made him an obvious, if not universally acceptable, person to consult. George was in a very different position : it was only four years since he had abandoned practice : that, however, was quite irrelevant in the circumstances of the time. The Provisional Government included people like Kevin O'Higgins and Patrick Hogan who had been in College at the same time as George not many years before. They remembered (there is an inference in the recollections that it was Hogan who first suggested his name) his distinction in the legal subjects. He was invited to submit comments on the drafts of the committee. 'I was not officially informed of the identity or even of the existence of the second consultant'. It seems an odd way of doing things; though one imagines that the word 'officially' should be strictly interpreted.

His part in the shaping of the constitution has been very fully covered by Mr Brian Farrell on whose account what follows has been based.[1]

> . . . In a typical desire to avoid a purely destructive and negative criticism, Dr O'Brien set himself the task of incorporating some additions and alternative proposals. . . . In all he offered critical comments on 49 of the 81 articles in Draft B. During its consideration of the document the Provisional Government accepted 26 of his suggestions in whole or in part, involving adjustments to some 20 articles.

To summarise the principal points that emerge from Mr Farrell's study, he 'articulated an assumption generally associated with a British emphasis on parliamentary sovereignty, that the constitution "should fetter as little as possible the freedom of the legislative body which it creates".' Joining for once with Alfred O'Rahilly, who was a member of the original committee, he criticised some of 'the more radical implications of the draft in the lives of individual citizens'. On the suggested provisions regarding religion, he suggested that the committee had not gone far enough towards securing equality. On the provision of free education he feared an incursion into family rights. He also criticized some of 'the more radical implications of the draft in the field of property rights'. He also procured an amendment of the draft in the limitation of the rights of the State over natural resources. This represented a considerable contraction of the claims made in the Democratic Programme published by the first Dail in 1919. Mr Farrell remarks that

> These criticisms expressed more than the natural caution of a conservative reacting to advanced ideas; they also sprang from a well-informed awareness and intelligent anticipation

1. *The New Irish Jurist*, 1970 and 1971, especially 1971 at p. 345 etc.

of the difficulties and complications created by the random inclusion of undigested reforming ideas in the constitution.

Lastly, George expressed himself as 'personally in favour of the abolition of the death penalty'.

He was soon to be asked to give advice to the Government on a variety of issues that were much more immediately controversial. Later in 1922 the Provisional Government appointed a Commission on Agriculture to advise on the policies that should be adopted by the new State. One of its members, Sean Hales, TD, was shot dead in December as part of the declared policy of shooting members of the Free State Dail. George was invited to fill the vacancy. He accepted and plunged into a sea of troubles.

The framing of economic policies was very far indeed from being a technical examination of possibilities and a conscious choice between one priority and another. In 1922 Ireland was essentially an old country setting up for itself as a new state. It had only too much history and too little economics to consider. At that time, every adult of nationalist sympathies knew two things about Irish economics. The first was that the population had been halved in eighty years : the second was that the process of depopulation still continued. There seemed to be no reason why emigration should not go on for ever; no reason why the population of the island should not fall below four millions as it had already fallen below eight millions, and seven, and six, and five. (The fact that population within the borders of Northern Ireland was increasing did not provide much comfort).

Every Irish leader, constitutional or militant, had assured his generation that the immediate cause of this disaster lay in the loss of self-government. O'Connell had told his monster meetings of the prosperity that would follow Repeal of the Union. When Parnell declared that no man had a right to place limits on the march of a nation, he was speaking precisely of the fiscal powers that a Home Rule parliament would sooner or later acquire. Three weeks before he went into the Post Office, Pearse wrote that

in a free Ireland . . . gracious and useful industries will supplement an improved agriculture. The population will expand in a century to 20,000,000 : it may even in time go up to 30,000,000.

E*

The matter argued itself. In a properly governed (that is to say, in a self-governing) country, the flow of people off the land would be absorbed in the growing industries of the cities just as had happened earlier in England and elsewhere. As things had been, but would be no longer after self-government, people went from the Irish countryside to the cities of the United States: what was internal migration in happier lands became emigration in Ireland. The lack of employment in the cities flowed from the lack of manufacturing industries. That, in turn, was the result of the free-trading policy of the United Kingdom which ruled out any prospect of small Irish industries receiving any protection in their early years. It was no wonder that the most abiding part of Griffith's programme for a Sinn Fein Ireland was his insistence on the need for industrial protection.

In agriculture also, matters had been distorted and again by the British connection. Tillage had declined: cattle raising had grown. By the early 1890s the rising number of cattle had exceeded the falling number of human beings. Moreover, although farmers exported heavily to Great Britain, Ireland did not feed itself. Before 1914 it was pointed out that the volume of agricultural imports was not all that less than the volume of agricultural exports. There seemed to be an unanswerable case that the first business of an Irish government should be to impose industrial protection, its second should be to encourage tillage.

All these beliefs were held by many people (and by many who supported the Treaty) not as the result of detached analysis but as an instinctive reaction to what they and their parents had been told by their leaders. George himself was not immune. The last sentence of the *Economic History of Ireland in the Eighteenth Century*, published in 1918, runs

> It is surely impossible to resist the conclusion that there is some connection between the legislative independence and the economic prosperity of Ireland; that Ireland can never be a rich and prosperous country until her independence is restored.

The chairman of the Commission on Agriculture was Professor Drew. Other members were Sir John Keane, Thomas Johnson, Joseph Johnston, FTCD, and a few politicians and farmer representatives.

The Commission was aided by the Department whose members, from T. P. Gill down, all gave evidence. Service on this Commission introduced me to a new circle of people and taught me a great deal about the problems of Irish agriculture. I do not think that I added much to the value of the examination of witnesses, the discussions or the report, but I learned a great deal. The Commission was of more use to me than I was to it. To have the policy of the Department explained and defended by its principal officers was equal to attending a first class course of lectures on agricultural economics by leading experts. The knowledge which I gained proved useful in the College, in the Senate and on later Commissions. The foundations were laid in my mind of those general principles of Irish agricultural policy in which I have continued to believe in spite of all the agricultural protectionism that has been so loudly preached. These were the principles which formed the basis of Hogan's policy with which I am proud to have been associated. I attempted to explain and justify them in my obituary article on Hogan in *Studies*. . . .[1] The final Report recommended the extension of the existing schemes of the Department rather than a radical change of policy. . . . The signatories of the report were vilified and attacked in certain sections of the press as 'ranchers' and Hogan was entitled in those quarters 'the Minister for Grass'. The course of events has completely vindicated the correctness of our views. The European Recovery Programme assigns to Ireland precisely the role assigned to it by our Report : the intensification of the production of livestock and livestock products based on the maximum possible consumption of home-grown feeding stuffs supplemented by cheap imports of raw materials.

He was writing in the early 1950s when the European Recovery Programme was in very recent memory. He would not have found much to change in the circumstances of the European Economic Community nearly thirty years later. To produce more grass would be thought nowadays to be the highest patriotism. He was never more than intellectually interested in the problems of Irish agriculture; and it may be thought that his detachment appears clearly in the article in *Studies* to which he refers.

1. *Studies*, September 1936.

Almost immediately, he got himself into still worse trouble on issues which were not so clear.

Before the Agricultural Commission had ended its labours I was invited to act on another body. The first suggestion of this new activity was conveyed to me one day when I was riding in the Phoenix Park with E. J. Riordan, who had become an official in the Department of Industry and Commerce. 'Ted' had been secretary of the Irish Industrial Development Association for many years and was greatly interested in exploring the possibilities rendered available by the Treaty to foster new industries. He was by nature a protectionist. He asked me if I would be willing to take part in a small committee to investigate the position impartially and to suggest how a policy of industrialization might be most successfully begun. I was very unwilling to accept this invitation. I already had the Agricultural Commission on hand and I did not see why I should undertake another job of completely unpaid work. Ted, however, pressed me so strongly that I could not refuse without giving him personal offence and I ultimately consented to act. If Ted had foreseen the outcome of his enthusiasm I doubt if he would have been so pressing. . . .

The Fiscal Inquiry Committee was composed of five members, later to be known among protectionists as 'the Five Sorrowful Mysteries'. T. A. Smiddy returned from the United States to preside; the other members were C. F. Bastable of Trinity, J. G. Smith of Birmingham, George, and R. M. Henry; all economists except for Henry who was professor of Latin in Queen's, Belfast.

My old *bête noire* Oldham was, I believe, greatly offended at not being included. He provided comic relief the day he came as a witness when he demonstrated to us on a blackboard, which he had brought on the top of a cab, the elementary theory of international trade. He was careful to explain that he was not addressing himself to Bastable who knew it all already, which was rather hard on the rest of us. To Professor Smith he was brutally rude. I think he mistook him for me.

The secretary of the Committee was T. Barrington, formerly in the Department of Agriculture, later in Industry and Commerce. He was a very able man who had written some excellent papers for the Statistical Society. He had a mind of his own on questions of economic policy and differed deeply from the Committee. From the beginning our relations were strained. Before the labours of the Committee were ended, Barrington had come to sit in a separate room.

The Fiscal Inquiry Committee was a much more one-sided investigation than the Commission on Agriculture, in which there was a clear difference of philosophy between the majority and minority reports.

The bias of the Committee was heavily in favour of free trade. Professor Bastable set the tone of the discussion. Nobody was better able to expose the fallacies of a protectionist argument. He was a survivor of the great days of Victorian liberalism when free trade was regarded by British, economists as a religion rather than a policy. His reputation as a writer of the standard book on international trade was very great. . . . I fell in with the views of my seniors. . . . But I am not sure that we did not attack the problem from the wrong angle. . . . I have already expressed the view that the law of comparative costs should continue to govern agricultural policy. Irish farming simply cannot afford to be deflected from its natural advantages for sentimental reasons. But in regard to manufacturers, some concession might perhaps have been prudently made to sentiment. . . . There was a widespread desire, not only among the businessmen who would have duly profited, but among the public generally for some attempt to revive Irish industry. If the Committee had indicated the directions in which such an attempt could be most safely and least expensively made, its reports would probably have received more respect and would have led to positive action. I was interested to learn from Professor J. G. Smith, who visited me many years later, that he agreed with this view.

Much more than an economic judgement was involved. It is probable that the first government would have proceeded slowly with industrial protection no matter what the Fiscal Inquiry Committee might have recommended. Its commitment to agriculture was very deep. The Fiscal Inquiry Report, however, not only formalised the difference of opinion between industrial protectionists and agricultural exporters but it gave that difference an intellectual basis which made it irreconcilable in the lifetime of the first government. It also did much to determine the length of that lifetime. Priority for agriculture worked well in the short patch of relative prosperity (relative, that is to say, to what had gone before and what was to come later) at the end of the twenties. When the depression came it was politically imperative to be seen to be doing something to maintain employment. For that aim, protection by tariff was the instrument that lay nearest to hand. By then, however, protection had been rejected by the government and had been eagerly seized by the opposition. It must be seldom that such a valuable card is so lightly thrown away.

This was to affect George's relations with the party that he had advised. At the beginning of the 1930s it was said that he would be made a member of the Senate as soon as a suitable vacancy arose. Not so long afterwards there were many who blamed the electoral defeat of 1932 on his economic advice. Ever afterwards he was to be associated with the doctrines of the 1920s. Naturally enough, he received no sympathy from the incoming party. He did not look for any. In the forty-two years of life that remained to him, that incoming party would be in office for thirty-five. He was isolated.

It must be remembered that his advice was not confined to the Commission of Agriculture and the Fiscal Inquiry Committee. He also served on the Select Committee on Wheat-Growing which reported in 1928. This was an instructive example of how these issues were debated. In 1927 Mr de Valera's new party, Fianna Fail, entered the Dail and settled down to establish itself in the public mind as the alternative government. It was strongly in favour of encouraging tillage.

In itself, this was not or need not have been a contentious issue. Hogan's own policy for agriculture involved the extension of tillage for animal feed. But it was clear enough that many farmers would not till unless they were paid to do so, as they had been paid during the first war. Hogan would have none of that. Mr de Valera would. The real division came over the insistence of Mr de Valera on the extension of tillage by the growing of more wheat.

This flew in the face of economic orthodoxy on the ground that, on Irish soil and in the Irish climate, almost any other form of tillage would be more useful than wheat. It was a heresy that George could not accept, especially when it was preached not only by Mr de Valera but by Alfred O'Rahilly, then Professor of Mathematical Physics and Registrar of University College, Cork. In his private affairs, Alfred O'Rahilly could be the kindest of men : he would go out of his way to assist even those who had written or spoken against his views. In public, there was no mercy for his opponents : *caritas non conturbat me* might have been his motto. George always refused to take him seriously. This was the deadliest insult that could be offered, which was why it was offered.

At any rate the case for wheat-growing was sent to a Select Committee for consideration. The details of the discussions need not detain us. The reports were quite predictable. One, against wheat-growing, was signed by, among others, three ministers (Blythe, Hogan and McGilligan) and George : the other, in favour of wheat-growing, by, again among others, Mr de Valera, James Ryan and Sean Lemass.

There were only two points of interest. The first was that the Select Committee was the first time that representatives of the two parties had sat at the same table since the Civil War. The second was that during the discussions Sean Lemass, whose interest in wheat-growing cannot have been obsessive, based an argument on what were patently wrong statistics. George pointed out the mistake privately before either Hogan or McGilligan, who would hardly have been so charitable, could swoop on it. It was a very small courtesy but one which was not common in those days. It is doubtful if he would have done as much for anybody else on the Fianna Fail team : but he had always a rather different feeling about Lemass. If indeed Lemass had become head of the government rather earlier than he did, it is likely that George would have accepted any invitation to advise that might have come his way.

The immediate result of course was to confirm him in his stance of a defender of the status quo. The pattern was to be repeated in the Derating Commission a couple of years later. Agriculture, it will have been observed, was not one of his compelling interests. Agricultural de-rating came lower still, if that were possible. However, he signed the same kind of report, with the same kind of co-signatories and with much the same set of adversaries on the other side of the table.

This was the last commission to which he was appointed by the first government. It did not end his giving offence to those who would shortly come into power. His articles in *Studies* kept the fires burning. The Jesuit quarterly had taken on a new lease of life after 1922. Its issues were filled with articles on the various problems facing the new state. Its editor, Father Connolly, was a man of immense charm, kindness and ruthlessness in the pursuit of contributors. George had no chance against him. Between 1923 and 1947 he wrote twenty-six articles. This was not at all as many as Alfred O'Rahilly who wrote about everything, nor as many as Michael Tierney was to contribute in later years. But George must be ranked as one of the most frequent and certainly one of the clearest contributors of his time. His first article, on William Conner in 1923, seems derived from his *Economic History of Ireland from the Union to the Famine*. It may also have owed something to the book which he certainly contemplated but did not pursue, *The Economic History of Ireland from the Famine to the Treaty*. The second, in 1925, was on the rather unexpected subject of *Dr Samuel Johnson as an Economist*. Later that year he was on *The Budget*. This got him going. For the next twenty years he was in and out of *Studies*. Some years he appeared in all four issues. His subjects varied from the balance of payments (a new concept to the nation) which he explained—with greater complacence than he was afterwards to show—in 1925, to the perennial problems of the railway system, arterial drainage (not a subject close to his heart), unemployment and emigration. These were the staple topics of the time : they were discussed in the light of the circumstances then prevailing. The only occasion on which he dealt directly with the issues which flowed from the controversies of the 1920s was in the obituary article on Patrick Hogan. This was a formal and unyielding apologia for the policies which Hogan had implemented as Minister for Agriculture; policies which George had recommended in one commission after another, for which, before and after 1936, he was under attack.

His articles were by no means only on Irish subjects. Especially during the war, he wrote widely on developments in Great

Britain, on full employment, on cheap money and on the death of Keynes. The atmosphere of that time is so long lost that it is hard to explain the value of those articles. There was then an almost complete lack of comment on economic affairs, domestic or foreign. At home, the Central Bank had not yet begun the series of reports which infuriated or delighted the post-war years : abroad, people were engaged in war work and anyway paper was short. In *Studies* George explained issues that people wanted to know more about and were anxious to learn how, if at all, they might be related to future policies in Ireland. These articles were waited for by the public; they also gave their author a special pleasure. In his articles as in his lectures, he was a superb expositor. He knew that, and he liked it. Moreover, anybody would like being asked to write by Father Connolly who was a very special kind of editor. Lastly, he felt that by writing for *Studies* he was paying back some part of what he owed to Father Finlay and to the Jesuits in Belvedere. It was a very pleasant part of his life. The association had weakened somewhat before Father Connolly retired in 1950; by then George was concentrating on his speeches in the Seanad.

There was a quite different type of Catholic publication with which his relations were not so happy. It has already been noted that the later 1920s witnessed a fortunately short-lived outbreak of professional Catholicism. It did not last long but it was virulent while it lasted. This intolerance mingled politics and religion and infused both with a plentiful stream of personalities. It attacked institutions such as Trinity College and the Royal Irish Academy and indeed any other Royal foundation in sight. 'The upstart Cromwellian crew that built mansions in Dublin from 1700 to 1840' exactly expresses the material and the human objects of their invective. More modern creations of the Anglo-Irish such as Plunkett House and the Abbey Theatre were equally offensive to them. Those who were engaged in the direction of these institutions were denounced as foreigners, or anti-Irish, or proseletysers.

There were several such publications vying with each other at the end of the 1920s, one run by a very distinguished Order indeed. (Even the Jesuits were not immune from this curious fever. A couple of them expressed opinions on Irish life which, in Father Conmee's day, would certainly have landed them on the next train to Tullabeg or, in extreme cases, on the next boat to Australia.) The special object of their invective, worse than any foreigner or proseletyser, was any Catholic who in any way mixed with his fellow countrymen of a different religion. This lowest circle included people like Dan Binchy, Myles Dillon and, above all, Michael Tierney whose gallant resistance to the Censorship of Publications Act incurred undying hatred and eventually cost him his seat in the Dail. It is hardly necessary to say that George was also included.

His principal assailant was the *Catholic Bulletin*. This was a remarkable monthly publication which deserves to be restored to memory and indeed merits a critical analysis. Its cover depicted the Cathedral of Armagh and the Rock of Cashel. The suggestion of Faith and Fatherland was somewhat diminished by the fact that it was in no way under official ecclesiastical supervision. It may indeed have been a standing embarrassment to the higher echelons of the Church in Ireland (or, at least, so one hopes though there may have been exceptions) just as it must have been to its publishers who were bound by a contract made in more settled days.

Its contents were an extraordinary mixture. Each issue commenced with a general review of events which soon turned into vituperation of individuals and institutions. The *Bulletin* had a rather agreeable habit of giving soubriquets to those whom it hated most. Thus, Tom Bodkin was Don Whiskerando, Walter Starkie was 'the Trinity Catholic decoy-duck' or otherwise Don Gualtero Fitzwilliam Starkie and Dan Binchy, on being appointed Irish Minister in Berlin, became Don Antonio de Berlin. The references became increasingly arcane; eventually it was only close students of the *Bulletin* who could follow who exactly was being attacked. Each issue contained articles from continental centres, especially Rome and Paris. These were often well-informed and balanced. They were followed by an article or two on Irish history and a closing section for the young, especially those of the young who wished to improve their Irish.

This led to some extraordinary results. A highly competent discussion of the Young Plan for German Reparations was followed by 'Charlemont and Catholic Claims' and 'A Compendium of Catechetical Instruction'. An informed and dispassionate comment on the fall of M. Herriot's government in 1925 was succeeded by an article on how Sir Henry Sydney brought about the defeat and death of Shane O'Neill. Later, the controversy about wheat-growing was enlightened by an article citing the decrees of Pope Celestine IV on compulsory tillage in the Papal States in 1290. That did not exhaust the *Bulletin*'s interest in Italian affairs. An issue of 1930 contained the following. 'Daily we are asked is the Duce a Catholic? We reply in the affirmative. He himself has never tried to conceal his religion'.

This may give the impression that the *Bulletin* was a source of innocent merriment. So it was, to those who were not attacked. George had little hope of escaping. To be sure, he first figured in a reasonably favourable light. Discussing the vacancy in the Chair of National Economics in 1926, the *Bulletin* noted 'the woeful misuse of the chair since 1909'. Kettle's 'heart was set on other things'. Oldham's tenure had been 'a total perversion of the whole purpose of the work paid for by the people of Ireland in respect of the Chair of National Economics'. George would not have disagreed with that, any more than with the conclusion that 'There is hope in the recent appointment of Dr George O'Brien'. But a rider was added that the chair must be placed on foundations which were not suspect. 'These foundations are not to be found in Plunkett House, the Abbey Theatre, among the Associated Aesthetics or Big Business'.

This was a pretty full list of George's associations; it must have been written by someone who knew a lot about him. It strengthens the suspicion, always held by his victim, that part at least of the *Bulletin* was written by that enigmatic character, Father Timothy Corcoran, S.J.[1] George and he were to be colleagues in the College for many years but it does not appear that they had much to say to each other. This may be explained by the later comments of the *Bulletin*. By 1929 George had become 'Economist-in-Chief to Green Grazierdom'. In the next year it referred to an article of his in *Studies* as 'the Doleful Ditty of Doctor George O'Brien . . . our Economic Hamlet'. This sally amused several of his fellow sufferers.

It did not amuse him at all. None of the references amused him. He believed that his students read the *Bulletin* every month

1. Father Corcoran was Professor of Education, in which capacity he did a great deal to denigrate the teaching of Newman on the idea of a university.

and that they distrusted him as a result. He was quite mistaken in this. Certainly, copies of the *Bulletin* were brought up to Earlsfort Terrace as they appeared and were read to the last page. Student interest in the Catholic press was perhaps greater then than it has been ever since. But it did not in the least affect the student view of George. There was a lot to be said for having a professor who was mentioned in public discussion. There was even more to be said for being attacked by a particular type of attacker.

George did not see things in that way. His special way of counter-attack was to make highly offensive and wounding personal references to those whom he suspected of being his traducers. It is not possible to be more specific in this matter. Those whom he attacked may be dead but their children are still alive. But the principle on which he worked was interesting. He would make remarks, in quarters where they were certain to be repeated back to the victim, about such things as physical disabilities. This method had a dual advantage. It was hitting under the belt and, therefore, doubly painful. Better still, he could not possibly be sued for any remark of that kind. He was always very conscious that he could be a good mark for damages in a defamation action while his adversaries were not. It was not magnificent but it was war. He made no bones about what he was doing or why. There were many facets to his character.

He was to serve on one more major commission, the second Banking Commission which was appointed in 1934 and reported in 1938. Invitations were issued with liberality. The *Economist* noted with some awe that the membership consisted of

> the Chairman of the Currency Commission . . . the permanent head of the Department of Finance, the Chairmen of the Industrial and Agricultural Credit Corporations, the Chairman of one bank and directors of two others, the Professors of Economics of the three University Colleges of the country, a Roman Catholic Bishop, representatives of Labour, and finally, two external experts.

George did not expect to be asked to serve by Mr de Valera's government. He was pressed by Lord Glenavy, then a director of the Bank of Ireland, to accept if an invitation was issued. The banks felt that they had not paid proper attention to the proceedings of the first Banking Commission which had met and reported in 1926. They decided that, in view of the times and of the change of government, they would be wise to take no chances and to marshal all their forces. At this time George was anxious to maintain close links with the Bank of Ireland; accordingly he agreed to act. He did not do so with any enthusiasm.

> I accepted the invitation with great reluctance. I was nervous and unwell and was beginning to develop strong views on the subject of unpaid service on Commissions. During the whole period of the Commission's sittings, I was more or less ill.

The circumstances of the meetings did nothing to improve his condition. The Commission met in a room at the top of 1 College Street.

> 72 steps, no lift, an incredible noise from drays rattling over cobble stones, and trams clanking along, grinding, shuddering to a halt. To hear, the windows had to be closed even in summer and there was no central heating in winter, only a coal fire.

That was Per Jacobssen's memory of the four years. George added that the meetings invariably started half an hour or more after the time fixed. Worse still, they might go on until nine in the evening or even later so that a meal in Jammets was problematical.

Nevertheless he enjoyed these meetings. Per Jacobssen, then of the Bank for International Settlements, and Theo Gregory, of the London School of Economics, were the two 'external experts'. It was a great joy to him to have people of such distinction in Dublin where he could talk freely to them about all kinds of issues. Occasionally he would bring the pair of them down to the Statistical Society. It was a night to remember when that happened. There was a faint air of the Congress of Vienna about the Banking Commission, once its members had escaped from College Street.

He took a large part in the examination of witnesses and in the drafting of parts of the report. His special responsibility was Appendix 15, *A Note on some aspects of Papal Encyclicals in relation to the Terms of Reference of the Commission*, of which he was co-author with the then Bishop of Raphoe, Dr MacNeely.

This was not a topic usually to be seen in reports on banking and currency systems, but the appendix had its uses in the Ireland of the 1930s. George himself was not very interested in Papal Encyclicals, but he was almost certainly given the job in order to keep out Alfred O'Rahilly who was also a member of the Commission. Appendix 15 revived antagonisms that had been dormant since the days of controversy over wheat-growing.

I think it was this appendix that finally roused Alfred O'Rahilly to dash off his minority report, his large volume *Money* and his incessant articles in the *Standard* attacking the Commission in general and me in particular. O'Rahilly's behaviour was exactly the same as it had been in relation to the Constitution Committee many years earlier. He had not matured or mellowed in the interval—nor had he shed any of his vanity.

George always took the view that he would not reply to these attacks. He was sure that a vigorous reply would simply increase the circulation of the *Standard*. His line was that he did not read the *Standard* any more than he had read the *Bulletin*, though he was certainly remarkably well informed on what they said about him.

One last quotation may close this account of the years of controversy.

Alfred afterwards calmed down. His fire was directed against Darwin, Marx, and H. G. Wells and he forgot about his great monetary reforms in which, of course, he had never been genuinely interested. One of the peculiar things about O'Rahilly was that, while he was waging his campaign against me in the *Standard* he was writing friendly and cordial letters about University affairs. He apparently lived his life in separate compartments, a Jekyll and Hyde sort of existence. The situation was like the wars in the eighteenth century when belligerency did not lead to the complete severance of personal relations. The age of chivalry survived in Cork. When I meet him nowadays he is quite friendly. He has forgotten all about his attacks on me and would be surprised to be told that I had anything to forgive. I have forgiven; but I have not forgotten. One does not forget being bitten by a mad dog. But the mad dog frequently forgets that he has bitten his victim.

The Banking Commission was his last major appearance on committees of enquiry. He was pressed into service once again when a further Commission on Agriculture was appointed in the autumn of 1938. He would not have consented were it not that the chairman was Timothy Smiddy for whom George, like many others, would have done anything to help. But the Commission soon showed that it would never get anywhere, so great were the antipathies between opposing interests.

On the outbreak of war the Minister immediately dissolved the Commission on the grounds that its terms of reference were not relevant to war-time problems. Hitler was responsible for so much evil that any little iota of good that he did should be brought to the notice of the recording angel. One good deed in the Fuhrer's very naughty world was the ending of the Agricultural Commission.

From the spring of 1922 to the autumn of 1939 had been a long time. It had brought George a great and continuing volume of criticism, and it must also have brought some degree of personal unhappiness. Writing later of the Commission on Agriculture and the Fiscal Inquiry Committee, he was unrepentant.

This was the first occasion on which I was forced by intellectual conviction to take the realistic line in Irish economic policy. This made me unpopular in many quarters, but has been completely vindicated by the course of events. Ever since the Treaty I have ranged myself with the economists who accepted Ireland as it was rather than with those who wished it to be in some ways different. I accepted the facts of geography and history instead of attempting to charm them away. I was among the physicians who prescribed a hard diet for the Irish patient and the surgeons who were prepared to recommend a painful operation, not among the faith healers and the Christian Scientists. This was the intellectual rather than the emotional approach to Irish economic problems. It was based on my legal training which taught me to see facts as they were and not as I would have liked them to be. I have been taught at the bar to discuss any case on its strict legal merits and to avoid considering the abstract rights and wrongs of the parties or the social consequences of judicial decisions.

This approach attuned with my somewhat cool nationalism which was devoid of emotion and sentiment. . . . My life may have suffered from an over-intellectual approach to private and public problems. In private life this approach may have led to wrong interpretations, but in public life it tended to correct, if not popular, policies. Every country needs a corrective, an antidote against the hysterical outbursts of screaming fanatics. There must be a sane section in every society. But the sane section is in danger of being disregarded and of missing fire if it fails to take note of the irrational emotions and impulses on which political action is mainly based. All through my life I have believed unduly in the force of reason and have under-estimated the forces of hatred, revenge, cupidity, and ambition. I think that this cool rational outlook, derived from my Victorian childhood, has helped to preserve a little sane detach-ment in economic policy since the Treaty, but it has earned me the reputation, in wide circles of being unpatriotic if not corrupt and venal.

That is as uncompromising a statement of belief as could be found anywhere. One is left musing on the strong streak of maso-chism that ran through the policies of the 1920s. George himself, as a professor, fully recognised the difference between Economics and Political Economy. It was perhaps a pity that he, and those whom he advised, were not equally conscious at that time of the danger of ignoring the human emotions. But if there was ever a decade that was obsessed with sound finance, balanced budgets and strict adherence to priorities, it was the 1920s.

For himself, the result was that he was left on his own. A great deal of mud had been thrown at him and some of it stuck. He had been asked to advise on what he thought were economic issues. They turned out to be political issues. The politicians did not mind in the least. They could and did exchange insults and they thrived on them. George could not. To end this chapter as it began, the professor of National Economics who entered Uni-versity College in 1926 carried with him a much heavier load than academic honours.

10

Return to the College 1926

By the middle of 1926 he had achieved his ambition and had obtained the Chair of the National Economics of Ireland in University College. In academic as in other professional circles, preferment is rarely unvexed and simple. In his case there was no simplicity and plenty of vexation.

It will be remembered that Tom Kettle, the first occupant of the chair, had been killed in France in 1916. In the next year the College proceeded to fill the vacancy and advertised it in the usual way. At that time, in 1917, George was at home between his two visits to Glasgow. He had not yet abandoned the Bar; but he enquired about the procedure of application and went so far as to obtain testimonials. He approached his three law professors and the then Attorney-General, James O'Connor. He did not approach Father Finlay, the professor of Political Economy, or any other economist. In the event he did not proceed with the application. The chair went, after a closely fought contest, to Charles Hubert Oldham who was already in the College as Professor of Commerce and Dean of the Faculty of Commerce. As things turned out, George was never to be on happy terms with the holders of those two titles but that will emerge in its place.

Nevertheless, he came to feel that if the Bar had to be abandoned, the College might provide an acceptable substitute. This was to happen, after considerable delays. The outcome was happy for him. His mother, however, could hardly have been content with the prolonged uncertainty nor, in the end, with what she must have regarded as the descent from a profession to a professorship.

The more he thought about it, the more promising it seemed. An academic position would provide a secure income and a career that did not involve travel or being civil to solicitors. Certainly, his best qualifications lay in the law subjects; but there was no sign of any approaching vacancy there nor was one to occur, as it happened, until 1924. The position seemed to be much more promising in Political Economy. Father Finlay was now approaching seventy. He showed no sign of waning vitality, but it was reasonable to hope that sooner or later he might welcome an assistant. It was worth a try, especially as no other path of rehabilitation or advancement was apparent. He decided to take an MA degree by dissertation as his first step. Being the kind of person he was, he began by consulting the entry under 'Political Economy' in the College calendar. It listed a number of suggested theses, several of them being on issues of economic theory. One other suggestion was 'The Economic History of Ireland in the Eighteenth Century until 1815.' This, with the terminal date deleted, was what he chose.

It is many years since the College calendar provided lists of suggested dissertations. It is surprising that it ever did. Professors are notorious (some perhaps more notorious than others) for a lack of interest in what is said or not said about their subjects in the calendar. This did not matter greatly because in those days and for long afterwards until it was reformed no one would have dreamed of consulting it for more than the most elementary information and, even then, what was read would have been treated with considerable reservations. Why George should have approached the pages of the calendar as if they were pages of the Sibylline books, Heaven only knows. It was another instance of that innocence which had obscured the difference between pass and honours degrees. A more normal person would have sought the advice of his professor.

For once, innocence was abundantly rewarded. The suggested theses were under the heading of 'Political Economy', so that he approached the professor of that subject, Father Finlay. Many things would have been very different if he had acted like a reasonable man and, in view of the subject of the proposed thesis, had enlisted under the new professor of National Economics. It was a remarkable chance on which to found a professorship of thirty-five years.

His description of what happened says much about his feeling for Father Finlay.

The first time I ever saw Father Finlay was when, as a boy in Belvedere, I attended a retreat which he gave in Gardiner Street. I was very impressed by his cold intellectual handling of spiritual questions. But I had no premonition that the preacher was to become, one day, my kindest friend, that he would open the door to my second and successful career, and that I would succeed him in his professorship. I attended his lectures in University College but I do not suppose that he identified me apart from the other undergraduates. . . . I did not see him again until, four years later, I went to consult him regarding my thesis. He was a very busy man, with endless interests outside the College. If he thought about me at all, he probably regarded me as a nuisance, as one of those young graduates who, instead of getting on with their careers, hanker after other academic distinctions and degrees. However, he did not discourage me, and I call to mind his example when I am tempted to discourage young graduates who seek my advice in similar circumstances. Though not discouraging, he was by no means enthusiastic. His manner was, as I have said, distantly civil. The first time he realised that something more than the ordinary M.A. thesis was afoot was one day when I brought him some chapters in typescript to report progress. . . . When he saw the amount of work I had done and estimated the size of the thesis when it would be finished, he advised me to publish it and present it for the degree of D.Litt. I had never heard of degrees on published work but I decided to act on his advice.

The thesis was finished, as has been said, in an incredibly short space of time, and was presented to the University for a doctorate. The Senate nominated the two most eminent economic historians of the day, Sir William Ashley of Birmingham and Dean Cunningham of Trinity, Cambridge. Sir William was unable to act but the Senate awarded the doctorate on the report of Dean Cunningham. Accordingly the degree was conferred in 1919.

His reactions were mixed. On one hand : 'No member of my family attended. My doctorate was not regarded with favour. It was a sign of my failure as a barrister'. On the other : 'I had now taken two appropriate steps towards an academic career. I had published work to my name and had become a doctor. But I had to wait many years and had to publish many books before I attained my reward. I learnt to practice the twin virtues of perseverance and patience in a quite unusual degree.' Junior staff members in any university may reflect that he had remarkably little to complain about, but to the end of his days he never saw the matter in that light.

Whatever about patience, his productivity was remarkable. *The Economic History of Ireland in the Seventeenth Century* followed in 1919; in the next year he wrote a long (and rather biased) introduction to E. J. Riordan's *Modern Irish Trade and Industry*; in 1921 the *Union to the Famine* appeared. He certainly thought of a sequel; some notes for it survive; but it came to nothing. Instead he published *An Essay on Medieval Economic Teaching* in 1920, in the middle of his historical work. It must have been a thoroughly satisfying subject because he was able to draw on legal principles to a considerable extent. Another essay, on the *Economic Effects of the Reformation*, which appeared in 1923, was highly thought of at the time. He published a text book, *Agricultural Economics*, in 1929 based on his lectures in the Albert College. In the same year he published what was perhaps his principal contribution to economic analysis, *Notes on the Theory of Profit*. Many years afterwards George Shackle delivered a public lecture in the College. He went out of his way to remark on the importance and the distinction of that short but acute analysis. George, who happened to be present, was delighted. So, for his sake, was everybody else. Shackle was perhaps the most distinguished, but certainly not the only, teacher of economics to praise the *Notes*.[1]

In those straitened days there was no possibility of new posts being created in the College. Appointments came only from the death or retirement of the incumbent. As a former Fellow of the Royal University, Father Finlay was not under any obligation to retire at a fixed age. 'I was sometimes tempted to blame him for failing to make a vacancy, but it was only a temptation to which I never consciously yielded'. (Few junior staff will believe that one). In fact, the greatest single bit of good luck in his life was that Father Finlay did not retire at this time. If he had done

---

1. He also edited *The Bank of Ireland, 1783–1946* which was written by F. G. Hall and appeared in 1949. Reference is made later to his two other books, *The Four Green Fields* and *The Phantom of Plenty*.

so, Oldham would presumably have determined the consequential arrangements. No place would have been found in them for George. Oldham detested him.

George rarely started a quarrel, but if one were forced on him he would retaliate with every weapon he could find to hand. One technique which he occasionally used, and has not previously been mentioned, was to say something about his adversary which appeared flattering on the surface but on examination would be found to contain a deadly insult. Oldham never received anything approaching a kind word, even decades later. At the risk of digression, an extract may be given from George's recollections.

I have contemplated writing a book called *The Boriad*, modelled on Pope's *Dunciad* in which I would lampoon some of the bores I have known. . . . (Oldham) was the prince, king, archangel, very God of bores. He was unfortunately a biter as well as a barker, a peculiarly vicious and tiresome brute. . . . I avoided a personal meeting with this monster with great dexterity for many years. . . . But I observed him at a safe distance and heard many accounts of his exploits. My study of him taught me that the perfect bore is composed of a mixture of extreme vanity combined with a keen interest for his pet subject. Alfred O'Rahilly for example is vain, but he is not a bore because he is not really interested in any subject outside himself. . . . It is the combination of vanity with enthusiasm that makes the perfect bore. Oldham possessed both qualities to an almost unlimited degree. . . . At some remote period in his youth he had mastered the doctrine of comparative real costs. This had come as a revelation that coloured and moulded his whole life—something like the illumination experienced by St Ignatius Loyola during his illness. For fifty years this simple —over simple—doctrine was shouted through Dublin. I say shouted advisedly because, in addition to his vanity and his enthusiasm, Oldham possessed another ingredient of the complete bore—a loud voice.

If George could write in this vein when Oldham had been in his grave for twenty-five years, it seems safe to assume that he said much worse things at the time. The acoustics of Dublin being what they were, and no doubt are, it seems probable that the Professor of National Economics came to hear what was being said about him by the young aspirant to academic honours.

In fact this set-piece seems a bit over-done. Oldham's surviving students agree that he could be a bore and that he could be opinionated. But he had some very good students in his classes; though it may be, as George would certainly have said, that they would have been good anyway. He was a person of some distinction. As a young man in Trinity he had been a friend of Maud Gonne, Yeats and Douglas Hyde. Then and later, he was that unusual type in Irish life, a Protestant home ruler. Later still, he laid the foundations of the Faculty of Commerce in College. He was President of the Statistical and Social Inquiry Society and a frequent (and emphatic) contributor to its discussions. His stamping-ground was the Contemporary Club which met to discuss matters of public interest every week in Lincoln Place. This club, it will be readily understood, was about the only club in Dublin that George never entered.

For all that, Oldham was eleven years younger than Father Finlay. If he had been the survivor, it is hard to know what would have happened to George. But the luck held. In 1926, early in the Hilary term, Oldham died suddenly. As George put it, with some unction, 'my enemy had been taken and my friend survived'.

Economics had not then become a profession. There were very few graduates in the subject. George possessed outstanding qualifications and he was readily available. This was important because the term was in progress and lectures had to be given. George was summoned by Father Finlay and then by the President. He was appointed *locum tenens* pending the involved working of the machinery of appointment. He gave his first lecture on Monday, 1 March. There was not then, nor ever afterwards, any stage-fright. As regards the formal appointment, no opponent appeared. He was recommended to the Senate by the Governing Body in June on the proposal of Father Finlay, seconded by Patrick Semple. It is recorded that Mr Patrick Belton dissented but this opposition, whatever its reason, left no scars. In July the Senate accepted the recommendation.

Arthur Cox organised a party to celebrate the appointment. It comprised William Butler, Charles Bewley, James Geoghegan, Joe Walsh, Ted Riordan, Tom Bodkin, Kevin O'Higgins and Paddy Hogan. Writing years later George reflected on the variety and mutability of life. Butler and Riordan were dead as were

O'Higgins and Hogan, the one murdered, the other killed in a road accident. James Geoghegan was cast out from the circle of his friends because he espoused the cause of Fianna Fail and contested the Longford bye-election of 1930 in its name. What was much worse and quite unforgivable was that he did so successfully. George quarrelled with Bewley and Walsh over their attitude to Nazi Germany. With Bodkin he remained on cordial and affectionate terms (*exceptis excipiendis*, as it were), until the end; but their meetings were infrequent after Tom left Dublin for Birmingham. He continued

> the sole survivor of this little party who remains at the same time alive, resident in Dublin and a friend is Arthur Cox. I have referred to the peculiar tenacity of my relations with Arthur—our apparent mutual affection and suspicion. The list of friends who gathered at a turning point in my career is a curious reminder of the central place he occupied in my intimate circle.

The College to which he returned after fourteen years was outwardly unchanged but inwardly transformed. The interval was short enough but it had been filled with great events. The College of the 1920s had to adjust itself to a new society with values and aims which were different from and more varied than the old. This foreshadowed what was to happen on a much larger scale when the number of students began to increase rapidly in the later 1930s.

The structure and government of the College did not reflect these changes. It was what later came to be called the 'old' College. The original officers were still there. After seventeen years, Doctor Coffey was still not much more than half-way through his presidency. Arthur Conway was still Registrar and would not move into the presidency until 1940. In the College office, John Bacon, devoted, kindly and too often frustrated by his chief, dispensed good advice and friendliness until his death in 1939. On the academic side, the Deans enjoyed a security of tenure which only retirement or death itself could disturb. Patrick Semple was Dean of Arts from 1909 until nearly the half-century: Pierce Purcell was Dean of Engineering for longer still. Their tenure was as tranquil as it was secure. No ambitious colleague would have dreamed of challenging their re-election (when, that is, anybody remembered to re-elect them). Still less were they likely to be called on by the President to serve on an infinity of committees. Doctor Coffey kept affairs in his own hands. The left hand might rarely know what the right was doing; but Deans and Professors, no matter how senior, would be no better off.

This stability, if that is the proper term, induced an air of timelessness. It seemed as if the College, trusting to the barrier that the Green imposed between it and the city, had decided to ignore the changes that had taken place in Castle Yard and Upper Merrion Street. In 1926, when the parliamentary party was already a memory, John Dillon still sat in the Governing Body. As late as its issue for 1931–32 (though no later, even timelessness had its limits) the calendar began its list of Governing Body and Academic Staff with the unyielding prefix:

Visitor
HIS MAJESTY THE KING

No less retentive, the preamble to every College Statute until 1934 commenced with the words: WHEREAS *His late Majesty King Edward the Seventh was graciously pleased....*

The language of administration may have remained the same but everybody knew very well that a lot had changed since 1914. In that year the College, like the country, had been Redmondite. Its members, staff and students, would have been willing to work the Home Rule Act if it had been brought into operation. Many of them volunteered for service in the war. It was quite in keeping with the mood of the times that the President of the College and no less a College personage than Johnnie McArdle should have acted as sponsors of the Inns of Court Officers Training Corps. For some years, until 1920, the calendar carried a list of those who had joined up. There were nearly five hundred of them, of whom about one in every ten was recorded as having been killed or having died on active service.

This was overlain by Easter Week and its aftermath. College graduates had taken part in the planning of the rising: College graduates had fought in it. The College shared the reaction of the country to the executions. The feasibility of a sovereign Irish republic, the wisdom or unwisdom of a rising while the war was still in progress, were beside the point. Certainly, there were unspoken reservations, which were to appear in 1922, but for the moment they were not apparent.

On top of all these things came the civil war. That blood-stained division affected almost every institution in the country, down to the smallest co-operative creamery or sports club. It affected the College especially severely because so many of its graduates had been, in one way or another, connected with Sinn Fein before or after 1916. Many of them were active participants in the civil war. Many more of them found their sons or their younger brothers engaged on one side or the other, often on the side that they opposed; they opened their newspapers to read of the killing, not always in combat, of their relatives or of their friends.

The bitterness of that time took years to disappear; in 1926 it was hardly below the surface. For years to come the College was to be haunted by memories of those who had died between 1914 and 1923. Today, they are insubstantial shades and the tragedy of their early death has faded. But for many years their memory was still fresh in the hearts of those who survived, to whom it may have seemed that some part of themselves, and perhaps the more generous part, had died too.

Officially, of course, the College took no side in the Civil War though later parliamentary elections suggested that a majority of the staff and the graduate body were pro-Treaty into the 1930s. Dr Coffey's unswerving policy was to insulate the College from the turmoil as far as possible. It was probably the only policy that could give hope for a future in which the killing and the destruction would have ended at last, but it led to some odd results. Mr de Valera was Chancellor of the University but for years he was virtually forbidden to enter the College. Close relations with graduates was discouraged. This was explicable as long as some graduates on one side or the other might have injected their bitterness into student life, but a temporary expedient was allowed later to harden into a settled attitude to the great loss (it may be thought) of both the College and its graduates.

In the meantime, a new State had been established, whatever might be thought of its title-deeds. It had to provide itself with a civil service. The tasks now to be undertaken went far beyond the experience of the outgoing regime, many of whose members had no intention of serving the new State in any circumstances. Ministers turned to the universities, in particular to the College,

F

to fill the gaps. This was done amazingly successfully in view of
the hasty enlistment. It has often been said that the structure of
the civil service was one of the greatest of British legacies to the
new State, but the men to staff it had to be found in a great
hurry in 1922. The College graduates were an invaluable source
of supply. This happened less than twenty-five years after one of
the best disposed of Chief Secretaries for Ireland had reported his
inability to find Irish nationalists or Catholics of sufficient ability
to discharge the much more limited responsibilties that fell to
Dublin Castle at that time. The Jesuits, and the College in its
first ten years, had done good work.

The College now seemed to stand in much the same position
to Merrion Street as Trinity had so lately stood to Dublin Castle.
The new government was dominated by its graduates. Suddenly
it seemed that the College had become the official university, all
the more so as Trinity took some time to adjust itself to altered circumstances. In 1926, there seemed no reason why all this should
not go on, if not for ever at least for a very long time indeed.

Optimism was strengthened by the rapid growth in the number
of students. There had been a fall immediately after the war but
a new increase began about 1927 which was only occasionally
interrupted during succeeding decades. The students came from
all over the country : in the 1920s only about a third of them
came from Dublin and the surrounding area. There was an
interesting change in the courses that they pursued. In its early
years the College had been dominated by Arts and Medicine.
In the inter-war period there was a marked expansion in Science,
Engineering and Commerce.

This was certainly a sign of development, but the position of
the College was not so happy if it were looked at from other
angles. In some respects, it was isolated. It was regarded with
suspicion by many of those who had opposed the Treaty; it was
deeply distrusted by many churchmen. At its foundation in 1908
it had been described by Cardinal Logue as 'a Godless bantling' :
the phrase represented a view widely held by those who had
hoped for an advowedly Catholic University instead of a college
that was formally neutral in matters of religious belief. In this
matter the College got the worst of both sides; on one, its critics
argued that it was too much identified with the Catholic Church;
on another, it was too little. These things mattered in the 1920s.

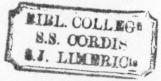

There was another sense in which it was isolated. Around the time that the Treaty was signed there were a number of people in academic circles who expected, indeed hoped, that royal foundations such as the Royal Irish Academy, the Royal College of Surgeons and the Royal College of Physicians would be abolished or, at the least drastically remodelled, by the new state. This implied an attack on institutions which for very many years had been closely associated with Trinity College. In the circumstances of Irish history, they had not had comparable associations with University College.

Accordingly an attempt was made to found a National Academy which would clearly replace the foundation of 1785. One of the movers in this project was Father Corcoran. He organised some meetings to discuss it among members of the College staff and graduates. George was one of those who was invited to attend; his name was put forward as a possible member of one of the sections of the new body.[1]

It is clear that he was not attracted by the invitation. If he had to choose between Father Corcoran and Father Finlay, who had seen to his election to the Royal Irish Academy, there was very little doubt where he would stand. In the event, the project fizzled out, largely on account of the loyalty of College people such as Arthur Conway, John J. Nolan and Felix Hackett to the older foundation. It is an interesting example of the uncertainties of the time and of the pressures placed on the staff and graduates of the College. More than that, it might be said, it showed the manner in which they resisted such pressures.

The most abiding difficulty of the College, which was to grow still worse with the years, was its finance. The new state was established precisely when Whitehall was increasing the grants to British universities to meet post-war conditions. The example of London was not followed in Dublin. The new administration, seeking a prickly excellence in all things, strove above all for economy and a balanced budget. It pursued these aims with a single-minded devotion and remarkable tenacity in matters where a less heroic austerity might have gained (or retained, as its term of office lengthened) support.

This was reflected in the provision made for the College. In

1. This is mentioned on pp. 407–409 of *Letters to W. B. Yeats*, vol. ii, edited by Finegan, Mills Harper and Murphy. The Macmillan Press, 1977.

1926, the year in which George joined the staff, the College of Science and the Albert Agricultural College at Glasnevin were made over to University College. It soon became obvious that the change was not accompanied with a suitable increase in the endowment provided by the state. That endowment was then increased from £42,000 to £82,000. The number of students was then 1209. The endowment was not increased again until 1946 when the number of students was 3362.

The College was not indeed the only example of the low priority given by the first two governments to university education but its elder sisters had the advantage of having been already housed and equipped. Granted the continuous increase in the number of students, the problem of accommodation could not be solved even by heroic poverty. The founding Act of 1908 had envisaged the building of premises for the College. Plans were drawn up for a quadrangle of buildings. This quadrangle was to serve the needs of fifteen hundred students. (In 1909–1910 there were 530 on the College roll). In the event only one side of it— that facing the Terrace—was built. It bears the date of 1914, no year for starting anything. For just under fifty years thereafter, until the College was at last looked after by the state (under a Fianna Fail government, it is proper to record) the students who by then numbered seven thousand had to do as best they could in this one wing and in the buildings behind it which dated from the exhibitions of the mid-nineteenth century.

One result of this public economy was a depressive effect on salaries. The point comes logically here and it is useful as a guide to one aspect of George's life. In 1926 he was paid £800 as Professor of National Economics. In 1930, when Political Economy was added to his duties, the salary for the combined chairs was set at £900. This annual salary remained unchanged until 1946 when he received a bonus of £70 and then another of £100. In 1947 the salary was increased to £1,200 and in 1951, after twenty-five years as a professor, to £1,600. None of his colleagues fared any better; the junior staff, on the whole, fared worse. It was no wonder that the President's Report for 1946–47 should have contained the comment :

The condition of being hard-up which was normal to the College since its foundation, and which its members had learned to bear with a certain amount of cheerfulness was changed by the rising costs of the war years into a state of grim and unrelieved penury.

In 1926, however, the worst of these frustrations still lay unsuspected in the future. The shooting was over at long last; the College could look forward to peace and progress. There was an exhilarating feeling of occasion, of the opportunities and challenges presented by the new state, of being able to do things for the first time. The dreams of 1912 were revived among the students in Arts and Law who began to think of the constituencies that they might represent in the 1930s. The engineers could take a deep and justified pride in the planning and construction of the Shannon Scheme and the national grid. Nothing like that had ever been attempted in Ireland. Among the traditional faculties, the Medical School enjoyed a re-birth of energy. It must have seemed good to be alive in that false dawn of the later 1920s before depression wrecked so many hopes. It must have seemed even better to be a newly-appointed professor of the National Economics of Ireland.

It was not. He was taken aback by what he found.

One would have fancied that a young bachelor entering a big College would have received a welcome from at least some of the staff. I do not think that I received a single invitation from anybody connected with the College—except from a few of the medical staff whom I already knew and visited—for over ten years. . . . I used at one time to think that my colleagues disliked me for some reason, but I have come to the conclusion that their attitude was one of indifference rather than of dislike.

Such thoughts led him, as those who knew him will have already guessed, into a lament for the absence of commons and a high table. This was a complaint that he nourished for years. He would not allow himself to be talked out of it. It was in vain to point out that the College had not the money to finance such amenities, being forced (with increasing difficulty as the years went by) to save every penny to maintain the academic establishment. He would reply that a high table would not cost all that much and that the true reason was that the government of the College did not want it and would not have it even if it could be afforded. (In this, he was probably right). It was also argued that if there were a high table, it would certainly be attended with remorseless regularity by precisely the people whom he wanted most to avoid. He would admit some justice in that but in a few minutes he would return to the charge that not only did the College not have a high table but, what was far worse, it did not want to have a high table. Finally, it would be pointed out that he was running a kind of high table, in exile as it were, in the Royal Irish and that he had full control over who should be there, which was a great deal more than he could hope to have in the College. He was still inconsolable.

The fact was that the staff whom he joined were almost all people who were considerably senior to him. Their circles were already well formed. He was in the unusual position of having obtained a chair without any previous stint of lecturing in the College or anywhere else. There had been little opportunity to get to know him. Granted also the range of activities that have been described in previous chapters, his colleagues were unlikely to think that he stood in much need of company.

This sense of distance from the staff never completely disappeared. Even in later years he kept as far away as he could from the normal run of academic politics. He flattered himself that he achieved thereby some degree of independence and that his opinion was the more greatly valued because he kept above the ebb and flow of argument. This may not have been true. Because he was absent, his opinion was not canvassed; because he kept aloof, he was not relied on by any group. Certainly this saved him inconvenience and unpleasantness; but there were many decisions to which he might have contributed usefully if he had cared to do so. There were occasions on which he felt himself or his interests to be directly imperilled. Then he would stand and fight very vigorously indeed. Normally, however, he was inclined to withdraw, to leave matters to be decided by others in his absence. This attitude persisted long after his standing in the College was unquestioned. It consistently told against his spasmodic attempts to obtain better staffing in his department: what new appointments the College could afford went to subjects whose professors were more combative. All this, it still seems, was a great pity for the College and for himself. Nevertheless, what was to be important and fruitful was that, ill at ease with his colleagues, he paid special attention to his students.

The Professor 1926-34

His primary obligation was to deliver three lectures a week on the National Economics of Ireland. This course extended over two years of the primary degrees in Arts and Commerce. These classes sat together. In any morning class, therefore, he was lecturing to the second and third year students in Arts in the honours groups (mainly in Political Economy and in Legal and Political Science), the second and third year students taking a pass Arts degree and the second and third year students taking a Commerce degree. (In Commerce, as in Medicine and Engineering, there were no separate pass and honours courses; honours depended on the results in a common examination.) It goes without saying that this arrangement made for an exceedingly varied class as well as what was thought to be, by the standards of those days, an exceedingly large one. It was no small test of his nerve.

He had also two evening classes given to second and third pass Arts (there were no honours courses in the evening classes) and second and third Commerce, all of them again combined. These evening classes in some Arts subjects and in Commerce had been revived some years earlier. This revived a tradition that dated from the early years of the Catholic University.

The decision to revive these courses did the College much honour. It was an acknowledgement of the duty of a university to offer courses to those who could not become full-time students. The evening students whom George met were 'men and women of mature age, most of them teachers or civil servants. There were over a hundred of them and they formed a large and critical audience'. So they have always been since, although their numbers have grown so greatly. They always were and are exceptionally pleasant and rewarding people to lecture. Admittedly it is not always that one begins an evening lecture with enthusiasm,

but any initial hesitation is removed by the thought that the class
has taken considerable trouble (sometimes travelling from towns
as far away as Kildare or Castleblayney each evening) to come
and listen. George got on very well with all his classes but he
got on exceptionally well with the evening people. Certainly, they
interfered with his usual dinner in one club or another but that
was acceptably replaced by a quiet meal in the upstairs back
room in Jammets or, later, in the Unicorn or, later still, in the
Golden Orient in Leeson Street. These meals were also a convenient way of giving hospitality without having to spend the
whole evening on it. But the evening classes did not exhaust his
responsibilities.

> I was invited to give a lecture a week to the students in the
> Faculty of Agriculture on agricultural economics. As I could
> not find a suitable textbook I wrote one myself, and it received
> excellent reviews. The Faculty of Agriculture was . . . situated
> at the Albert College, Glasnevin, and I have always enjoyed
> going there one day a week. The staff were more friendly than
> in Earlsfort Terrace and there was more of a team spirit. . . .
> . . . The time came when, instead of fearing, I positively en-
> joyed my lectures. I felt that I had really made a successful
> fresh start.

In the summer of 1930 Father Finlay retired from the chair of
Political Economy. It was decided to join the two chairs; and
this was done by Statute XVI of the College which came into
effect months later. In February 1931 the Government Body,
on the proposal of Father Finlay seconded by Agnes O'Farrelly,
decided to forgo the usual procedure of advertisement and
recommended George's appointment directly to the Senate. The
Senate made the appointment in the following month. George
had been lecturing in both subjects ever since the previous
October; and it is hard to think of anybody who could have
successfully contested the new chair against him or who would
have tried. Technically, however, the procedure was irregular;
and it was to cause him some unnecessary anxiety in the future.

He was now at the head of a rapidly growing department. He
had to give a further four or five lectures a week to morning and
evening classes. He was given the assistance of a statutory lecturer, whose time had to be divided between Political Economy

and Commerce. Given the smouldering hostility between the professors of the two subjects, this was an impossible situation for everybody. It came to an unhappy end in 1939.

Ten or eleven hours lecturing a week for twenty-five or twenty-six weeks of the year cannot be presented as an intolerable burden, even when the office work and the growing weight of examining are counted in. It would not have been regarded as intolerable in the 1930s. George never claimed that it was. He did point out, with great justice, that the lecturing depended almost completely on him and that if anything were to happen to him even in the shape of a passing indisposition, the morning and evening classes would come to a full stop. This was to provoke a revival of anxiety and strain when, in the middle of the 1930s, his confidence was temporarily weakened. Apart from the lecturer, he did not receive any assistance at all until 1936 when the writer was brought in on a strictly part-time basis. From 1941 onwards he and I, greatly assisted by Alexis FitzGerald, did our best to cope with ever increasing numbers. It was not until as late as 1951 that the department was put on a satisfactory basis.

He always held strong views about the duties of a professor and of the kind of person that a professor should be. His views on what kind of a professor he himself was were equally clear and dispassionate.

The personality with which my students were confronted was that of a man of the world who had been introduced into the College to lecture them on economics rather than that of a great economist who had emerged from the seclusion of his study. I may perhaps express my opinion that there is much to be said in favour of the sort of professor that my students encountered. A professor is a teacher not a research worker in a laboratory. He should be an interesting teacher rather than a deep original scholar. . . .

A professor transmits to his students far more than the information conveyed in his lectures, much of which can be derived from textbooks. He conveys his outlook and valuations on all sorts of subjects. His lectures are coloured by his own personality, which is the result of millions of influences derived from his background, his contacts, his reading and his reflections.

F*

Every activity that improves a professor in any respect will improve his competence in his vocation. Very few departments of his life are without their bearing on his professional duties. I have always interpreted the phrase 'whole-time professor' to mean a man who does not engage in any occupation that might prove a distraction from his teaching without producing some compensating enrichment of his own personality. It does not mean a man who never leaves his College or never reads any books but those on his special subject. . . . I have always drawn a distinction between activities that are competitive and complementary to my professorship. Among the latter I have included work on commissions and in the Senate, writing and journalism connected, even remotely, with my subject, and business and social contacts. I think that the sphere of complementary activities can be particularly widely defined in the case of economics, which is concerned so greatly with the current problems of the world. My predecessor, Father Finlay, was a man of good general education, friend of many people drawn from all ranks and classes, and a man of the world rather than a dry-as-dust pedant. Nobody meeting him would have taken him for a professor. I hope that nobody would have taken me for one. . . .

I am afraid that I have always been, at heart, a little contemptuous of academic success. I regarded my career in the College as a second best, a comeback after my failure at the Bar, which I looked at as my first love. During the first years of my appointment in the College, I was immensely pleased to have made a fresh start and to have a regular professional standing. I hope I treated my new position with respect. . . . I was determined to make my new position a success and to demonstrate to the world in general and to my mother in particular that I was not destined to be one of the world's failures.

To put it mildly, the foregoing represents a remarkably detached attitude to academic life in general and to a professorship in particular. His colleagues could hardly be blamed if they suspected that he took the College a little less seriously than they did themselves. The same detachment marked his approach to lecturing.

I honestly do not think that any student of mine would accuse me of being a bore. Even if I were to possess the first qualification for bores, vanity, of which I think I am comparatively innocent, I am saved from that species of offensiveness by lack of enthusiasm for my subject. I am essentially tolerant. I do not wish to force my views down the throats of my students. If they disagree with me I do not care. I am paid to teach, not to make converts or reform the world. The emotional enthusiasm which would be in place at a revivalist meeting is out of place at a university lecture.

It came down to this : he was paid to lecture in Political Economy just as, if he had stayed at the Bar, he would have been paid to appear in Court. The one needed the same care and responsibility as the other. He would check his authorities; he would plan the sequence of his argument; he would consider if it might be made more acceptable by the use of some well-judged analogy. It was his job to do the best he could within the accepted conventions of professional responsibility. There is much the same to be found in university lecturing. The professor accepts a responsibility to give the lectures, to prepare them properly and to deliver them in such a manner that the argument can be understood. It is his duty to state the issues fairly, to point out the implications of each course of policy, to provide the class with all the means that are available to understand what is involved. It is no part of his business to identify himself with one policy or another.

This is a very high statement of duty and behaviour. It needs qualification. The implication that students will be easily influenced by what they hear in lectures over-estimates the powers of the lecturer and under-estimates the intelligence of those who are lectured. In the specific case of students of economics in University College it has never seemed that they have been particularly impressionable : their constant characteristic has been a cheerful and rather mocking cynicism. They may go astray in their opinion but they will not be easily led astray. Further, it must be admitted that it is difficult to lecture with detachment on matters which are the subject of acute political controversy. This was happening in National Economics all through the 1930s. When George's lectures reached such topics as the salvation of the country by the growing of more wheat or the powers of compulsory acquisition of land under the Land Act of 1933 they suddenly became orations, indeed philippics. But when such issues, with their echoes of past commissions of inquiry, had faded into the background they were not replaced. That this was so was not the least of his services to the College and its students.

Essentially, he did not think of himself as teaching a class in the sense of forming their minds into a given pattern or along particular lines of thought. To attempt to do so is one of the temptations which beset anybody whose lecturing lies in the field of the speculative subjects. It was not a temptation to which he yielded. All his life he disapproved of 'viewy' people who felt that they had discovered the answer to this or that, and that it was their duty to impart their solution to every captive audience in sight. Fundamentally, this lay at the root of his dislike of Oldham and, later, of Alfred O'Rahilly, not that there was any lack of a *casus belli* in either case. He was a professor, not a crusader. He would have thoroughly agreed with Jowett : ' Preaching is not teaching . . . and teaching should never become preaching'.

More deeply still he believed with Newman that the acquisition of knowledge was not at all the same as education and that the object of a university education was primarily to inculcate

a habit of mind . . . which lasts through life, of which the attributes are, freedom, equitableness, calmness, moderation, and wisdom; or what in a former discourse I have ventured to call a philosophical habit. This then I would assign as the special fruit of the education furnished at a university.[1]

From the beginning to the end, thirty-five years later, he took his duties very seriously.

I was now in a position of great responsibility. I was entrusted by the authorities of the leading College in the country to mould the minds of those of the younger generation who had chosen economics as their field of study. These young people would, in their later lives, be influenced by what they had learned from me. Many of them would occupy positions of public importance, in politics, in the civil service or in journal-

1. Newman. *The Idea of a University*, 1910 edit. Fifth Discourse.

ism. I would infect them with my point of view, with which they, in turn, would infect others. I have sometimes been rather frightened by the responsibility of my position in the College, moulding the minds of young people at their most impressionable age. Plato likens teaching by the spoken word to planting trees in the souls of some listeners. Elsewhere he says that a philosopher is the parent of progeny of the spirit. Henry Adams develops this idea in a passage that impressed me deeply when I read it. 'A parent gives life, but as parent gives no more. A murderer takes life, but his deed stops there. A teacher effects eternally, he can never tell where his influence stops'. A professor is a mirror in which the opinions of countless thinkers and writers is reflected. They may be refracted as well as reflected. A professor may be a transmuter rather than a mere transmitter. . . . I was in a position to colour opinion. It is interesting to attempt to assess how I would colour it. Economics is a subject that allows for a considerable latitude of treatment. There are parts of economic discussion, conducted even with the most correct academic detachment, where the personality and opinions of the lecturer must intrude. Different people regard the same problem from different points of view. What was my point of view? What were the principles, biases and prejudices that coloured my outlook as a professor?

There follows a long discussion on how his approach to economics was shaped by influences in early life.

I breathed in my childhood the air of Victorian liberalism. My father had worked his way up in the world from small beginnings entirely by his own thrift and energy. His undoubted personal virtues had resulted in a hard-earned material reward. He deserved his success and was entitled to hold what he had gained. That his profits should be confiscated by penal taxation would have appeared to him not only unjust but intolerable. If he had succeeded in business it was because he had given better value to his customers than his competitors had done. He owed nothing to the favour of any politician or planner. He provided the public with what they wanted and he had reaped the appropriate reward. Business people were paid what they were worth. Profit was the sign, not of exploitation, but of acumen and good service. Business failure, bankruptcy and unemployment were the penalties of the losers in the race. They were regrettable but inevitable casualties in a competitive society. It was right and proper to buy in the cheapest market, even if it was the labour market. Protection was regarded as something that had been discarded wherever enlightenment prevailed and trade unions were weak and comparatively powerless. These were the unspoken assumptions of my childhood. They coloured my whole outlook on life. I did not know it at the time, but my attitude was very akin to that of the great classical economists who had coloured the whole background of late Victorian thought. . . . The business background of my childhood, the professional assumptions of my youth, and the self-reliant character of my own career, unquestionably coloured my outlook on economic problems. I became an individualist, a believer in enterprise and self-help. If I had suffered from want and insecurity I would probably have been more conscious of labour problems. During my period of involuntary unemployment I enjoyed an ample income. I was never made aware of the pinch that people feel when they cannot find a market for their service. When I did finally secure paid employment, I was appointed to a position with security of tenure for my life-time. Perhaps this made me insensitive to the fear of unemployment. It may even have dulled my awareness of the keenness of competition in business. I had attained my position by my success in the competitive struggle; but, having obtained it, was rather like a monopolist, protected from further competition. . . . Indeed I am not sure that this detachment, this absence of emotional feeling was not overdone. It may have misled me on certain occasions when I was asked to direct my mind to topical issues with political bearings. . . . This blindness to the background enabled me to examine problems coldly and rationally and to arrive at correct and unprejudiced solutions. But the value and the weight of my advice were reduced in the eyes of the public and the politicians because I had failed to take account of popular emotions. My attitude to every problem was coloured by my own over-intellectual mode of living. I saw every problem as an examination question to be answered or a case to be decided.

This long quotation may illustrate his philosophical approach to that part of human affairs with which Political Economy is concerned. With the subject itself, he was not greatly concerned in his earlier years. When he came to renew his undergraduate acquaintance with it in the library of the RDS, it was as part of his campaign to get into the College. He was not doing so on account of any particular interest in economic issues : he would have much preferred to have had a law professorship in his sights. Neither then nor later did he believe that Political Economy was a subject of fundamental importance to a civilised society. Archbishop Whately is credited with the statement that 'next to sound religion, Political Economy is most essential to the well-being of society.' George was the last man in the world to agree with such claims. Much more would he have agreed with Keynes, in the preface to *Essays in Persuasion*, that 'the day is not far off when the Economic Problem will take the back seat where it belongs, and the arena of the heart and head will be occupied, or re-occupied, by our real problems—the problems of life and human relations, of creation and behaviour and religion'.

The circumstances in which he prepared himself to lecture greatly influenced his approach to the subject. His legal training was dominant. In the early years, he argued from what were then regarded as the authoritative text-books, Mill, Marshall and Pigou. The manner in which he interpreted the texts was instinctively legal. *Pacta sunt servanda*. Certainly contracts might be unjust because, as in the very convenient example of the Irish landlord and tenant system, the two parties had not equal bargaining strength. It was then the business of the State to step in and see that justice was done. That might, and did, apply to a growing number of activities in society. But in general people should keep their word and the State should keep the ring. People should be left to get on with their own business.

This had become rather less than contemporary and rather less than Marshall or Pigou. Even Tom Kettle, in a famous essay in *The Day's Burden*, had written with greater imagination of the kind of society that a free Ireland might become. The strict limitations on George's approach sprang from his initial studies. He was to modify them as he grew older, notably under the influence of the *General Theory*. He never completely abandoned them. He could never bring himself to be much interested in schemes of social regeneration, whether they were Marxist or Papal.

This attitude should not be attributed solely to a conservative frame of mind. It derived at least in part from his concept of what Political Economy was about. He never entertained extravagant views of the contribution that it could make to society. He would have firmly agreed with Mill's statement that it was

> . . . not a thing by itself but a greater whole, a branch of Social Philosophy, so interlinked with all the other branches, that its conclusions, even in its own peculiar province, are only true conditionally, subject to interference and counteraction from causes not within its scope, while to the character of a practical guide it has no pretensions, apart from other classes of considerations. Political Economy, in truth, has never pretended to give advice to mankind with no lights but its own, though people who knew nothing but Political Economy (and therefore knew that ill) have taken on themselves to advise, and could only do so by such lights as they had.[1]

Of course, George was aware of the development of the mathematical approach to economics during his lifetime. It was not that he thought it valueless. It was rather that it offended his view of Political Economy in two ways. In the first place, it made the subject increasingly arcane, which so good a communicator as he was would feel to be a serious fault. In the second place, it obscured what he believed to be a fundamental element in his subject, that Political Economy, Philosophy and Law sprang from the same root and should not be severed from one another.

> Modern economics has lost some influence by its having become esoteric, a study to be pursued by the initiated, not comprehensible by the general reader. The great classical economists, like the great historians, were all literary men whose works were read with pleasure by a wide public. Modern economics and modern history have taken a wrong turn in the direction of pedantry and dryness. In very recent times, a reaction in the right direction seems to have begun. My own leanings have always been in favour of the literary approach to economic discussion. I have always discussed economic problems

1. *Autobiography*, Columbia U.P. 1924, pp. 165–166.

in literary rather than mathematical language. I was a believer in the liberal, humanistic, tradition expounded so satisfactorily by Newman.

To put the matter in another way. He did not in his heart believe in the kind of economic engineering which became fashionable in the 1950s and 1960s. He was sceptical about the lasting effects of programmes and planning. He was not inclined to join in the worship of growth. This emerges very strongly from the presidential address which he read to the Statistical and Social Inquiry Society of Ireland in 1942. *Economic Relativity* discloses an extraordinarily wide range of reading in the economic literature of the day. It is infused with the over-riding thought of the necessity of priorities, of the proposition that Political Economy is a matter of choosing how to use scarce resources. This comes out most strongly in his last book, *The Phantom of Plenty*, which is clearly a statement of personal belief.

Most deeply of all, he believed that in the last resort a country's prosperity rested on the character of its people. He agreed, again with Mill, that

> The worth of a State, in the long run, is the worth of the individuals composing it, and a State which . . . dwarfs its men, in order that they may be more docile instruments in its hands even for beneficial purposes, will find that with small men no really great thing can be accomplished; and that the perfection of machinery to which it has sacrificed everything, will in the end avail it nothing for want of the vital power which, in order that the machine might work more smoothly, it has preferred to banish.[1]

This, it may be thought, is not only Mill. It is Sir Horace Plunkett and Father Finlay.

Fundamentally Political Economy had its social uses, still more its political uses, but its claims should always be carefully scrutinised. He would have thoroughly agreed with Keynes: 'Economics is essentially a moral science and not a rational science'.[2]

The students who listened to his first lectures in Political Economy in the autumn of 1930 were not conscious of these

1. M. Packe, *John Stuart Mill*, London, Secker & Warburg, 1954 at p. 406.
2. *Collected Writings*, vol. xiv.

reservations. They did realise that the whole style of lecturing had changed. This was only to be expected. Father Finlay was eighty-one when he retired : George was thirty-eight when he replaced him. What has since been called 'the generation gap' was obvious.

He was a professor for what may be described, by present-day standards at least, as the unusually long period of over thirty-five years. During that period the number of his students increased enormously. For one reason or another the interest of Arts students in the 1930s and subsequent decades lay in the field of economics rather than, as previously, in classics or philosophy. It is obviously impossible to write with detachment on these matters : one can only say that from George's earliest years, there was a constant stream of talented students who looked for an inspiring teacher in Political Economy and felt that they had found their ideal in him.

That stream flowed without pause throughout the years of his professorship. As happens in any university the stream was broader and deeper in some years than in others but it never dried up. This was not a matter of solely academic importance. The people who graduated in the 1930s and later decades were exactly the people who were of an age to contribute to the great expansion of economic activity, and, therefore, of national self-confidence, in the 1960s. They were extraordinarily good people and it was a matter of great importance that they should find a teacher worthy of them. It was their good fortune, and the nation's good fortune, that they found one. It was the saving grace of George's life, which made up for so many defeats and disappointments, that he could give them exactly what they and their times required. Throughout all his professorship, even in the very last years when his interest may have been on the wane, he was regarded as one of the very best and most stimulating lecturers in the College. He was articulate, he was audible; he was incisive—the three gifts without which the greatest authority becomes useless as a means of communication. He had an extra-ordinary gift of providing a metaphor or an analogy which would drive a point home more effectively than any amount of logical reasoning. There was one other thing. After the early years he was never content to lecture from the then accepted textbooks. He kept up with what was being written. At one level he lectured on *The General Theory* in the session of its publication. At another, he would go out of his way to refer to some useful article that had just appeared in the *Economist* or the *New Statesman* and *Nation*.

This point goes deeper than may be thought. It has been said that students were often cynical, that their instinct was *nil admirari*. But it may be suggested that, especially in the 1930s and 1940s, the two decades which concern us at present, their minds had been influenced by what they had learned at school and in their homes. They were children of their time, and the time was one of certitude in Church and State, to use the phrase that brings back the atmosphere of those years. This acceptance spilled over into everything in life, and into those aspects of life with which Political Economy was particularly concerned. It was a revelation to learn in George's lectures that in fact everything had not yet been settled, that economics was still a speculative subject, that battles were still being fought. This, of course, is what universities are about; but such questionings were rare anywhere in the inter-war and war-time periods. He showed that there were at least two sides to most propositions, that the difference was rarely between what was wrong and what was right. His lectures were a drawing up of blinds and a letting in of the light.

As time went on and classes grew larger, the lecture hall was the place of communication. It had not always been so. In the earlier years he had made a point of arriving early, before the previous lecture had finished, so that he might exchange a few words with waiting students. This was not done without an effort. He might well have said with Jowett that 'I ought to get rid of shyness, which has detracted at least one-third from my life'. He could not get rid of it, he was determined not to yield to it. And so he joined the waiting groups (*Don't run away, now, don't run away*) and conducted a conversation which was not made any easier by his habit of circling around the corridor rather than standing still—the sign, if it had been understood, of his shyness.

What he had to say on these occasions might or might not be memorable. It was certain that it would not be any matter of shop, which was for the lecture, or any matter of sporting activity of any kind in which he claimed complete disinterest. It was rather like Froude's memories of Newman at Oxford who

did not enter on such important (*sci.* religious) questions, although they were in the air and we talked about them among
ourselves. He, when we met him, spoke to us about subjects
of the day, of literature, of public persons and incidents, of
everything which was generally interesting.

There was not much perhaps to these brief meetings except the
one thing that was really important. Students felt that George
was interested in what they had to say, that he was interested in
talking to them and that it was not his fault if he could not talk
to them all. They were pleased with this feeling and, therefore,
with him.

In any college at any time there are staff whose grace of manner, or whose associations in sport or in political life, give them
a special influence. George could hardly claim any of those
attributes, and yet he commanded influence and respect among
many of the most able students that the college could boast. It
is not easy to see how this happened. The explanation may well
lie in his line of approach. He had the gift of making students
feel that they were, or rather could be, of importance, that life
held out possibilities that they had never envisaged but that they
could realise if they used their talents. He built them up in their
own estimation at a time in their lives when they were still unsure
of themselves. By a deep irony he did for them precisely what he
could never do for himself.

He took to some of them more than to others. Those whom he
thought to be particularly promising would find themselves
invited out to dinner. It might be cynically said that this was not
quite so much of a compliment as it looked, in view of his constant dining out. But if they made the grade, as it were, they
found themselves dining out not only with George but with his
friends or with some visitor from the *Economist* or *The Times*.
To dine with people much older than oneself, who were 'in the
thick of things', to use his own constant phrase, was an immense
experience for young people. They had now joined the succession
of George's 'swans', the young gentlemen whom he extolled to his
friends as being of almost limitless promise. It must be admitted
that some of his older friends eventually got a little tired of constant exposure to these shining talents and more than hinted to
him that a couple of swanless nights might be no harm for a

change. George's promises of reform would never last for very long. As the years went on and classes increased in number out of all reason, it became increasingly difficult to conduct these ante-class conversations or to select suitable swans; but he coped until the end of his professorship. After he had retired it was a point of honour with his successors that they would bring a couple of the promising people of their time to meet him. This delighted him. It seemed as if in the company of young people he could shake off the demons of shyness and nervousness which plagued him throughout life.

Two things should be added here. His interests were not confined to the swans. He was interested in many parts of student life. If the L. & H., or some club in which he knew a student to have a particular interest, appealed for funds, his subscription would be one of the first to arrive. This generosity did not go unremarked among those who decided who should be elected to the vice-presidencies of student clubs and societies. As a result he found himself to be the President of the Commerce Society and of the Swimming and, later, the Sailing clubs. In such circumstances he was not content with a cheque. He would give the committee a dinner in the Moira, or the Wicklow (reviving old memories) or the Bailey. The host would usually go home before his guests had thought of leaving the table but a good time was had by all.

The second point was that his sympathy was not confined to dinners. It was freely given in circumstances that were more grim. One example may suffice for many that could be given. One of his most brilliant students fell victim to an incurable disease. He had just embarked on a professional career which was full of promise. He was not reconciled to death. To visit him was a trying experience. I met George one day leaving the nursing home. He was pouring with sweat and trembling. He said that he could never bring himself to go back, much though he felt that he should. But he did, many times more. There were many professors in the college who would have done most of the things that have been described in the foregoing passages, but they were especially difficult for George to do on account of his peculiar temperament. By some intuition, students realised this. It was no wonder that they liked him very much indeed.

George was engaged in many other activities throughout the 1930s which, as they were related to the College and to his chair, should receive mention at this point. First of these in time came the foundation of the Finlay Lecture on topics of interest to students of economics. It was endowed by a public subscription designed to mark the great work that Father Finlay had performed in so many areas of national life. The launching of an appeal for subscriptions in the circumstances of 1931 seemed foolhardy, but it was a great success. As his successor in the chair, George was closely associated with the venture. Its success, however, was very largely due to one who is inseparable from any memories of the College at that time and will reappear later—Dr J. C. Flood.

> . . . Flood was primarily responsible for the foundation of the Finlay Lecture. It was his energy and organising ability that made possible the accumulation of the large sum of money, collected on Father Finlay's retirement, by which the lectureship is financed.

Very few people indeed could maintain unbrokenly good relations with Flood even when they made the attempt. It was quite typical that he should have had such a quarrel with his colleagues that he refused to attend the function at which Father Finlay was presented with his portrait by Leo Whelan. It was not the last time that George was to find himself engaged in hostilities on that front. But the Finlay Lecture was most successfully launched. Keynes gave the first lecture, on 'National Self-Sufficiency', in the Physics Theatre in Earlscourt Terrace in April 1933.[1] Finlay Lectures have usually been well attended but this first one surpassed them all. Almost all the members of the new government were present. Headed by Mr de Valera, they sat on one side of the theatre as far removed as possible from the members of the government whom they had replaced. It was assumed, for some reason which is lost to memory, that the lecturer would denounce the pursuit of protection by high tariffs which had contributed to the Great Depression. The smiles and self-confidence were therefore much more obvious on one side of the theatre than on the other. But as Keynes proceeded to show himself unexpectedly friendly to the erection of economic defences, above all when he declared that 'were I, an Irishman,

---

1. The text will be found in *Studies*, June 1933.

I should find much to attract me in the economic outlook of your present Government towards greater self-sufficiency', the smiles faded from one side and appeared on the other.

The lecture was followed by a dinner that evening to which George invited, on Keynes's prompting, some of the best known wits of Dublin. It was, by George's account, a total failure. There were too many wits and Gogarty talked too much. Worse still, Keynes was called to the telephone in the middle of the meal. When he came back, he said: 'You may be interested to know that the United States has just left gold'. The short silence that was felt to be appropriate was broken by Gogarty: 'Does that matter?'

Nevertheless, the Finlay Lecture became an institution. It bestowed its benefits in many directions.

The Lecture, in addition to being a fitting memorial to my very kind friend and distinguished colleague, has become one of the leading public events of the year in the College. We have been lucky in securing some of the leading economists— amongst others, Keynes, Stamp, Ohlin, van Zeeland, Robbins, Hayek, to deliver the lecture. This has given our students the opportunity of hearing distinguished people lecture, and has afforded me an opportunity of making acquaintances that I would not otherwise have made. It has given the College some publicity abroad, since some of the lectures have been re-printed and translated into other languages, always with a reference to their original delivery in the College.

The Finlay Lecture is still delivered but it now alternates with the O'Brien Lecture which was established when George retired. They are a great ornament and inspiration to the teaching of Political Economy in the College.

At much the same time he made the acquaintance of Geoffrey Crowther. The circumstances afford a small sidelight on the fears of the time. In 1932 the Bank of Ireland decided to obtain the services of an adviser skilled in contemporary economic thinking. The reason did not lie so much in its financial position, which was excellent, as in the possibility that the new government of Mr de Valera would interest itself in banking and currency issues. Some of its members had already shown themselves interested in the then fashionable doctrines of Major

Douglas. George found the adviser—Geoffrey Crowther.

It was while he was in Dublin (in the summer of 1932) that he was asked by Sir Walter Layton to act as his secretary and this introduction led him to the editorial chair of the *Economist*. I had been appointed Dublin correspondent of the *Economist* in 1929. . . . When Crowther came to Dublin he had no connection with the *Economist* nor had he any knowledge of the identity of their Irish correspondent. He referred one day to the excellence of their Irish letter and it was then that I revealed the fact that I was its author. In after years Crowther rose to be editor of the paper. He never ceased to be kind and friendly. He wrote me numerous complimentary letters about my communications and made a gracious reference to me in the preface of his *Outline of Money* which increased my esteem with many generations of students.[1]

Those years of the early 1930s were perhaps the happiest he had known since childhood.

I had not only made a second start, but was making a great success of my new career. The summer of 1932 and the spring of 1933 marked the culminating period of this happy stage in my life. I was well established in the College, and no longer suffered from any anxiety about stagefright recurring. . . . My health was good. The anxiety condition was improving. My radius of movement was widening. I paid a couple of visits quite far in the country. I gave no thought to religious things or indeed to any of the deeper issues of life. I was very happy and thought that everything would go on in the same way indefinitely.

There are several things to be said about this passage. His radius of movement may have been at its widest, but it was still short indeed. A journey as far as Moyvalley was the furthest he got. It is a reminder of the confined limits within which he had to live. Again, it was deeply typical of him to relate the sunny summers of those years to his condition. He was always finding symbols and making them as suggestive as anniversaries. At the time he did not rejoice in the sunshine as much as the reader

1. 'I owe the greatest debt of all to Professor George O'Brien, without whose encouragement the book would never have been written.'

might suppose. Sustained good weather was indeed good for the terrace of the Irish before and after dinner; but it was also good for the growing of wheat. It vexed him that Mr de Valera enjoyed not only the support of the electorate but also, as it seemed, the favour of Divine Providence.

Still, he could not be thinking of Mr de Valera all the time. There were plenty of more pleasant things to do. High among them, and most acceptable to a sociable man, was the entertainment of visitors to Dublin. They came mostly from London. The English connection was still very close. It was not much more than a decade since it had been closer still. Even in the 1930s and later, Irish foreign policy was not much more than an exercise in Anglo-Irish relations. There was a constant stream of visitors to Dublin to ascertain what the next development might be and assuredly it did not dry up during the years of war in the next decade. After they had paid their visit to Merrion Street, *ad limina* as it were, they sought out George. There were many reasons why they should. He was well known in the circles of what later became to be known as the Establishment through his writings, his association with Horace Plunkett and the *Irish Statesman*, his regular contributions to the *Economist* and occasionally for the *Sunday Times*. The visitors might be revenants from the British government of Ireland, like W. G. S. Adams, or enquirers into the affairs of the Irish Free State, like Keith Hancock, or visiting lecturers, like Arnold Toynbee. These are examples; there were others, like Evelyn Waugh, but unfortunately neither man seems to have set down his impressions of the other. All of them found themselves at a table in the Irish where George, always a good host, exerted himself not only to answer their questions but to elicit snippets of gossip on public and, on occasion, highly private affairs. Sometimes he was inclined to boast, with much justice, that he was a remarkably well-informed man even if he had never left Dublin. These evenings were pleasant and informative with the exception of the ghastly evening when Toynbee dined. The news had just come through that Anthony Eden had resigned the Foreign Secretaryship; and the guest was too sunk in gloom to make more than a pretence of conversation. It was rarely like that. One of the later visitors was Hayek, who gave the Finlay lecture in 1945. He was credited with having made two observations after his return from Dublin. One was that the city reminded him instantly of the Vienna he had known before 1914. The other was that George had the best cellar of any professor of Political Economy that he had ever met. All this filled George's life and gave him plenty to think about. Indeed it insensibly moulded his ways of thought, and one example may appropriately balance what was said at the beginning of this passage. By dint of having to explain Mr de Valera's policies, he came to understand, if not yet to sympathise with, the feelings that inspired them. This was a lengthy process—it had to start a long way behind scratch as it were—but it was to gather momentum when war broke out.

It was not only a matter of feeding visiting lions. He would be dining out anyway. He was always a man who would be going out. Probably he was always so : certainly he rarely spent an evening at home in the last forty years of his life. One imagines that the habit began when home was an uncomfortable place and the attractions of the Arts Club were all the more persuasive. But even when he abandoned the Arts Club, it persisted. What follows is true of any period of his life after the 1920s.

It must be said in passing that those who did not know him well and those who did not know him at all may be misled by these references to his dining out. It was not quite as it may appear. He was not a man who ate or drank heavily. He may have been such in his youth : there were periods in later life, usually signs of increasing strain, in which he seemed to be dining more amply than usual. They never meant much because the 'usual' was so modest. His demands were essentially one dish, preferably of fish, and a half-bottle of wine. He ridiculed the convention of white wine with fish. Many younger people learned many things from him. They never failed to learn to drink red wine rather than white, burgundy rather than claret and never, never, to pose as an authority on vintages. But wine there had to be, at all costs. One of the best known stories of his senatorship relates to very early days when he and Fearon found themselves faced with an hour's adjournment of the Senate. They had some qualms about walking down the street to the Kildare Street club and decided to try the Oireachtas restaurant. They ordered steaks and a bottle of wine. They then noticed that everybody else was drinking tea. Hurriedly, the story goes, they asked for the wine to be served in a tea-pot and poured into tea-cups. The episode was noticed by a colleague who did not fail to pass on the story. George never denied it; but he usually changed the subject as soon as possible.

He organised his friends with care and, so far as possible, distributed them over different nights. In the earlier days his companions were usually older than himself, men like Edmund Curtis and Harry Monahan. Harry was legal adviser to the Land Commission and was understood to be the only man in Ireland who could find his way through all the Land Acts. He had an acute sense of observation and humour and an equally strict sense of the proper standards of personal conduct. George reserved his more scandalous stories and his more speculative observations for nights when Harry was absent. Then, increasingly as time went on, there were his junior colleagues in the College. There were those who had come into his life at different times, such as Terence White who must have been his oldest friend of all. There were visitors from England who came over more regularly than those noticed earlier, such as Patrick Ryan of *The Times* when governments changed every three years or so or John Vaizey when he was engaged with Paddy Lynch in the writing of the first volume of the history of the Brewery. There would be others again who came out of contacts with the Management Institute or the Statistical Society or whatever body he happened to be concerned with at the moment. He brought all kinds of people together. He was a great catalyst in days when divisions were much sharper than they have since become.

The result of all this was that no one who knew him would have dreamed of ringing him at home in the evenings. He was bound to be out with the Sunday party or the Wednesday party or the Friday party or one or other of the gatherings which succeeded each other during the year with all the regularity of the old liturgy. The one place he certainly would not be was at home.

This was a puzzle for some of his friends. After his mother's death he had spent a great deal of time and money in refurnishing his house; indeed the account of why he did so and of why he chose this or that fill a surprisingly large amount of recollections. It was clearly a great emotional release for him. But even

when he had done as much as he wished he did not spend all that
much time with his creation.

To begin with, after he had become master of the house, he
had a long succession of domestic difficulties. 'My poor mother',
it seems, had coped with such matters better than he had realised.
In his later years he was very well looked after indeed by John
Lynch and his wife Bernie. That being so, some of his friends
thought that he might have acted as host occasionally. That he
did not, was part of the defences that he had built for himself
against his insecurity. In fact he was a most hospitable man,
always asking people out to one or other of the evenings that
have been described. But he insisted on retaining his freedom.
His hospitality was always given outside his house, where he
could always decide when it was time to go home. If he did not
like the way in which the party was turning out, that might be
very early indeed. And, above all, he wanted to be sure who
would be at the table. It was no wonder that he was practically
never seen in the gregarious surroundings of the Dolphin even
in its greatest days. Doctor Johnson's tavern chair, the throne of
human felicity, was not for him. He never enjoyed such self-
assurance.

Even when, in 1932 and 1933, the sun shone most warmly he
was conscious that the dark might come again. He always knew
throughout his life that his comfort was insecure. Referring elsewhere in his recollections to that happy and promising time, he
remarked. 'The sleeping dog was in a very sound slumber during
those years.' In the margin he later pencilled a note: 'None of
the sleeping dogs were dead! Some woke later than others.' It
is dated 5 March 1956; soon after he had suffered a third, and
even more serious, breakdown.

It was not for nothing that the last sentences of the last
quotation should run as follows:

And yet, though I did not know it, the tide, which had been
flowing so strongly, was beginning to turn. Full tide had been
reached. I was about to go through a period of strain and
unhappiness that in many ways resembled my previous condition at the Bar.

12

The Professor: the Middle Years
1935-46

HIS immediate anxieties arose out of the College. They did not come in any way from his students with whom his relations were warm and happy; they came from more senior people. First among them must be placed John Charles Flood, who has already made an appearance in connection with the Finlay Lecture. George's first impressions bear quotation.

> The mention of Dr Flood . . . awakes a train of recollections which is mostly disagreeable. I became aware of the existence of this extraordinary individual when I was examining for the B.Comm. for the first time in 1926. Among the appalling schoolboy and schoolgirl scrawls I found the hand-writing of a mature character, and answers not dictated by the Oldham catechism, but possessing some degree of original thought. On inquiry, I was told that the author of this paper was Dr J. C. Flood who went from faculty to faculty collecting degrees. Shortly afterwards I was introduced to him. He was then about thirty years of age. He was apparently the sort of person who hangs about universities, afraid to mix with people of his own age—a Triton amongst minnows. He was obviously pleased to meet me and made the first advance towards developing a friendship. Needless to say I responded. He was the first person connected with the College who took any notice of me and I was glad to make a new bachelor friend. He asked me to dinner and I asked him back. I think that he liked me as much as his perverse disposition allowed him to like anybody.

This is not the most promising beginning to the description of an acquaintanceship and the account grows still more acid before it ends in the severance of relations nearly twenty years later.

They were two men who could not possibly get on together.

Flood was to enter, to general astonishment, the Order of Saint Benedict, a couple of years after the second war. He died in Ealing Abbey at the age of eighty towards the end of 1978. This settled at long last one of the many mysteries about him, which was his age. In the middle of the 1920s he had become Auditor of the Literary and Historical Society. He was an exceptionally fine and compelling speaker. He concerned himself with the affairs of the Society for many years afterwards, long after the average ex-Auditor had abandoned his interest. He was obviously older than the average member. What had he been doing in the years between?

It was understood that he had served in the French army during the first war. This conveyed an agreeable association with Hilaire Belloc, then still much in fashion among the more traditionally minded members of the Society. What neither they nor anybody else could understand was how a youth, generally understood to have been born in Bristol, could have got there. He never unbent so far as to explain; just as he never spoke about his war experiences, whatever they may have been. His story was accepted; which was much more than could be said for other Tritons of his time who claimed to have been the life and soul of the IRA before the Truce.

What was quite certain was that he came to College and obtained a very good degree in Medicine. This was followed, quite unusually, by degrees in Arts, Commerce and Law. It was said that he enjoyed one of those post-war grants which enabled ex-servicemen to follow university courses but did not lay down any terminal date. However that may have been, in 1929 he unsuccessfully contested an appointment in Medical Jurisprudence against the late Jock McGrath. From then on, the members of the Faculty of Medicine, and especially Dr Coffey, were the objects of his unceasing abuse. He took up a position in the Main Hall to the right of the doors, so commanding the route by which the President would pass to his office. Every day at the appointed time, he would deliver some calculated insult which the President could not help but hear.

He did some practice and held a junior appointment in a hospital which, it need hardly be said, was outside the usual sphere of College influence. Whatever about his professional attainments, he had an imposing manner. He was certainly one of the best speakers of his time—and in College we heard them all. His presence was imposing, he had a magnificent head and a fine chiselled face. When he wished, he could be extraordinarily charming; he could as easily be unbearably offensive. He possessed a remarkable capacity to divine what remark might wound his listener most deeply. The charm and the insult could be mingled together in the same conversation. One never knew what to expect but it was always necessary to be wary and very necessary indeed to be careful what one said to him. He had a genius for making trouble. Having said all that, it must be added that those who knew him in College (the members of the Faculty of Medicine, no doubt, excepted) have cherished a curious affection for him ever since and remember his monologues in the Main Hall as one of the experiences of their youth.

The apparent ambivalence is easily explained. Those who had learned their trade in the L. & H. learned also how to deal with him. One of his ploys was to approach his victim with the words 'Everybody is saying . . .' followed by some unkind remark. The accepted way to reply was 'Yes, Flood, it occurred to you this minute'. This could end the ploy because it was almost always the literal truth. Coarser people would use coarser words and relations would be suspended for some time. To talk to Flood was usually dangerous and, for those who could cope, always exciting.

For George, it was always dangerous. He had none of the defences which his more cynical juniors could erect. There was a streak of naiveté in his character, which was never more apparent than in his dealings with Flood. He believed whatever Flood took it into his head to say, whatever that might be. George might like or, more usually, thoroughly dislike it, but he would accept it as having some relation to the facts.

This was the more unfortunate because there were some things said that George took very seriously indeed. One such was that the new government, when it had settled down, might revise university charters and so endanger academic security of tenure. It seems most unlikely that anything of the sort occurred to Mr de Valera who, besides being Chancellor of the University, was always scrupulous to respect existing rights. It could not be denied, however, that several of his followers made highly critical references in the Dail to George's lectures. By a refinement of cruelty the point was sharpened by the suggestion that possibly George's appointment to the combined chairs in 1931 was irregular and might be successfully challenged. This worried him very deeply indeed. Any of his students could have told him how little importance should be attached to Flood's baiting; but then he was not, nor ever had been, the kind of person who could see that for himself.

His most immediate concern in College, however, was his relationship with the colleague who was then Professor of Commerce and Dean of the Faculty of Commerce. This was Bernard Shields, universally known (and often with an affection which George did not share) as 'Barney' Shields.

Not the least advantage of academic life is that colleagues who do not like each other can avoid meetings without too much difficulty. This did not and could not apply to George and Barney. Political Economy was indubitably in the Faculty of Arts as it always had been since its teaching, first provided by Newman, had been revived in 1899. In 1911 the first Statute of the new University College provided for the establishment of a Faculty of Commerce. Its institution must surely have been due to a feeling that Irish youth should have access to instruction which would assist a career in the commercial world.

It was not then as easy as it has since become to determine exactly what courses should be provided to attain that end. It must have seemed obvious that some economics would help, so Political Economy was made a subject in the new Faculty. Ever since it has attempted to preserve a precarious balance between Arts and Commerce. Accountancy was another subject that seemed appropriate. So far so good; both subjects could claim a formal discipline. The third major subject was Commerce. It covered, to go by the syllabus contained in the College calendar (not always the most trustworthy source, it may be remembered), economic geography, domestic and foreign trade, statistics, business organisation, scientific management and industrial welfare, trade unions and industrial disputes, and the economics of transport.

It might be thought that all this would give everybody so much to do that they could keep out of each other's way. Unfortunately George was hardly in the College before he gave offence. He was on very friendly terms with John Hooper and Roy Geary who were in what was then the Statistics Branch of the Department of Industry and Commerce. He got much help from them in the preparation of his courses in National Economics. This suited him and still more his students. It also suited the Branch, who were able to inform the Department that they had developed a new and important activity. It was suggested that some part-time lecturing in Irish statistics might be given by members of the Branch. Barney protested vigorously and successfully. Statistics formed part of his subject, not George's. For the rest of the many years in which they were colleagues, the two men disagreed about almost everything. The fortunes of war varied. George usually won what might be called the set battle-pieces, but there was an unending series of raids and ambushes with which he could not be bothered and which he usually lost. This did not necessarily damage the work of the Faculty, but it greatly annoyed him.

His relations with Shields became something very near an obsession. It must be said that, so far as one could see, Barney did not spend half as much time thinking about George as George did about him. He didn't mind in the least what George said about him as long as he was left free to get on with his own work. That work, it needs to be said, he did very well, and he had a series of very good students, such as Jim Beddy, Jerry Dempsey and Todd Andrews. He got on well with his classes. They indeed were fond both of him and of George if for different reasons and in different ways. It is an unedifying episode over which even George's admirers must refuse to be drawn into partisanship.

The accumulation of these anxieties, unnecessary as they may have been, preyed on his health during the middle 1930s. It was in no way as serious an attack of depression as he had had twenty years before or as he was to have some twenty years later still, but he had few remedies to hand. To travel, to get away from his house, might have been a remedy, but it was not possible. The best he could do was to spend the Long Vacation under a different roof, and this he did. Every year at this time, as soon as the lecture year had ended he would retreat to the Marine Hotel at Malahide. The north county, then still unspoiled, held a deep attraction for him. He could spend the days perhaps golfing,

G

more likely walking around the by-roads or along the strand at Portmarnock. He could be sure of congenial company, John Nolan the Professor of Experimental Physics and soon to be Registrar of the College; Edmund Curtis the historian; A. J. McConnell and his wife, Hilda. To add variety some swans might be asked down for dinner or even to stay. These were pleasant interludes in a period of much worry. Years later he would speak of them with affectionate recollection.

During one such summer, he wrote what is perhaps the most widely admired of his books. It owed very little to his circumstances. For some time past he had felt very fatigued and depressed. The escape to Malahide was more eagerly awaited than ever in the summer of 1936.

I asked Paddy Byrne to come to Malahide with me and we spent about six weeks there together. He was the perfect companion in the circumstances. He was intelligent and sympathetic. A bad nervous breakdown had driven him out of the Jesuits. He understood my difficulties. We spoke the same language. The rest did me good and I was able to resume lectures in October.

I found an amusing and agreeable occupation during this summer in writing. I had the same curious mental energy during my months of minor breakdown that I had had many years earlier after my more serious nervous crisis. I was told by a doctor friend that periods of nervous fatigue are frequently accompanied by intensive intellectual alertness.

The Four Green Fields is a relatively short book of about 60,000 words but it is most closely argued and garnished with a wealth of analogies. It is perhaps the best written of all his numerous books. He enjoyed writing it immensely.

Unlike my economic books, it did not entail any laborious research. The raw material was derived from easily accessible histories and biographies which I would read at home. I did not introduce any footnotes or any other apparatus of erudition. I wrote, so to speak, with the writing pad on my knee. I let myself go, for the first time. . . . The result of my 'abandon' was that I was able to take care over the literary form of the book. I had lots of leisure and I took plenty of time over writing and revising the little book, which was the perfect companion for a period of convalescence. The book was very well received and, indeed, established quite a reputation.

The argument of the book is so highly, perhaps too highly, concentrated that an attempt to summarise it would be both impertinent and unsuccessful. Its importance lay in the date of publication. When it appeared the economic war was still in progress. The Irish Free State was still in existence : it was still technically a Dominion. George's point was that the major Irish interest should be to re-establish friendly relations with Great Britain. But, he argued, in Anglo-Irish relations there were three parties not two—the Free State, Great Britain and the majority in Northern Ireland. That majority, he held, had in the past prevented the growth of good relations between the two countries. Northern resistance to Home Rule had not only wrecked the Redmondite party but had also contributed to its replacement by separatist feeling. The North, he argued, stood to gain nothing by improved Anglo-Irish relations and in fact had no interest that could be served by any such improvement.

What then was to be done or what could be done by any government in Dublin? The underlying thesis was deeply pessimistic. He did not believe that any improvement in the prosperity of the Free State, even if it came at last to be more prosperous than the North (which seemed an unlikely prospect in 1936), would lead to any change of heart in Belfast. Northern Ireland was founded on ascendancy. The principle had been variously stated in the past and might be differently stated in the future but it over-rode all other factors. There was nothing that the Free State could do. There was nothing that Great Britain could do as long as it remained a Protestant state. The best course to follow, both in London and in Dublin, was to remove the causes of controversy that then existed and to prevent partition poisoning Anglo-Irish relations. Not even that achievement might change the situation. 'Indeed, insoluble is not too strong a word to apply to the problem of Irish unity, so long as the *data* of the problem remain unchanged.' Forty years later, the reader may consider how far the *data* have changed and whether the changes, and there have indeed been some, have brought a solution nearer.

It was a deeply pessimistic book. It held out no easy road to unity. Worse still, its message was that there was almost literally nothing that nationalist Ireland could do (coercion being ruled out) to improve matters, as long as the spirit of ascendancy remained vigorous. The best it could do was to cultivate its three green fields; but it need not expect to discover envious stares from across the boundary ditch.

It was a brilliantly argued book, so brilliantly that it was an immediate success. George was always rather surprised at that, perhaps because he knew so well that under all the brilliance which aroused such admiration, he had prescribed no remedy for partition because in his mind no remedy then existed. When the present troubles began in the north at the end of the 1960s, several friends suggested that a second edition would be a great public service. He thought otherwise. He did not think that the essentials of the problem had changed.

His reaction to this success was curious in some ways. It inspired Major-General Montgomery of Fivemiletown to found the Irish Association with the aim of improving north-south relations by better personal contacts. Naturally, the General strove to involve George in these efforts. Equally naturally George completely refused. He was interested in the subject as a matter of Anglo-Irish relations and as a theme of the nineteenth century. He was not particularly interested in partition itself. His desire for closer links with the North was tepid to say the least. He did not look forward with longing to any development that would bring Belfast closer to Dublin. When, in later years, he spoke about the *Four Green Fields* it was to boast that he had written a book about modern Ireland without mentioning the name of Mr de Valera. On occasion, he would go further and enact a little pantomime in which Mr de Valera would take up the book and turn at once to the index to find that he did not appear under 'd' nor, to his astonishment, under 'V'.[1] The whole episode is remarkable from many points of view. But it gave him something to do when he was feeling low and brought him much praise after too many years of abuse.

This pleasant anxious being was interrupted by the outbreak of war. It was the occasion for his final rupture of relations with

1. George knew, perhaps better than his listeners, that there was no index to the book.

Charles Bewley. George, like everybody else, was aware that Bewley, during his years as Irish representative in Berlin, had become deeply pro-Nazi and anti-Semite. In August 1939, Bewley, now retired from Berlin, arrived in Dublin. He was on his way to New York. There, he intended to publish a selection of the dispatches which had passed between him and Mr de Valera in the preceding seven or eight years. These dispatches, he was convinced, would wreck Mr de Valera's reputation as an upholder of Irish interests against Great Britain. (One's memory of his account of their contents does not recall issues more profound that the question of whether the Legation should fly the tricolour on the King's birthday and similar trivia obviously thought up by Bewley himself.) He was quite certain that Great Britain and France would give in to Germany, that there would be another Munich. He expected the further growth of Nazi power. He looked forward with relish to the extension of anti-semitism and totalitarianism into the democracies. He was altogether intolerable.

When war, contrary to his expectations, did break out, the journey to New York was cancelled. Bewley returned to the Axis countries. Few things, it must be said, gave George more pleasure than to learn years later that he had been interned by the Americans. He was cast down by the news that Mr de Valera had magnanimously interceded to obtain his release. He was furious when Bewley, back in Dublin, called on him. It was made quite clear that relations had been finally severed. There was a hard side to his nature.

Like everybody else who remembered the circumstances of twenty-five years before, he gloomily set about providing against the shortages that war might be expected to bring. These measures were not as successful as they deserved to be. To begin with, he went out and bought two new suits. When this news got around the town, it inspired Arthur Cox (who was hardly renowned for sartorial elegance) to remark that 'George must expect a Thirty Years War'. Coming from where it did, the remark was a bit hard but it must be confessed that George's standards of dress, however high they may have been in the days of the Arts Club, steadily deteriorated as he grew older. He had no sense of colour. For years he sported a cardigan and muffler of a peculiarly ghastly shade of mustard. At much the same time as he bought the suits, he bought a sports coat of the best Donegal tweed but of a very brilliant shade of blue. I first saw it in the Yacht Club. He was anxious to know if it looked too striking for a man touching fifty. Just as I was beginning an insincere answer, Harry Barniville passed us. 'That's a great coat, George. Where did you shoot it?' Dinner that night was dreadful. Barney, who was the kindest of men, could never have dreamed of the anguish he caused. We left early. The sports coat was not seen again, which was just as well.

His other act of prevision was equally ill fated. With the advice of Raymond Brooke, he bought many cases of wine and whiskey when these essentials of life were still available. He lamented that he could not possibly afford such extravagance but comforted himself that he could now contemplate a long war with equanimity. To salve his conscience completely he had an air-raid shelter built in the garden for his mother, his aunt, their nurses and the domestic staff. If bombs fell, he pointed out, they could go to the shelter and say their rosaries; he would remain in the house and specifically in the cellar. Neither the shelter nor the wine was used. His domestic staff contained one who tampered with the cases and their contents. By a refined turn of ingenuity she did not content herself with drinking one bottle and then another. She took a couple of glasses from each and topped up with water. The precious stock was almost completely contaminated before this grievous loss was discovered. If, however, Hayek is to be believed, some of the damage must have been made good by the end of 1945.

There were more serious matters to be thought about. At an early stage of the war he was asked by the *Times Literary Supplement* to help them out with reviews while their usual contributors were on war work. He welcomed this very much : it helped to occupy his mind : it kept him abreast of contemporary publications. Later, as the foreign correspondence of the *Economist* dried up in the wake of successive German occupations, he found himself writing much more frequently for that journal. Again, he was very glad to help Geoffrey Crowther. He was a man who never forgot any kindness.

Another invitation, however, was declined. For years previously George had been in close touch with Forrester, an agent for Methuen & Co. His frequent visits to Dublin were memorable occasions. Around this time he suggested to George that the tedium of wartime might be relieved by the writing of a history of Ireland under the Union. (A general survey rather than a professional study was contemplated.) George thought about this for quite a while. He was implored to accept by many of those who knew him best. In the end he declined.

This was not due to indolence. The causes lay deeper. Then and long afterwards he was disposed to cry down his economic histories. Writing in the early 1950s he stated that

> I have not looked at any of my historical works for years. I am afraid of my more mature judgement finding them unsatisfactory. I have read so much and learned so much in the last twenty-five years that I have become more self-critical and censorious. I like to think that these early efforts were as good as they were said to be by contemporary reviewers and I prefer not to court disillusion. These poor neglected children of my youth were the means of introducing me to a secure and happy career. They served the purpose for which they were designed. I doubt if I shall ever look at them again. I may be guilty of ingratitude to them but I am at least innocent of any vanity about them. They are the foundations on which my whole academic position has been constructed. Like other foundations they are buried underground.

He could be disarmingly frank about himself. He had written his economic histories for a very specific purpose. He had written them in a very short time. That carried implications of which he was well aware though he was not pleased when others, junior to him in age though certainly better equipped professionally as historians, spelled them out. He would never argue the matter; though he might mutter that his critics had not yet written all that much themselves. It depended a little on the personalities concerned. There were several historians whom he greatly admired and liked; there were others whom he neither admired nor liked.

At any rate, he did not accept and Methuen's commission was then offered to P. S. O'Hegarty. It cannot be contested that P.S. brought out many facets of the Irish nineteenth century that George would have missed. There remains a feeling that the matter might, with equal truth, be put the other way around.

The effect of the war was, of course, to restrict still further his freedom of movement. Curiously enough he found that 'soothing and pleasant. Travel had become practically impossible for everybody. When all my friends were sealed up I felt less conspicuous. I was less tormented in the summer by innocent inquiries about holiday plans.' (This, it may be said, was one thing that was certain to send him into a rage. Many hapless students, thinking to make conversation, asked him each June if he planned to go to France or Italy. They were shaken by the paroxysm that invariably followed.) However, the Irish was still there, even if there were no cars and the last tram for Dublin left at 8.45. Indeed its attractions were increased because Sir John Maffey, the new British Representative and two members of his staff, Douglas Craig and Norman Archer, were now frequent diners. They dined no doubt partly for relaxation and partly to hear what people who were outside official circles were saying. Sometimes they would bring down visitors from London. On such occasions, the dinner would not have got far before the subject of neutrality was introduced. No more determined nor more logical defender of Mr de Valera than George could have been found. His listeners might not have gone away converted, but they would not leave without realising that the case for neutrality rested on something firmer than a sterile Anglophobia. In his own line, George was as strong an advocate of the national policy as was Tom Bodkin in the correspondence columns of *The Times*.

Around this time he was brought into the full tide of English economics. The story is worth telling at length, both for its own interest and as an encouragement to those tempted to despair of tracking down papers that have been long lost.

During one of the sad and boring summers of the war I had an agreeable distinction of an unexpected kind. I had heard very little from any of my friends in the Brewery for a long time. One day I received an invitation to lunch at the Brewery. I met, on this occasion, a member whom I had not met before, C. K. Mill. This gentleman, who was a kinsman of John Stuart Mill, was married to the daughter of J. E. Cairnes. This marriage, one might say, united two great economist families. Mill told me that he had found, in his father-in-law's house in Raheny, a box full of letters between J. S. Mill and

J. E. Cairnes. He invited me to inspect them. I paid three or four visits to the charming house where the box was found. The correspondence was interesting, especially because of its reference to Irish affairs. I communicated with Professor Hayek who was editing the works of J. S. Mill. Hayek suggested that I should write an article about the letters for *Economica*. The preparation of this article, involving, as it did, research in the National Library on Irish history, provided me with an occupation at a time when I was in danger of being depressed. The same box in Mr Cairnes' house contained a brown paper parcel labelled *Ricardo Letters*. These proved to be the long lost letters of Ricardo to James Mill. They had been lent by J. S. Mill to his friend Cairnes, shortly before the latter's rather premature death. The Cairnes family had neglected to return them and they had been forgotten for over seventy years. Hayek notified this new find to Dr Piero Sraffa who was editing the complete edition of Ricardo. Dr Sraffa came to Dublin to inspect the letters which proved to be of the greatest value. Keynes, who was immersed in Treasury business, found time to write to me enthusiastically about my discovery. When Sraffa's edition of Ricardo's works appeared, some years later, my name was given honourable mention in the preface in the company of some of the most eminent economists. The finding of this box, therefore, was a boon in more than one way. It gave me an interesting occupation in a period of boredom, it procured my admission to the pages of *Economica*,[1] and it brought my name to the attention of every serious student of economics owing to its inclusion in the great edition of Ricardo.

Nearer home he maintained his contact with economic issues through his association with the Statistical Society. That body enjoyed one of its most flourishing periods in the years between the wars. This was largely due to the energetic secretaryship of Roy Geary, partly also to interest in the statistics, all quite new, which Roy and his chiefs, John Hooper and then Stanley Lyon, were beginning to turn out from the Statistical Branch. There was a full programme of papers read each year. The discussions might attract an interesting collection of men, people of the

1. *Economica*, November 1943.

H

standing and controversial capacity of George Duncan and Joe Johnston, T. J. Kiernan and Henry Kennedy, T. A. Smiddy, Kenneth Edgeworth and Lord Glenavy. Any evening on which some of these might be expected to be present was an evening to mark and later to remember.

George began to attend the Statistical after he had become professor. He was never seen there before that. Oldham was a constant attender and tended to dominate proceedings. It was no place for George. But once the coast was clear, as it were, he attended regularly and, as a matter of course, became a member of the Council and later one of the honorary secretaries.

He read two papers, both of which will repay reading today. The first, in October 1940, was entitled 'Some Recent Developments in Economic Theory'. This was a wide-ranging and closely argued defence of the record of economists during the years of the Great Depression. He laid stress on the wide area of their agreement and suggested that several obvious issues of contention were due rather to differences of terminology rather than of concept. He defended the individualist system against its critics on the right and left, the right being more vocal at that time than it has been ever since. In particular, he insisted on the ethical content of economics.

His presidential address, 'Economic Relativity', was delivered in 1942. This was a long essay to re-assess the scope and purpose of economic science. He considered and defined the limits of usefulness of statistics and the statistical approach. Against them, then growing in fashion, he upheld the traditional instrument of economic enquiry, deductive analysis. Fundamentally, he held, in economics 'the principle of scarcity rules'. This part of the address looked forward to the theme of his last book *The Phantom of Plenty*. Taken in all, his logic was cast in a formal mould and was essentially bleak. He did not share the then fashionable hope that at the end of the war the world would be able to forget the incidence of costs.

These are necessarily short and inadequate summaries of these two papers. Indeed they are not intended to be summaries but rather as indicators of his themes. It is of course possible to query the precise manner in which they were enunciated : for example, he dealt with the place of statistical enquiry on a philosophical rather than a practical basis. What does stand out from them is the intellectual strength of his approach to economics. He viewed economics as a whole and in its relationship to other human values. He attempted to reconcile different definitions or varying lines of thought. Perhaps he was over-anxious to do so : there is a faint echo here and there of the barrister who must attempt to bring conflicting decisions within the four walls of his argument. He is always searching for the underlying and unchanging principles. Lastly, must be mentioned the extraordinarily wide scope of his citations. This is not to be appreciated without reading either or both of these papers. It is sufficient to say here that the anxiety to keep in touch with what was being said and written was one of the characteristics of his approach to his subject whether he was lecturing in the College or reading a formal paper to the Statistical. He lectured his students on Keynes's *General Theory* within months of its publication. More esoterically, he also referred them to Morgenstern's *Theory of Games*. It was no wonder that those students who wandered into the Statistical to hear him read a formal paper or contribute to a discussion felt deeply proud of him.

Although it anticipates a little, this seems the best place to refer to *The Phantom of Plenty* which was published in 1948. Its argument was that the great economic progress which had filled the nineteenth century was exceptional and unduly costly in terms of the use of resources. The further growth of resources could not be taken for granted. It was therefore fallacious to assume that the problems of production had been solved so that only those of distribution remained. To speak of 'poverty in the midst of plenty' was to ignore the growing pressure on the sources of supply. The Malthusian dilemma had been made irrelevant by the progress of invention and the discovery of new natural resources in the nineteenth century; the twentieth century should not expect that such good fortune would continue indefinitely.

The issue is, of course, one that can be endlessly debated. It is also as much a matter of technology as of economics. The striking feature of the *Phantom* was that it appeared when it did, at a time when the mood of the post-war world assumed so strongly that, after the damage of the 1940s had been made good, the only obstacle to renewed progress lay in the field of distribution. It was not, therefore, at all a fashionable work though its clarity of argument received much praise. Thirty years later, under the pressures of the emergence of OPEC and greater interest in the environment, it may receive greater attention, as indeed it has already had from the Club of Rome.

The *Phantom* was George's last major publication. His opportunities for exposition in the College of course continued for many years to come. Unexpected events in the year of its publication were to give him a wider audience.

13

The Professor: the Later Years
1946-55

His mother died in June 1946. This was a turning point in his life. It removed a continuing strain on his emotions. He could now re-assess his circumstances and consider what he wished to do with the rest of his life.

> As long as my mother was alive, my main ambition was to keep going and to avoid another breakdown. I must, at all costs, prevent a second failure. . . . She was the only person who vividly remembered my first breakdown and the only person who feared a repetition of that dreadful experience. To every observer except her, I was not the unsuccessful barrister but the successful professor.

Now the ghosts had been lain that had walked with him for thirty years.

The immediate path of release lay through the by-paths of academic politics. It was known that by September 1947 Arthur Conway would reach the statutory age limit and retire from the presidency of the College. As that year came in the possibility of a contested election seemed remote. It was widely assumed that John Nolan, who had been Registrar since 1940, would succeed Conway with as little fuss as Conway had succeeded Coffey. Interest was centred on who would be the new Registrar, not on who would be the new President. As things turned out, the possible future of the minor post influenced the future of the major.

George had become very close with John Nolan, whose integrity and independence of judgement he greatly admired. He had some reason to believe that if Nolan became President, he might well become Registrar. The belief was strengthened by an approach from Michael Tierney.

In July Michael Tierney asked me to meet him some day to discuss the question of who would succeed Nolan as Registrar. He indicated that there were certain people in the College who would welcome my appointment. I gave him a rather non-committal answer and indicated that I would be prepared to consider taking a full-time registrarship if it could be arranged as I was a bit tired of lecturing. I asked him if he had any intention of being a candidate for the presidency. He said that he had not, that he thought Nolan had earned it and that he might be a candidate when Nolan's term of office had expired.

All this was duly reported by George to Nolan. As the election approached, Nolan was not helped by some injudicious statements and claims on the future made by some of his junior supporters. He was positively damaged by the zealous support of J. C. Flood. These things did not go down well with senior and influential members of the Governing Body who would have the first opportunity, before the Senate, of casting a vote.

By the end of August Tierney had been persuaded to change his mind and to stand. His supporters, it can be said with some certainty, were not so much hostile to Nolan as to some of his supporters. The immediate result of the now certainty of a contested election was to bring another candidate into the field, Harry Barniville, who as a sitting Senator for the University and a person of immense influence, was clearly a formidable candidate. The contest was now wide open. George had always been on good terms with Tierney but he felt that Nolan had the prior claim. He proposed Nolan at the Governing Body in October. Three months earlier this would have seemed to be not much more than a formality. In the event Nolan secured the greatest number of votes of the three candidates; but the lead did not look decisive enough. It was not. The Senate appointed Tierney who thus entered on a long and stormy pontificate.

It was a curious election. It seemed so at the time and it was to appear even more curious as time went on. The result was heavily influenced not only by the preference of the electors for any one of the candidates but, in an almost equal degree, by their dislike of some supporters of each of the candidates. Nolan, who bore his unexpected defeat with great dignity, was perhaps the greatest sufferer of the three. Apart from that aspect of the matter, there was a feeling that the College needed vigorous leadership. This pointed to Tierney; and it certainly was not belied by events. There was another strain of thought which was very prevalent at the time, that the result represented a victory for the academic body over the academic politicians. Tierney entered into office with the greatest goodwill even from those who felt that Nolan had been harshly dealt with by fate. Most certainly George thought so; though he soon came to realise that the registrarship would have been a bad exchange for lecturing and meeting students.

I must say that Tierney bore me no grudge. He treated me with the greatest politeness and friendship and took me into his confidence. We had known each other for many years. We had been fellow sufferers at the hands of the gutter press on several occasions. We used to meet at AE's tea parties in Plunkett House. I had reason to believe that he approved of my work on account of excellent reviews of my books which he had written.

This harmony was not to last. A vacancy arose in one of the law chairs in which George and the President supported different candidates. The contest attracted much attention. The President's candidate was not successful. George was very conscious that he had been on the opposing side twice in a relatively short space of time. Other events, still in the future, were to increase the coolness. But, it should be added, the two men always felt that they had a lot in common. The memory of the 1920s was still strong.

In any case, George soon had a new interest which diverted his attention from College politics. The later stages of the presidential election coincided with important developments in national politics.

During 1947 a new party, the Clann na Poblachta, led by Sean MacBride, had been formed and attracted wide support. Other parties had arisen from time to time but had not been able to survive for long or to command widespread support. This was not true of the Clann, or at least seemed not to be true at the time. In the autumn of 1947 it captured two seats at by-elections which was more than either of the traditional opposition parties had been able to do in years. Mr de Valera announced that he would ask for a dissolution of the Dail early in the new year of 1948.

George was not interested in what might happen in the Dail or whether or not there might be a change of government. His association with the heirs of Mr Cosgrave's administration had grown very tenuous indeed. He had been impressed by Mr de Valera's maintenance of neutrality after 1939. He had never been much of a party man at the best of times; he was not one now in any sense. In this, there was an unexpected link between him and his great exemplar. 'Since 1832' Newman wrote to a friend in his later years, 'I have had no politics.' George cannot have been aware of this saying because he would certainly have quoted it frequently if he had. If the date were advanced by one hundred years it would have exactly represented his thought.

What interested him was a possibility much nearer home. A dissolution of the Dail would mean an election to the Seanad. The three seats allotted to the National University would be open to contest. The three sitting senators were Helena Concannon, Harry Barniville and Michael Ryan. Mrs Concannon was as definitely Fianna Fail as Harry Barniville was Fine Gael. M.J. never advertised his politics but it was generally thought that he would be Fianna Fail if it came to the point. None of them spoke often in the Seanad, if a considerable under-statement may be made. Still more to the point was that Michael Ryan had been elected at the previous contest in 1944 when he put out an over-confident Michael Tierney. George had always assumed that Tierney would seek his revenge at the first opportunity. Now, however, he had ascended above the battle. The path was open.

Moreover 1948 was a bad year for sitting candidates. There was the general post-war feeling of new possibilities and opportunities. Everybody in the Oireachtas suddenly seemed to have been around for a long time. New candidates were as immediately attractive as new parties.

George always claimed that the first encouragement came from a group of students whom he met one morning over coffee. They told him of their feeling that the University, and more particularly the interests of its graduates, was not properly represented in the Seanad. It does not seem that he needed much encouragement.

There was a great amount of support available. He had now

lectured for over twenty years to classes that had grown in numbers all the time. It was not simply that there were a lot of them : they were also the kind of people who carried influence and would look out for votes for him. Moreover, he would appeal strongly to those voters who were of much the same age as himself. Then there were those deep (and largely unfished) pools of voters, the school unions. There were many graduates who had been at CUS : there were even more who came from Belvedere. He became an assiduous attender at their annual dinners : he kept in touch with their activities. It was true that he was not well known in Cork or Galway; but then the bulk of the votes was in Dublin. Standing as an independent, he could not hope for formal party support; but a candidate who stood clear of the long feud between Fianna Fail and Fine Gael was exactly what many graduates wanted to have and was also the kind of person they thought a university representative should be. All in all, his potential support was formidable if it could be got out. But his true strength lay then and always in the fact that he was not only well known but also that he was highly respected and well liked.

This came as rather a surprise to him. He was not prepared for it.

The real importance of the election was that it showed me that I had the confidence of the general body of graduates. It demonstrated that what I had interpreted as unpopularity was really indifference. The aloofness of my colleagues and their failure to entertain me or to invite me out were signs, not of any personal dislike but of their peculiar unsociable method of life. This was the first time I had ever asked them to do anything for me and they responded generously. I could not help feeling a certain satisfaction. I had never made the slightest concession to popular opinion. I was known to be 'rightist' in economics and politics, pro-British and a believer in free trade. I had friends in Protestant and Unionist circles, and was a member of the Kildare Street Club, reputed—unjustly—to be the headquarters of all things anti-national. My hostility to the Irish language movement must have been well-known. Although I had never written or spoken a word offensive to religion I had never played up to Catholic sentiment. . . . I was entitled to draw the conclusion that I had been returned on the ground of personal integrity.

The beginning of the quotation suggests that he did not then understand, any more than had been the case twenty years earlier, that people can be well thought of without being asked out to dinner every night. The ending is very true. His election brought him a deep satisfaction and a great access of self-confidence. He owed a very great deal to those who organised his campaign and worked in the areas where there were votes to be got out, to people like his agent, Alexis FitzGerald, to Tom O'Rourke, to M. P. Linehan. But essentially he was elected for what he was. It was his own doing, not even the most devoted support could have brought him home otherwise. For him, the best of all was that he had been elected in his own constituency, in the University. It was only human that he should confide to a friend his delight that at long last he had done something that Arthur Cox would have loved to do but had not done. (In the event, Arthur was later to join him in the Seanad but as a member nominated by the Taoiseach, John Costello).

He was a member of the Seanad for just under seventeen years. It was a period of comparative instability in Irish politics; and elections were unusually frequent. He had to defend his seat in 1951, in 1954, in 1957, in 1961 and finally and unsuccessfully in 1965. In each of these elections until the last he got in comfortably. He took his responsibilities seriously and gave good value. He also developed some of the arts necessary to retain parliamentary seats.

While I always took an independent line when it was called for, I never felt called on to trample on the feelings of my constitutents when I could achieve no practical good result. For example, I did not feel bound in conscience to speak my mind on the language issue. To have done so would have injured my own position without any equivalent gain. I fell, I am afraid, into the temptation of wooing my electors. I have always been polite and friendly to students, but I confess that I became even more friendly when they became my future constituents with votes at their disposal. I have carefully revised the register of voters and have tried to get all my own ex-students to register. I suppose that this shows over-confidence in one's popularity but I am inclined to think that a majority of the students whom I have lectured would give me a vote, if not a first preference. I think that I can claim to have acted well as a representative of the University. I spoke on a large percentage of the few debates we had. Whenever any question touching on the university or its graduates arose I spoke at some length, and can claim to have kept the Seanad awake to the standpoint of my constituents. I pressed the claim of the College for additional endowments to the point of being accused of caring less about the country than about my own constituency. I spoke in debates when legal and economic issues were involved, and have thus linked together my two professions with my political career. My old love for the law prompted me to take an active part in discussions on legal questions. . . . I attempted to keep alight the legal respect for individual rights. I preached the doctrine of the rule of law. I had a horror of totalitarianism in all its forms. I knew that every man would be a dictator if he dared and that the only way to curb human cruelty and ambition was by maintaining legal and political liberty absolutely intact.

The foregoing passage must have been written about 1951, towards the end of or just after his first term. It is a very candid account of how he approached his duties. Perhaps the best example of how he met a highly embarrassing issue was provided by the debate on the Republic of Ireland bill in 1949. It was a matter which he approached with distaste. He had never been ideologically a republican : equally he had no particular monarchical sympathies. He took it for granted that sooner or later the country would formally declare itself a republic. But he thoroughly disliked the manner in which the intention to repeal the External Relations Act was announced and he disliked even more the manner in which it was assumed that the repeal necessarily involved the withdrawal of the country from the Commonwealth. This, again, was in no way due to any attachment to imperial connections as such. To his mind, it could never be to her interest that Ireland should be obliged always to deal with Great Britain directly and by herself. Ireland had gained greatly from the support of the Dominions in the 1920s when her policy had been directed towards dismantling the structure of empire.

It would gain even more in a post-war world in which India and other newly self-governing countries would be full members of the Commonwealth. Their presence would provide abundant opportunities for Irish statesmanship and initiative. To throw such opportunities away seemed to him to be feckless.

Nevertheless, there was nothing to be gained by opposing the repealing legislation. What he could and did do was to employ a highly pragmatic approach. His enquiries were not on matters of principle but were of high practical importance. What, he asked, was to be the position of Irish professional graduates, past and future, in the United Kingdom and in the still extensive British possessions? What was to happen to Commonwealth trading preferences? What was to be the effect on Irish membership of the sterling area? What was to be the position of British companies registered in Ireland? All these questions were, as it has since turned out, even more to the point than he could have known. They were exactly the questions that civil servants in Dublin and London were anxiously discussing. It was a considerable advantage that at least one member of the legislature should lift his eyes from the issues of the past.

Until the later years he was a frequent speaker. He had set occasions, such as the Central Fund bill, the Finance bill, the Appropriation bill and, earlier, the Supply and Services bill. He was always, as might be expected, a clear and fluent speaker; one parliamentary reporter remarked that 'there was always a verb in each of his sentences'. Sometimes indeed the speeches closely resembled lectures which was natural enough as he often used the one as raw material for the other. He did not hesitate to inform the Seanad of the trend of contemporary economic thinking; in his very first speech he was hardly on his feet before he quoted from the *Economist*. In his earlier years he referred often to the majority report of the Banking Commission. This led him into some difficulty because speakers for Fianna Fail, notably Mr Aiken and Mr MacEntee, had no difficulty in pointing out that the policies of the first Inter-party government bore no great resemblance to the recommendations of the Commission. But his speeches were well received by his colleagues. He was much more acceptable in his parliamentary career than John Stewart Mill of whom Robert Lowe remarked that 'the hon. gentleman for Westminster is a great deal too clever for us in

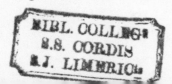

this House.' Nobody thought that way about George, which may help to explain why his parliamentary career was considerably longer than Mill's.

There were some threads that ran through all his speeches. There was his deep suspicion of administrative law; one of his very last interventions was on the subject of delegated legislation. He served for a long time as chairman of the Seanad Committee on Statutory Instruments. He was always ready to defend the dignity of the Seanad if some action by the Dail appeared to impugn it. Anything that related to the professional bodies or the universities aroused his interest at once. He attacked the proposal in 1959 to abolish proportional representation; and he was proud of the fact that it was rejected by the Seanad before it was rejected by the country. He protested against the destruction of Lower Fitzwilliam Street by the Electricity Supply Board. After much heart-searching he came out against the infliction of the death penalty. Above and beyond these matters, he proposed measures which were later carried into effect; an enquiry into the incidence of income taxation, the limitation of testamentary freedom and the institution of premium bonds (this last before it was suggested in the United Kingdom). Almost always he was on the side of the angels. He made a habit of asking his friends for their opinion on matters in which he intended to speak and then making up his mind for himself on what he would say. Prominent among such advisers in the earlier years was Brian Inglis, then parliamentary correspondent for the *Irish Times*.

There were other matters on which he was less successful. Two of his most abiding complaints were that members of the Oireachtas were debarred from membership of State companies and that members of commissions of enquiry were not paid for their labour. Ministers of successive governments were impressively unanimous in the belief that these proposals would not improve the standards of public life. He remained unconvinced.

Another goal that he set himself was that he should be able to walk on grass from Burlington Road to Leinster House. This was a hard saying; but his disciples interpreted it as meaning that the public should be able to walk through Merrion Square, along the side of the National Gallery in Leinster Lawn and past the steps of the National Library into Kildare Street, an old right of way in his youth which had disappeared in 1922. Merrion

Square has been liberated; but the considerations of security which led to the closure of the short cut from Merrion Street to Kildare Street at the time of the civil war unhappily still prevail.

The Republic of Ireland Act had a further and unexpected effect on his affairs. As has been said, he did not approve of the measure and still less of the manner in which it was launched. Nevertheless he felt it his duty to put and defend the Irish case in the columns of the *Economist*. This was not easily done. Geoffrey Crowther had his own views and had no reason to hesitate in their expression. Matters came to a point where a contribution by George was accompanied by a retort from the editor. This was an impossible situation; and George resigned. He was pressed to change his mind but he stuck to his decision. The parting took place with much cordiality tinged with regret. His successor, whom he for all practical purposes nominated, was a member of his staff and continuity was preserved as far as possible. He greatly regretted the severance : he had always enjoyed writing for the *Economist*, and he felt affection and admiration for Geoffrey Crowther.

Up in the College, however, things were going his way. The academic staff was still small and many of those who had been the original appointees in 1909 were now retiring. He was now over twenty years in his chair and the change of president emphasised his seniority. He did not wish to be associated too closely with some of the policies that Michael Tierney introduced. With one of them, however, he was in enthusiastic agreement. The new President had no high idea of the academic standing of the subject of Commerce. He felt that its disappearance would not greatly impede the development of the Faculty along better lines. Accordingly he decided that the term of office of Barney Shields would not be further extended. This decision was certainly within his powers but it was one that had not previously been exercised. Certainly the President exercised it on his own initiative : long before his election he had been heard to express views, pungent as usual, on the subject. Most certainly George did not put it into his mind; though equally certainly he did not exercise himself to oppose it. From his point of view, there would be a double gain. He would be freed from a partnership which he had always actively disliked; and he would have the opportunity at long last of acquiring a satisfactory staff.

Matters did not progress as easily as he had originally hoped. There was some hesitation about ending Barney's term of office. Much worse, the President developed some ideas of his own on how Political Economy might be developed. For a while he toyed with the idea of infusing a strong element of sociology into the department. This was not welcome to George on academic grounds and, if certain contingencies had become actual, still less on personal grounds. On the other flank as it were an extension of statistical method was suggested. That would have been much more acceptable; the trouble was that the better the provision made for statistics the worse, inevitably, would be the provision for economics. Negotiations were long and delicate. Eventually, in the autumn of 1951 he acquired three statutory lecturers, John O'Donovan, Paddy Lynch and the writer. This was an enormous accession of strength especially as Alexis FitzGerald continued to lecture for a number of years. It put the department on a proper basis at long last. Nobody then foresaw that the continuing growth in student numbers would soon become so great as to recreate much of the accustomed pressures. But we were lucky enough to pick up Louis Smith, Gerry Quinn, Paul Bowe and later Garret FitzGerald as time went on. Things were never so bad after 1951 as they had been for a long time before.

George regarded the appointments as a great liberation. He was now able to extend the activities of the department and to delegate the lecturing. He had no longer to fear that the work would break down if anything, even temporarily, happened to him. He reduced his own lecturing though he regarded it as a point of honour to meet the evening classes. He could consider himself free for other things. The Seanad was, of course, his primary concern. Speeches in Leinster House and lectures in Earlsfort Terrace could run closely together; and he could reasonably claim that one enriched the other.

There were plenty of other things to be done. He found himself on the Governing Body of the College and later on the Senate of the University. These appointments were not altogether welcome. They largely depended on the nomination of the President who in his earlier years sometimes nominated George and sometimes, depending on the exigencies of College affairs, might not. George was never very enthusiastic about being on these bodies but, like everybody else, he did not care to be dropped. He found the routine of College business to be boring, the succession of appointments to be embarrassing. He was never a College politician and he knew that he would make a bad one. He had no doubt that he preferred his classes to his colleagues.

His feeling was strengthened as the character of the new administration took shape. He was never on bad terms with Tierney but there were many things with which he could not sympathise. The suspected moves towards some kind of reconstitution of the Catholic University left him quite cold. There was no Newman in sight. If the existing College was to be reorganised, he said, there was a case for giving it back to the Jesuits. He did not really mean this : he felt much gratitude to the Irish province but he was highly selective in his opinion about some of its members. It was an agreeable way of shocking some people. In the same way he held aloof from the great issue of the presidency, whether to move to Belfield or try to carry on in and around the Terrace. He did not much care for the idea of the move; but his feelings depended not on College politics but on his own memories. For him, to the end of his life, the College was not Belfield nor Earlsfort Terrace. It was 86 and Tom Kettle leading his little class down the steps into the May sunshine of the Green. To leave 86 was to go away from all that. Worse still, it might mean going away from the memory of Newman.

He did not enter into these or the many other controversies of those years. He was hesitant about criticising Tierney even when it became a kind of national occupation. He could and did criticise at times the style in which the College was being run. Even there, he was never quite sure of himself. He sometimes recalled what happened one evening when he had dined with Kate O'Brien in the Shelbourne. It was after some particularly provocative pronouncement by the President; one thinks it was at the time of the great business of the housing of the Palles Library. The two had denounced at dinner how the matter was being handled. They continued to do so when they stood talking on the pavement outside the entrance. Their voices carried on the evening air. Far enough to upset a young gentleman wearing a College scarf who appeared from nowhere. He addressed his elders : 'Arrah, don't be saying that. Damn Tierney but don't knock the poor old College.' They had no reply and they watched him disappearing unsteadily into the shadows of Merrion Row. According to George, who did not tell the story often or to many people, they felt curiously ashamed of themselves. The feeling lasted. If he had been an academic politician, he might have made an effective and popular critic of the administration. He was not; so he did not criticise in public although he knew that his silence might be misunderstood.

As the 1950s went on he was asked to help in a number of ventures outside the College. They involved matters which lay close to his interests as professor and senator. The first of these was the Irish Management Institute which was formed largely on the initiative of Sir Charles Harvey, then managing director of Guinness, with the warm support of Sean Lemass in 1952. Its primary purpose was, and is, to raise the standard of management in Ireland. George was invited to become one of the members of its executive committee and acted as such for a number of years. He never claimed any expertise in what was needed, but it was useful for him to hear the views of those who were more immediately concerned. As Dean of the Faculty of Commerce, he was responsible for what was by far the largest school of university studies connected with business management. He bore the discussions at the Institute in mind when it came to the revising of courses. It was always agreeable to him to attend these meetings, at which he met so many people who had been his students. Whether they were on the electoral roll or not, he was always genuinely glad to meet former members of his classes.

Some years later he was asked to take on a more active responsibility. The Standing Committee of the Irish Banks decided that it should publish a quarterly journal which would contain articles on matters of general economic interest and, when and if necessary, express the views of the banks. George was a natural selection to look after the venture, and he was delighted to be asked to act as editor. From the first issue of the *Irish Banking Review* in 1957 until his last illness he contributed the first article. In bulk they formed a regular and predictable procession; an article on the budget prospects, a second on what the budget tried to do; a third on the annual report of the Central Bank, and a fourth on the prospects for the new year. Factually, they were completely reliable; and they were most useful for generations of students. George was perhaps fortunate that the New Departure in our economic affairs heralded by Dr Whitaker's survey and the White Paper of 1958 appeared soon after he began to write. The spirit of the new policies was attuned to the beliefs that he had thanklessly defended decades before. Once again the emphasis was placed on the need to look outwards and to the export trade rather than inwards into self-sufficiency. The means of policy, it was true, would hardly have commended themselves to Mr Blythe; but the goals were those of former days. Further, the *Review* brought him into regular contact with old friends in the banking world.

Another activity suited his interests even more closely. In 1960 the Ford Foundation was persuaded, largely by Dr Whitaker and Dr F. W. Boland, to finance an Economic Research Institute. In 1966 the major financing was taken over by the Irish government and the activity of the Institute was extended to cover social research. He was elected chairman of the Executive Committee at once and served without interruption until his death. He was an ideal chairman, never unduly intrusive or demanding and always successful in finishing the proceedings at an acceptable time. The Institute was a source of much pleasure to him, more than ever after he had retired from the College. He called regularly to see how things were going and to discuss them with Maura Dempsey who acted as secretary for years. It gave him something to do and an opportunity to meet people with whom much of his life had been spent, like Roy Geary, and others, from Kieran and Finola Kennedy down, who had been among his students.

These appointments flowed naturally from his academic position. There was one other which did not. In 1952 he was invited to join the Irish board of Guinness. It was felt at the time that the mover in this proposal was Sir Charles Harvey who was anxious to strengthen the links between the brewery and life in Ireland. In comformity with a habit which grew on him in later years, George sought the advice of his friends whether he should accept or not. Needless to say, they had no difficulty on advising him how to act, to do (that is) exactly what he was going to do anyway. He was, of course, delighted with himself. He had always hoped for something from one of the older companies: the time had been when he had hoped for an invitation from the Bank. Guinness was an ample compensation; though there was always an impression that he was not an active member of the board. However that may be, it was a blow to him when he became a casualty in one of the boardroom reconstructions which occurred in the 1950s.

He acquired other interests on the invitation of former students, such as membership of the board of the Ashtown Tin Box company and of the car hire company which Dermot Ryan was building up in those years. These things gave him something to do, better still something that was new to do. Also, he liked to keep in touch with past students even when a Seanad election was not in the offing. In the case of Ryan's, it also brought him in touch with Sean Lemass for whom he had a respect which was not usually extended to the senior members of the party. What seemed more immediately attuned to his interests was membership of the board of Clonmore and Reynolds, the publishing firm which Lord Wicklow founded soon after the war. This appealed to him greatly. He was an admirer and close friend of Eleanor and Billy Wicklow. He was entranced by the varying success of the religious books which were published by the firm. He kept his friends informed (though not when Harry Monahan was present) of the varying fortunes of the hagiographical market and of how St Maria Goretti had captured the lead from the Seven Dolours. More practically, the firm published *The Phantom of Plenty*, which imparted some variety to its list.

All these things combined to give him, as it seemed, a happy and busy life in the 1950s. He appeared to have always something to do and somewhere to go. Ironically, it was at this time that he suffered the last, and in some ways the worst, return of depression. He never knew security.

14

Slowing into the Terminus
1955-73

His relapse into depression occupied much of the year 1955. It was much worse than the attack in the middle 1930s and it was both unexpected and unaccountable. It was a reminder to him, which he assuredly did not need, that his hold on even the modest happiness of ordinary life was as fragile as ever. To his friends, there was nothing in his circumstances that suggested any immediate cause. In the College, his classes were going prosperously and easily. He had just devised for his evening classes a course which provided a general summary of basic economic theory. It was (was) known to all as 'George's Round the Mountains Tour'. In the Seanad he had defended his seat successfully for a second time. Nevertheless, the old enemy struck again. This occurred in April; he was not fully recovered until the later months of the year. Distressingly, throughout part of that time, he was under treatment which included electro-convulsive therapy.

This happened when he was approaching his mid-sixties. When he returned he seemed to lecture as well as ever. He was still exact in meeting his engagements : few people can ever have sent so few apologies for unavoidable absence from boring meetings. But there was a change of mood. In other years he had counterattacked from illness with a burst of creative energy. He had done so in 1918 with the first of a long line of books. In 1935 he had been 'floated off', to use his own phrase, by the Banking Commission. There was no such rebound in 1955. He thought very carefully whether he should not retire from the College. The mood proved to be transient; but that it should have been entertained at all was significant.

He played the hand out. He had already reduced his lecturing as his staff increased; and some of the courses which he had been forced to make over when he became ill were not resumed when he returned. But he was scrupulous to honour his obligations to all his classes. He continued to lecture in the two subjects of his chair. He never abandoned his lectures to third year honours or to the evening students.

His friends were conscious that some day the last hand would be dealt and the last card played. Quite possibly they made heavier weather of it than he did himself. He had never been greatly interested in economic theory for its own sake : he was less and less attracted by the manner in which it was being developed and in which it was being expressed. Worse still, he perhaps did not get the same pleasure from lecturing as had been the case. This was not the fault of his students. They were still easy to get on with; they were as good as they ever had been; perhaps, if one pauses to consider names, rather better. The trouble was that there were now so many of them and he had never been completely at ease with large classes. The over-crowding of the lecture rooms in the Terrace had not reached anything like its worst point before he retired but it had become very bad indeed. He found himself addressing a public meeting, not lecturing to a class. Life had become less personal and more crowded. The stately procession of swans proceeded unvexed to the end but it was no longer so easy to make individual contacts. He did not like this.

He was due to retire in January 1962 on reaching the age of seventy. He did not wish to put everybody, the College, his col-leagues and his students to the difficulties that would be caused by a vacancy occurring in the middle of a session. He resigned in the early summer of 1961 so that an appointment could be made by October when the new College year would begin. It was a few months short of thirty-six years since he had been brought in to fill Oldham's place. Throughout all that time his lecturing had been at the centre of his life, his first responsibility and his greatest obligation. He might well have said with Jowett : 'The College is my real happiness and business.'

Years before his retirement he had reflected on the respons-ibilities of his position :

The vocation of a university professor is particularly exacting because one has such influence over the minds of the younger generation. To have the opportunity of moulding the outlook and the values of those who are starting their career in life is a great privilege. . . . The holding of a position such as mine in University College in recent years has been quite unusually responsible. The College has been, during my time of office, the principal breeding ground of the leaders of thought in politics, public life and the professions in the most critical years in the formation of the new Irish State. It is sufficient to recall the vast number of public and professional men that the College has produced in the first fifty years of its existence. It must continue to play an equally active—if not more active—part in future. . . . The mission of University College is not confined to Ireland. The College is the direct descendant of the Catholic University. . . . Even while it continues to serve many Irish students, its influence can extend beyond Ireland. Owing to the great dispersion of the Irish people, the College can, through its graduates, exert a good influence in many other countries. Ireland occupies a position of unique influence in the world today. It is the only country that is at the same time fully Catholic and fully liberal. It is the meeting ground of two great traditions, of the Roman Church and British democracy.

Such thoughts may not be much in vogue today. They are worth quotation nonetheless because they show once again how profoundly George was influenced by the thought of Newman. They show also another strain of thought, which will shortly surface for a moment, that Ireland possessed a special opportunity, if its people could rise to the height of it, as a country that was both Catholic and democratic. Lastly, the passage reflects how deeply conscious he was of his responsibility as a teacher.

When he retired, steps were taken at once to commemorate his long tenure of his chairs. Subscriptions for a memorial lecture flowed in from everywhere. The O'Brien lecture now alternates with the Finlay. Thus, the two names continue to be linked, as he would have wished. By an appropriate symbolism, the first O'Brien lecturer was Roy Harrod, who was chosen not only for his personal pre-eminence among English economists but also because he was the biographer of Keynes who had delivered the first Finlay lecture thirty years before.

The severance from the Seanad proved to be equally painless, so far at least as outward appearances could suggest. At the time when his successor took over, he was engaged in defending his seat for the fourth time. His success may have helped to ease things. His interventions thereafter became fewer though no less incisive when they did occur. It did not seem that he would be prepared to defend his seat again as strongly as would have been the case ten years before. There was perhaps some loss of will to fight. He was no longer in such close touch with the younger graduates; several of his principal supporters in the early days were now dead. In the event he lost his seat in the 1965 election to a new contestant. It was lost by remarkably little, which rather confirmed his friends in the belief that he was no longer all that interested. Nevertheless, they feared that he would take the reverse badly. Such fears were unnecessary. To one consoler, anxious to say something soothing, he simply remarked that Arthur Cox had just died and that, when all was said and done, it was rather better to be a live ex-Senator than a dead ex-Senator. He was indeed slowing into the terminus, to borrow once again from Newman, but he had not yet reached the platform.

Nevertheless, some slowing down there certainly was. He was still active during the day. He had always the Institute across the road where he could drop in to sign cheques, drink tea with the juniors and discuss the latest economic intelligence with an eye on what he might write in the next issue of the *Banking Review*. Some of his friends thought that he might have used his leisure in writings that would be less ephemeral. There were some topics that clearly would not now be approached. *The Famine to the Treaty* belonged to the years and expectations of his youth. *The Life and Letters of Sir Horace Plunkett*, which could have been a most valuable source for its period, and which he could have written with more understanding than almost anyone of his time, had been consumed in the flames of Kilteragh. From time to time, he talked about a topic that was half-formed in his mind—the influence of O'Connell and Newman in shaping the values of Irish Catholic society. To combine two such dissimilar political and cultural influences would indeed have been a triumph. But it never came to anything and he left no tentative notes behind. One never heard

him really get down to the argument. It remains an engaging
might-have-been. It was felt by some that he might have taken
the account of his life which he had written and recast it as a
survey of his times and friendships. It seems a great pity that
he did not devote some hours each week to a revised and ampli-
fied version; but the suggestion ignores the highly personal manner in which he looked at his writings. His views had been set
down years before and assuredly they had not been changed.

> I know that I was adversely criticized for not writing more on
> my own subject. But my conscience was clear. I did not regard
> publication as part of my duty as a professor. I did not even
> regard it as desirable unless I had something new and valuable
> to say. The books which I had published after I had left the
> bar were written with the object of securing an academic
> post. They were investments of time, energy and money which
> proved successful. . . . When I obtained my chair, I had no
> longer the same motive or the same urge to write. I had, so to
> speak, landed my fish. Besides, my principal duty was now to
> lecture and to influence students by personal intercourse and
> direction. . . . I had shown that I have the capacity to write
> bulky learned volumes if I wanted to do so, and there was
> no necessity to continue repeating the demonstration. I was like
> the dog that has shown that he can walk on his hind legs. He
> is not compelled to pass through life as a perpetual biped.

In this, as in other passages, one is left with a feeling that such
a weight of argument may mask some uncertainty. But if he did
so feel about writing on his subject, he was most unlikely to feel
otherwise about writing on himself.

In the last years, his day really began in the evening. There
was always somebody to dine with. His friends saw to that : so
did he. Their task was not always easy. One might ring up to
propose a meeting and be obliged to wait while a diary was consulted. Fred, it might be, was tomorrow night, Gerry the night
after, Louis or Paddy or Desmond or Garret the night after that
again. No, there was no date open. What about next week? It
might occur to one that most of his friends got on quite well
with each other and that once in a way he might be quite able
to dine and talk with two people at the same time. That was not
the point. To put down two people for the same night was waste-

ful. It was clearly better to have one one night and the other on another night so that the diary and his life was filled. This policy of full employment of his friends was openly avowed and altogether accepted. His friends understood that the horizons were closing in. They all owed him a lot for past friendship. They were glad to see him on any evening, the more so when they reflected that there would not be so many evenings left.

He must have shared that thought but as he passed through his seventies he seemed to be increasingly willing to accept old age. He had outlived most of his contemporaries. This did not disturb him. He had recruited many younger friends. Often he had been the architect of their careers. He could meet them on easy terms. He was fortunate enough to retain many of his interests. It was a great help that he retained his physical health : he enjoyed, to recall the Master again, 'the pleasant illusion of youth into old age'. In those later years he realised ever more clearly that, in spite of so many difficulties and trials, he had much to be thankful for—more, much to be proud of. The words that follow were written when he was approaching sixty : they may well stand for what he felt twenty years later.

On the whole I think I am entitled to congratulate myself on having rebuilt successfully after my collapse, and on having, with very little help from anyone, made a successful recovery. I am constantly reminded that I was a young man then, and that I am, if not an old, nearly an old man now. This realisation of increasing age is not entirely unpleasant. I have come to accept the inevitability of death with resignation. I feel that God has been very good to me in many ways, that one must take life on the terms on which it is offered, and that one must not regard with horror sharing the fate of all one's friends.

His friends were troubled less by the inevitable death than by the fear that he might suffer some disability which would impose inactivity and seclusion. That would have been altogether intolerable to him. Fortunately their worst fears were not realised. Into the first half of February 1973 he was around and active. His morning routine was to read the morning papers, walk down Haddington Road to Mass, and then to collect the English papers from Parsons, the bookshop at the canal bridge which was a constant port of call for him. On Friday, 16th, he collapsed in the

street on his way back from Mass. He was brought into Baggot
Street Hospital where it was recognised at once that he was in
the throes of a heart attack. For some days the reports were
deeply pessimistic, thereafter his condition improved though
never to the stage that he could be fully discharged. He spent
the summer in a ward. This was trying to him but he showed
remarkable patience to the many visitors who called on him.

He was allowed to return home in the late autumn; but it
was clear that there was little hope of a sustained recovery. He
must have realised as much; though he did not talk about it. In
his last weeks he spent his time reading Moore's trilogy. To one
visitor, in the last days of his life after Christmas, he talked of
how well Moore had recaptured the feel of the city before 1914,
how beautifully the Green was kept nowadays, how tall the trees
had grown, how he and Tom Kettle had walked there so often.
Salve may well have been the last book he opened. He suffered a
sudden collapse and on the last day of the year he ended a long
life that had been filled with disappointments and achievements
and goodness.

Index